China Online

The Chinese Internet is driving change across all facets of social life, and scholars have grown mindful that online and offline spaces have become interdependent and inseparable dimensions of social, political, economic, and cultural activity. This book showcases the richness and diversity of Chinese cyberspaces, conceptualizing online and offline China as separate but inter-connected spaces in which a wide array of people and groups act and interact under the gaze of a seemingly monolithic authoritarian state. The cyberspaces comprising "online China" are understood as spaces for interaction and negotiation that influence "offline China." The book argues that these spaces allow their users greater "freedoms" despite ubiquitous control and surveillance by the state authorities. The book is a sequel to the editors' earlier work, *Online Society in China: Creating, Celebrating and Instrumentalising the Online Carnival* (Routledge, 2011).

Peter Marolt is a Research Fellow at the Asia Research Institute, National University of Singapore.

David Kurt Herold is an Assistant Professor of Sociology at Hong Kong Polytechnic University.

Media, culture and social change in Asia

The aim of this series is to publish original, high-quality work by both new and established scholars in the West and the East, on all aspects of media, culture and social change in Asia.

China Online

Locating society in online spaces

**Edited by Peter Marolt
and David Kurt Herold**

Routledge
Taylor & Francis Group

LONDON AND NEW YORK

First published 2015
by Routledge

2 Park Square, Milton Park, Abingdon, Oxfordshire OX14 4RN
711 Third Avenue, New York, NY 10017

*Routledge is an imprint of the Taylor & Francis Group,
an informa business*

First issued in paperback 2017

British Library Cataloguing in Publication Data
A catalogue record for this book is available from the British Library

Library of Congress Cataloging-in-Publication Data
China online : locating society in online spaces / edited by Peter Marolt
    and David Kurt Herold.
      pages cm. — (Media, culture and social change in Asia ; 41)
    Includes bibliographical references and index.
    1. Internet—China—Social aspects.   2. Cyberspace—China—Social
aspects.   I. Marolt, Peter.   II. Herold, David Kurt.
HN740.Z9I5626 2015
302.23'10951—dc23
2014021199

ISBN: 978-1-138-80929-1 (hbk)
ISBN: 978-1-138-57792-3 (pbk)

Typeset in Times New Roman
by Apex CoVantage, LLC

Contents

Editors and authors

Editors

Peter Marolt has been a Research Fellow at the National University of Singapore's Asia Research Institute from 2008 to 2014. In his research and writing, Peter explores the frontier of New Media-augmented urbanity and the political significance of artistic aspirations and practices. He co-edited *Online Society in China: Creating, Celebrating, and Instrumentalizing the Online Carnival* (Routledge, 2011) and is currently writing a book on "Cyber China: making space for change."

David Kurt Herold taught and researched in China for over 9 years, before joining the Hong Kong Polytechnic University in 2007. His research is focussed on the use of informationa and communication technologies (ICTs) by humans. In particular, he studies the Chinese Internet, encounters between Chinese and non-Chinese online, the impact of the internet on offline society, and online education. His recent publications include *Defining the nation: Creating 'China' on a Bridge-Blogging Website* (2012); *Escaping the World: A Chinese Perspective on Virtual Worlds* (2012); *Through the Looking Glass: Twenty Years of Research into the Chinese Internet* (forthcoming).

Contributing authors

Jonathan Benney is a Lecturer in Chinese Studies in the Department of International Studies at Macquarie University. He has worked as a postdoctoral fellow at the Institute for U.S.-China Issues at the University of Oklahoma, a visiting researcher at the Goethe University Frankfurt, and a research fellow at the Asia Research Institute at the National University of Singapore. He finished his PhD at the University of Melbourne in 2010, and his first book, *Defending Rights in Contemporary China,* was published by Routledge in 2013. He studies contentious politics and political communication in modern China, with particular emphasis on new media, activism, dispute resolution, the role of law and rights, and the history of ideas.

Maria Bondes is a Research Fellow at the GIGA German Institute of Global and Area Studies' Institute of Asian Studies, and a doctoral candidate in Chinese

Studies at Hamburg University. Her research interests concern Chinese social and environmental issues, with a focus on environmental policy and activism. This includes the opportunities for social activism provided by the Internet and social media. She currently writes her doctoral thesis about the diffusion of environmental contention in urban and rural China, investigating the case of the recent wave of local opposition against waste incinerators across the country.

Alex Cockain is a Teaching Fellow at the Hong Kong Polytechnic University where he teaches courses in anthropology, sociology, media theory, social theory and social development. His research monograph entitled "Young Chinese in Urban China" was published by Routledge in 2012, and he has also been published in *The China Journal* and *China Information.*

Gabriele de Seta is a doctoral candidate in the Department of Applied Social Sciences at the Hong Kong Polytechnic University. His interest for contemporary China and underground cultures brought him to study the Shanghai experimental music scene in 2009–2010, while completing a MA in Chinese Studies at Leiden University, the Netherlands. His current research project is an ethnographic study of Chinese digital media users and their practices, with a focus on the dialogic construction of digital folklore across online platforms and communities.

Ge Jin is a human factor researcher at IDEO, the design and innovation consultancy. He is a PhD candidate in Communication at University of California-San Diego. His research mainly concerns how people incorporate the virtual and the digital into their everyday life. He was the first researcher to uncover the real money trade of virtual goods in online games in China. His documentary film Gold Farmers and articles on this subject have been widely quoted by academic and journalistic articles. He also regularly writes articles on topics like China's emerging middle class and online memes for popular media, including China Economic Review, Financial Times China, China Business Network, BBC and CNNGo.

Helen Kennedy is Senior Lecturer in New Media in the Institute of Communications Studies at the University of Leeds in the UK. She has published widely on various aspects of new and digital media, in journals such as Information, Communication and Society; New Media and Society; Convergence; The Information Society; and Media, Culture and Society. Her book Net Work: Ethics and Values in Web Design was published by Palgrave MacMillan in 2012. She is currently working on a monograph on social media data mining, for publication in 2015, and is also researching the reception of big data visualisations.

Xiao Liu is a Master student of Communication Sciences and research assistant at communication department in Université de Montréal, Canada. Her research interests focus on collaboration and knowledge circulation between users in the context of Web 2.0. Her articles were presented in ICA (International Communication Association) preconference and WSSF (World Social Science Forum).

Yu Liu is Assistant Professor at the School of Journalism and Mass Communication, the Florida International University. She received her Ph.D. in Communication from the University of Miami. Her primary research focuses on the social and cultural impacts of social media, specifically exploring diffusion of social media and how social media affects the civil participation and collective action. She is also interested in studying cross-cultural consumer behaviour.

Cuiming Pang is Assistant Professor at the Department of Culture Studies and Oriental Languages, University of Oslo, Norway. She received her PhD in digital media from the University of Oslo in 2012. Her research interests concern society and politics in China in general and digital media in particular. She is currently working on a project on communication and the formation of online communities in China.

Günter Schucher received his PhD from the Sinology Department of Hamburg University. He is a Senior Research Fellow at the Institute of Asian Studies, German Institute of Global and Area Studies in Hamburg. His research interests include social developments in the PRC and cross-Strait relations. His main research focus is on labor market issues and social conflicts. His recent publications include '*The Constricted Evolution of China's Rural Labour Market*' (2011), '*Do Rising Labour Costs Spell the End of China as a "World's Factory"?*' (2010); '*Where Minds meet. The 'Professionalization' of Cross-Strait Academic Exchange*' (2010). Together with Maria Bondes, he published '*Derailed Emotions. The Transformation of Claims and Targets during the Wenzhou Online Incident' in Information, Communication & Society* (2013).

Bingqing Xia is a PhD candidate in the Institute of Communications Studies at University of Leeds, UK. Her research focuses on labour and the quality of working life in the Chinese internet industries. Her main research focuses on in Chinese internet industries. Bingqing's background is in history and new media studies. She has presented her work at a range of international, annual and biannual conferences such as the Association of Internet Researchers, the International Association for Media and Communication Research, and the Crossroads Cultural Studies conference.

Qinghua Yang is a doctoral student in the School of Communication at University of Miami. She earned her first MA in intercultural communication from China. In 2011, she began researching instructional technology and media, while completing a second MA in Communication and Education at Columbia University in the City of New York. Her current research interests mainly focus on health communication and communication technology.

Part I
Deliberating online spaces

1 Grounding online spaces

Peter Marolt

The Chinese Internet has emerged as a growing field of research, and scholars have grown mindful that public spaces and activities in cyberspace are intrinsic to understanding social issues that exist offline, and vice versa. Online and offline spaces are increasingly recognized and rendered as interdependent and inseparable dimensions of political, economic and socio-cultural activity, and their interrelationship is driving change across all facets of social life. Continuing from our first co-edited book (Herold & Marolt, 2011), this volume carries on our investigations into the intricate specificities of the Chinese-language Internet, by illuminating phenomena and specificities of the Internet in China.

This volume emphasizes the connections between cyber and physical place-worlds and the people (a.k.a. 'netizens') who concurrently inhabit and perform in both these worlds. Online and offline China are conceptualized as inter-connected spaces in which human and institutional actors interact under the gaze of the – only seemingly monolithic – authoritarian state. The cyberspaces that comprise 'Online China' are understood as spaces for interaction that influence 'Offline China' and can be described as 'spaces of autonomy' (cf. Castells, 2012) in that they allow their users greater 'freedoms' despite the ubiquitous control and surveillance by state authorities. In a blend of online and offline contexts, China's online practitioners, as individuals or in groups, are creating and shaping autonomous spaces in which they engage in myriad social interactions, express ideas, produce shared meanings, etc.

The volume at hand presents and reflects upon the diversity of social and cultural practices and events taking place in China's online spaces and beyond. Contributors analyze how various actors utilize the Internet to create and re-create meaningful spaces, institutions and movements in their quest to shape their lives, and how these spaces propel or hinder the transformation of societal structures. Taken together, the chapters in the volume deconstruct the notion of the all-powerful and monolithic party-state while also avoiding to cast Chinese Internet users in a primarily 'political' role. Chinese cyberspace is home to many different users, groups, events, happenings, movements, artifacts, etc., and their goals and purposes are rarely 'political' in a narrow sense – even if they have an effect on politics. In the same way, 'the Chinese state' consists of many individuals, groupings, institutions, etc. that have different views on multiple aspects of 'Online

China', often at odds with each other. China's netizens are faced with contradictory, ever shifting regulations and 'harmonizing' state interventions that require constant choices, compromises, and great flexibility, in negotiating the boundaries of permissible online and offline behavior and action.

A less dichotomous re-conceptualization of both online and offline China and their diverse practices and networks of relationships allows for a deeper understanding of the importance of the Internet in today's China (and beyond). In this volume, we have integrated empirical findings and conceptual imaginings of the ways in which 'Online China' invokes the re-making of 'Offline China' (and vice versa) and how people create new, blended socio-cultural spaces in today's China. We found that the diverse practices that comprise the 'Chinese Internet' have profound implications beyond personal space: fostering self-expression, improving one's critical apparatus, broadening one's views, taking other people's thoughts and ideas seriously, forging relationships, etc. Slowly but surely, Online China thereby changes the country and the world as we know it, one micro-interaction at a time. This book is significant in that it examines the various ways in which Chinese netizens discover and live out their individuality despite the palpable atmosphere of political repression.

Framing and situating this volume

The relationship between information technology and societal transformation is multi-faceted, ever-changing and of unprecedented complexity. It is therefore hardly surprising that contemporary Chinese society changes far more rapidly than the capacity of scholars to record and interpret that change. There is a fast-growing scholarly literature confirming that the Chinese-language Internet is home to a growing sphere of free speech, that blogs and microblogs create an independent space for discourse, and how this aids the development of a civil society in China. Associated academic discourses have tended to portray Chinese people as passive victims of either China's party-state or globalizing economic forces. What results is limited by a control versus freedom paradigm in which, in a highly questionable practice (and practically by design), 'cyber-activist' becomes a synonym for 'cyber-dissident', without acknowledging (and still less engaging with) the various ways and degrees to which one can be active in cyberspace.

Another adaptation of these paradigmatic master narratives represent those who are not 'cyber-activists' as being all about entertainment and play. This may be in line with the preferred storyline (and political agenda) of the Chinese party-state, but the statistical fact that China's media, including the Internet, are dominated by entertainment does not mean that political debate or social transformation are absent. The widespread academic consensus about the Chinese Internet being all about entertainment that leads to some form of 'mindless escapism' or even addiction has to be taken with more than one grain of salt. Isn't it exactly such 'mindless' entertainment that creates the playful mood through which creative fountains of ideas can flourish? Since Wittgenstein, we know that "[h]umor is not a mood, but a way to observe the world", and Bakhtin (see Lachmann, Eshelman, & Davis, 1988) tells us that subversion of hierarchy and authority often happens by the means of "grotesque realism" and "carnival" – again mainly through humor. This suggests that the prevailing representations of netizens as entertainment-loving beings are merely imposed notions geared towards redefining their role as assisting those in power in reaching their goals. In a similar manner, larger social concepts such as capitalism or democracy may be useful as hermeneutic devices in understanding politics and the world, but they often create a fatal indifference towards the empirical; nor are they very helpful when it comes to grasping the complexity of a society and culture in which huge numbers of individuals are thinking very differently from what their governments say or do.

The terms of conventional scholarly debate of the 'Chinese Internet' are all-too-often framed as control versus freedom, domination versus resistance, or autocracy versus democracy. Perhaps for this reason, surprisingly little is known about the ways in which the 'online' and the 'offline' are related in everyday China, about aspirations and opinions of China's netizens, their levels of self-reflection and political maturity, or urban China's current status and future trajectories in the processes of social learning and transformation.

It is therefore of crucial importance to avoid reductionist perspectives and acknowledge the complex ways in which people support, oppose or ignore impositions of power and control. We cannot afford to lose sight of "people's ability to actively resist such impositions, and to carve out new, meaningful spaces for themselves" (Hil & Bessant, 1999, p. 41). This volume emerged out of a desire to heed these guidelines, as an attempt to provide a balancing 'view from below' that stresses the importance of empirical detail and diversity. In the process, we have found that grasping the existence and significance of specific events and particularistic resistances that are rooted in local identities and experiences is contingent upon learning about the everyday realities of the people involved. Judging the Chinese Internet merely on the basis of its content is just as misleading as focusing solely on censorship or the Internet's imagined emancipatory potential. The Internet should also be explored for specific conscious and intentional efforts and unintentional side effects at work at altering societal structures from below.

There is an upsurge of recent scholarship on Chinese new media that is slowly transcending the dichotomy of control vs. freedom. While appreciating that structural forces continue to exert strong pressures on social practices, these scholars point out that such morphological factors "neither wholly control nor wholly predict the outcome" (Williams 1974, p. 130; cited in Zhao 2008, p. 354). This recognition allows them to conclude and seek corroboration that "human agency and historical contingencies remain important" (Zhao 2008, p. 354). Nevertheless, apart from a few notable exceptions (Esarey & Xiao, 2008; Kluver, 2008; MacKinnon, 2008; Yu, 2006, 2007; Zhao, 2008; Zhou, 2005, 2006; also see Giese, 2006; Goldman, 2005; Qiu, 2004), Chinese Internet studies have yet to realize that agency can only be recognized if we are prepared to see it. We should thus embrace everyday life as a useful theoretical construct that helps us to *get away from thinking in terms of what media do to people, and toward how people actually use these media.* For example, Haiqing Yu examines digital media practices in the context of everyday politics in China. She affirms that the Internet has become an integral part of the daily lives of urban Chinese and that new media empowers people to narrate their own stories and make themselves heard, thus becoming "active participants in the production of symbolic values by being part of a culture of circulation" (Yu, 2007, p. 428). Yu concludes that "the seemingly apolitical media practices of the consumer masses turned out to be political in the end as they influenced the way people think about politics" (p. 424).

When people express themselves and thereby reveal their differences and distinctions, the resulting diversity creates a capacity for critical reflection and action (Arendt, 2001; Debord, 1967; Foucault, 1980; Goldfarb, 1998; Lefebvre, 1991). Furthermore, once people have created a shared public space for speech based upon different opinions, they become empowered to share a sense of the factual world, engage in a common course of action, and eventually re-create public life through social transformation. However, although the Internet provides opportunities for expanding the space for political participation in China, the actual realization of such a public civil sphere depends on intentional human action that move from a virtual 'e-sphere' into physical everyday realities. As the chapters in this volume show, such an emphasis on agency and space allows us to recognize qualitative changes in the ways people conduct and perceive politics, by demonstrating that the Internet and its various social media are an essential source of consciousness, expression, and action, and by examining related interactive links between cyberspace (imagined spaces) and city space (physical places). Through various 'media events', we can thereby catch a glimpse of the ways in which changing conceptions of politics create new spaces of expression and autonomy that are imbued with a potential of yielding shared meanings and political action different from traditional political forms and their institutional manifestations.

In the context of China, yet another difficulty arises: Qualitative research often wrongly assumes that research participants will tell you what most concerns them, and thus emphasizes the overt and seemingly obvious over the tacit, the implicit, and the liminal. However, in a context where many, if not most, important meanings and processes are not expressed openly, we need to "learn the logic of the experience we study, not to impose our logic on it" (Charmaz, 2004, p. 982). In order to do this we need to bracket our own views of reality and rationality and recognize that participants' views – as well as our own – are always relative to place, time, context, situation, and society (p. 982). In other words, we should always give first attention to the phenomena themselves, adapting our methods if necessary (Goffman, 1989).

Partly due to these complications, partly due to sheer size, there is very little grounded evidence about how the Chinese-language Internet is affecting peoples' everyday lives and larger cultural and social practices. Moreover, there is a clear dividing line in studies of cyber-culture between structural literature that favors abstraction in theories of cyberspace, and post-structural literature that examines closely the experiences of participants. Contesting current realities of knowledge production, I am convinced that grappling with the complexities of culture mediated in and through cyberspace requires us to do more than merely choose sides:

it compels us to develop alternative ways of seeing and conceptual models that help us make sense of people's idiosyncratic experiences and everyday perceptions of lives led in specific environments. By sharing netizens' thoughts on these effects and offering novel perspectives that make sense of them conceptually, this volume is conceived to fill some of this gap. After all, the expressions of its netizens may contain the only mature response to China's contemporary quandary, in the sense that their thoughts and ideas evoke and facilitate the envisioning of living spaces that are worth living in, in a civil sphere they can feel comfortable in. Bringing these expressions to the fore involves conscious (and thus observable) thoughts and ideas that can be linked to the vanguard of societal change and that open up our ways of seeing towards the less structural and monolithic aspects of social science. Remaining wary of an over-preoccupation with theory that overlooks (or ignores) the diversity present in the empirical realm and the individuality of Chinese people, what follows is hoped to reassert and invigorate the academic debate of the socio-political implications of the Chinese Internet. Along similar lines, Tai (2006) has found that the Internet has emerged as an emancipatory and empowering tool for Chinese civil society and has opened new opportunities for the revitalization of civil society forces. Even though the state still maintains a formidable presence in Chinese cyberspace, there are indications that the Internet marks a dramatic departure from previous types of communication technologies" (Tai, 2006, p. 289).

This trend suggests that we need to focus our attention on cyber-urban spaces and practices of 'performing place', on specific new modes of individual and shared agency, and on the 'spaces of autonomy' (Castells, 2012) in and through which these two come into focus, meet and augment each other. This edited volume is conceived around these issues.

The self and place: 'performing place' in the cyber-urban place-world

As cities, in China and elsewhere, increasingly "defy efforts to be classified into types, reduced to essential characteristics, and fixed by boundaries (intellectual or otherwise)" (Cherot & Murray, 2002, p. 432), we need new ways of seeing heterogeneous urban realities. What many Chinese urbanites face is not a deep structure and normative purity but instead, multiple orderings and nonlinear connections that call for constantly re-negotiated tactics and perspectives.

This holds true for Chinese netizens who, confined to maneuver within these orderings, create the spaces they need to attain their goals. It is equally true for the scholar who, in order to capture the vibrant pluralisms that are palpable throughout urban China, needs to engage with heterodox thinking drawn from various disciplines. Unfortunately, none of the established conceptual frameworks used in Chinese Internet studies leaves much room for action and agency rooted in urban everyday life, nor do they (explicitly) recognize that cyberspace and physical space have long become interdependent and augmenting dimensions of political consciousness and activity. In such a context of cross-pollination, the resulting "culture of real virtuality" (Castells, 1996, 1997, 1998) adds to the social and mental rhythms of organic social life, through evoking all kinds of fruitful interplay between them (Van Dijk, 1999).

I suggest considering that no particular perspective holds a privileged insight into the ways of the world. Living with diversity, it is helpful to understand the cyber-urban as both a consciousness-inducing cultural landscape and a pre-eminent site of socio-political interaction and exchange. To interpret these processes it becomes essential to incorporate multisensory 'lived' experiences into an understanding of how ongoing spatial redevelopments – both online and offline – affect an urban society at large. Moreover, if scholars involved in (critical) Chinese Internet studies want to understand and conceptualize the fluid and diverse individuals who broke loose and are at large in Chinese cyburbia, we need to assert the existence of an autonomous, active, self-assertive, situated, sensible, bodied self. This self is full of desire to create heterogeneous, exciting places which embody and thus create multiple identities that are no longer willing to give up their dreams. Perhaps Casey says it best: such a bodied self "is the only aspect of our being – individual or collective – capable of *performing place*, that is to say, making place a living reality" (Casey, 2001, p. 718; emphasis added).

I concur with Lefebvre that only through re-appropriating the City, and opening up our eyes to the myriad new ways of knowing, can we understand the everyday "rhythms" and "festivals" of urban society (cf. Lefebvre, 1991). What this edited volume aspires to infuse into the ongoing scholarly discussion is a conceptual sensitivity to geographical concerns. Chinese cyber-urban everyday life can be captured as a realm permeated with online *and* offline, cyber *and* physical, virtual *and* real places, lived in by *real* people imbued with a sense of creative and collective purpose. Such places function as incubators for intentional actions which are not restricted to those communicative actions that can be measured through sociological abstractions such as 'roles' and 'structures' (cf. Habermas, 1985). As Michael Gardiner suggests, the recognition of the importance of the everyday life standpoint allows us to "bear more accurate witness to the pluralistic, collective energies that constitute the minutiae of lived social relations, generate new forms of personal identity and express our corporeal needs and desires" (Gardiner, 2000, p. 208).

Living in or exploring a Chinese city comes with daily reminders that in our increasingly globalized place-world, we live with increasing architectural and (related) sensual-conceptual uniformity. The place-thinning we can observe (and that is often epitomized by erasures of the palimpsests of history) can be interpreted as a function of decreased bodily engagement that may be due to the rapidly decreasing public or private-public spaces (such as Beijing's *hutong* 胡同 'alleyways'). And the less we immerse our body/selves in creating new places, the less interesting our (physical) places will become. In Casey's words: "When the role of body becomes routinized, the place in which it is situated (and which it itself helps to constitute) lacks the intensiveness which makes a place not merely entertaining or instrumental but of intrinsic interest and central concern" (Casey, 2001, p. 719). Flattening and replacing the eclectic historical palimpsests of prior forms of living, this homogenous and homogenizing uniformity is constructed – through capitalist monuments such as shopping malls, office buildings, or gated residential communities – so that our bodies and selves feel at home and not lost in them. Casey concludes that self and place are mutually constituting, and that the body has become a mediator that actively engages place. If places become increasingly uniform (or "thin"), the same is true for personal identity. Casey therefore suggests that the more places are leveled down, the more selves should "be led to seek out *thick* places in which their own *personal enrichment can flourish*" (2001, p. 685; emphasis added).

Unfortunately, Casey suggests that it is what Bordieu called "habitus" that ties place and self together. He describes habitus as "the socially encoded core of our bodily self" (2001, p. 688), as a "middle term between place and self – and, in particular, between lived place and the geographical self" (p. 686). Yet although Casey recognizes that "a habitus is something we continually *put into action*" (2001, p. 687, emphasis in the original), he states that we are not the masters of place but prey to it; we are the subjects of place or, more exactly, *subject to place*. For him, such subjection ranges from docility (wherein we are the mere creatures of a place, at its whim and in its image) to appreciation (by which we enjoy being in a place, savoring it) to change (whereby we alter ourselves – our very self – as a function of having been in a certain place) (p. 688). Casey unquestioningly adopts Bourdieu's concept of self as a social product, as what Entrikin aptly termed a "strategizing maximizer of social capital" (Entrikin, 2001, p. 696). Therefore it is not surprising that in Casey's narrative, *an autonomous self would strive to overcome the thinness of place by becoming more responsive to geographic differences, rather than through actively pursuing change.* I contend that it is because Casey – like most scholars – has a very clear idea of action as inward-oriented that he fails to see the additional, outward-oriented component, that is that the body/self has the capability *to actively alter place and alter itself through the vehicle of an altered place.* Indeed, as individual subjects, we have the capacity and desire to *actively create* those "thick" places in which our selves can thrive and flourish. This is where the Chinese Internet (as virtual place-world) comes in – which I contend is so extensive and diverse *because* there is a lack of alternatives for personal enrichment in urban China's physical place-worlds.

Meaningful interpretation of lived subjectivity and agency rooted in the independent subject starts not from a universal conception of the subject, but rather by asking how we might understand a particular form of intentional subjectivity based on lived experience of the subject, through the study of an isolable, place-dependent practices, conducted by individual, intentional netizens ('free subjects'), rooted in an amalgamation of life in everyday (urban) China as well as its cyberspaces. When engaging the online, 'writing about' the world is intricately related to 'writing' the world. This way of seeing allows us to comprehend that cultural changes are not only on the way, they can also be seen through the Chinese-language Internet. Doing so allows us to appreciate that cyberspace contains, within its structure, the tools that allow for discontent and autonomy, dissent and resistance to representational manipulation and hegemonic repression – and also, as the recent National Security Agency scandals in the United States remind us, the tools to perpetuate repression.

Our human (and scholarly) capacity to envision depends on our ability to develop a phenomenal consciousness based on phenomenal experiences, that is, to make things known to our senses. The realities of place-based experiences are too varied to be consistent with any meta-narrative. While the 'network' has been identified as dominant organizing principle for society (cf. Castells, 1996, 1997, 1998), individuals continue to craft identities on their own, with one foot in their physical and the other in their virtual everyday lives. The manifold and vigorous online worlds that are developing in China are a perfect venue to scrutinize this.

In the various chapter analyses reflecting the empirical complexities of a current state of affairs, it becomes evident that engaging (with) the Internet is not only about *power* but to a significant extent about *reflexivity* and *autonomy*. Reflexively and autonomously, myriad Chinese netizens woke up and smelled the coffee. They reacted to and rid themselves of the imposed flattening of their physical place-worlds. They took action and shifted their focus from altering themselves (Lefebvre's 'social existence') to fit their surroundings to actively altering their surroundings (their 'spatial existence') and build an alternative and thicker place-world: the Chinese Internet. We as scholars should follow their lead – by continuing to deconstruct the reductionist structural power rhetoric prevalent in related academic discourse, in order to grasp what happened that hampered our understandings and scholarly intentionalities. Available knowledge about the Chinese Internet can be remixed, that is combined and recombined, endlessly. New knowledge, however, hinges on new ways of seeing, and thus on the recognition of the overlooked, silenced, marginal, and on the intentional agency of individual actors that are actively remixing their everyday lives in their cyburban place-worlds. These hybrid spaces are important as they make (conceptual) space for the interplay between the online and the offline across cities in China today.

The value of the ensuing narrative lies in offering a new way of seeing that allows for the revelation that the personal can be political, that society can emerge from – and be transformed through – individual action, without the need to coordinate and deliberate, or even be 'social' in an old-fashioned way. For China's netizens, the Internet has turned public speech into a daily act, and has thereby profoundly changed Chinese society. We should be prepared to find that change may come not through one revolutionary figure (China had that already) but through masses of young Chinese growing up in a cyburban civil sphere that is their fountain of ideas; a sphere with the capacity to empower them to make thinking expression – or eventually even solidaristic civic engagement – a regular habit.

We need to locate Chinese society in online spaces, to grasp in what ways the newly emerging hybrid spaces create shared meanings that are different from traditional culture and politics. These spaces are not less place based or a-historical, but the opposite, with thicker places permeated with meanings that are created by knowledgeable individual agents who find themselves living in specific places and circumstances that provide the context not only for their authorial idiosyncrasies but also for grasping the importance of individual thoughts and ideas. These emerging shared meanings can then help us grasp linkages between ideas and social transformation.

Understanding such linkages would then open up new trajectories for scrutinizing what kind of societal transformation is likely to occur in China. Of course the Internet is not a conduit to freedom per se; we need to look at individual agency, the roles intellectuals feel themselves capable of playing and actually play, and the institutional context (cf. Michael, 2000). At the same time, the act of 'being online' is not a solitary activity limited to cyberspace. It also has profound implications in the physical sphere: fostering self-expression, improving the critical apparatus, broadening one's views, taking other people's thoughts and ideas seriously, forging relationships, shared values and meanings, and new forms of institutions. Even if the majority of educated urban Chinese are not interested in overt movements for political change, this does not relegate them to the status of docile, entertainment-chasing consumers. Arguably, there can be no political subversion without preceding intellectual subversion, and only those who query dominant representations can engage in creating autonomous critical projects that depart from the orthodoxies promoted by the Chinese party-state. Ultimately, any societal transformation that is achieved without such a radical project is futile. It seems that China's netizens are well aware of this.

As Hannah Arendt observed when she interviewed Germans in 1950, people living in a dictatorship are incapable of recognizing reality (Arendt, 1977). A dictator has the capacity to turn lies into truth and vice versa, so what is important is no longer the truth but the dictator's opinion. Opinions replace facts. Dependency replaces autonomy. Facts are represented and treated as mere opinion. Although China may not fit the typical definition of a dictatorship, this emphasis on 'mere opinions' is still widespread in China. For example, virtually all critical Western media reporting on China is disparaged either as mere opinion or as having an underlying agenda. Yet with the onset of social media a focus on 'facts' and 'truth' is slowly becoming a trend, and China's bloggers and microbloggers are the trendsetters. It seems that the individual subject, through online diversity, may be capable of *action*, through overcoming the sensorial and spiritual impoverishment of (dictatorial) modernity, in which single-sensory phenomena are often accepted as 'real'. In the next section, I attempt to provide a preliminary link between this form of empowerment and issues of individual consciousness and agency.

Consciousness – agency for the Internet age

In cyberspace, we often see experiences as text: as the intentional expression of *thoughts and ideas*, and therefore as free and consciously reflected activities that underlie all discourse and action rooted in *agency*. While all discursive practices encourage people to shape their identities, active online participation requires explicit "linguistic acts of self-positioning" (Poster, 1999, p. 221). It is through such actions that individuals read and interpret communications and respond to them by shaping and transmitting articulated, textualized linguistic acts of their own.

Yet "the concept of 'agency' is difficult to interpret, as it combines action, mediation and power" (Kluitenberg, 2006). Furthermore,

> New hybrid spaces must be deliberately 'designed' to create free spaces within which the subject can withdraw himself, temporarily, from spatial determination. Given the power politics and the enormous strategic and economic interests involved, and the associated demands for security and control, it is clear that these free spaces will not come about by themselves or as a matter of course.
>
> (Kluitenberg, 2006, p. 14)

Pace Kluitenberg, *I find that agency – individual or shared – is to be understood not merely as a conduit through which greater structural forces are played out, but rather as the human facility to engage in meaningful intentional action.* This engagement enhances the capacity to influence events and create change in our own lives and beyond. *Human agents are then not mere recipients but interpreters and expressionists of information.* "Agents are normally able, if asked, to provide discursive interpretations of the nature of, and the reasons for, the behaviour in which they engage" (Giddens, 1991, p. 35). This authorial agency is what creates ideas and thoughts that are able to *influence*, that is wield transformative power over, subsequent discourse and action.

This individual agency is corroborated also by Donna Haraway, author of *Manifesto for Cyborgs*, who wrote that "[l]iberation rests on the construction of the consciousness, the imaginative apprehension, of oppression, and so of possibility" (Haraway, 1991, p. 149). Offering the new category 'cyborg', she defines it as a creature both real and imagined, born of differences, blurred boundaries, and conflicting multiplicity. For Haraway, the cyborg is formed as "a matter of fiction and lived experience [. . .] a fiction mapping of our social and bodily reality" (1991, p. 191). With this view, she puts forward a new way of thinking about how subjectivity is constituted that does not obliterate the authority of the subject. This flies in the face of the dominant narrative that subjectivity is something already there and thus to be discovered and excavated, rather than something constructed. In a Chinese context, Tai finds that

> [t]here has emerged a growing body of autonomous individuals who are able to develop independent opinions and consciousness free from the sphere of state influence, and they regularly contribute to online communications in debates and deliberations through their own writings.
>
> (2006, p. 290)

As Eric Paras (2006) shows in his seminal book *Foucault 2.0: Beyond Power and Knowledge*, the focus of Foucault's inquiries shifted from the "society of surveillance" (cf. Foucault, 1979), to the relation of the individual to herself. Paras argues convincingly that Foucault's untimely death and his lack of publishing major works during the last eight years of his life diffused the clarity with which Foucault moved towards the study of the subject as an independent phenomenon, as individuals constitute independent loci of experience, located firmly outside of mechanisms of power. Instead of power as the only guiding principle, autonomy and reflexivity emerged as the characteristics of a Foucauldian subject that was empowered to shape its own existence – in other words that possessed the liberty of action and was thus endowed with a basic humanity based in individual freedom. Conceptually, Foucault relied upon the deployment of what Paras terms a "prediscursive subject: that is, a subjective nucleus that precedes any practices that might be said to construct it, and indeed one that freely chooses among those practices" (2006, p. 14). This opposes Foucault's own former view that individuality is completely controlled by power, and that we are individualized by and through power itself (cf. Foucault, 1980). It also endows human individuality with free, independent subjectivity outside the mechanisms of power.

Granted, Foucault himself labored to undermine the ideas of liberty, individualism, "human rights", and the thinking subject, before he abandoned this hard structuralist position in the early 1980s. Yet, instead of welcoming the resurgence of a free and conscious subject capable of autonomous action and expression into the academic canon, many scholars ignore the inconvenient and messy subjectivity that is based on any possibility of autonomous activity of consciousness. They instead insist on the existence of a meaning-producing 'system' based on anonymous discourse, happening as a series of interconnected relations in which the elements (people and things) are a matter of indifference. Such practice may produce 'data' that can be 'analyzed', but it needs to be complemented by a scholarly outlook on individual action and agency that heeds the existence of a free and intentional subject imbued with autonomous consciousness.

To establish a connection between these abstract ruminations and the Chinese Internet, it is useful to consider Foucault's fascination with the Iranian Revolution of 1978–79. He said in a 1979 interview:

> In rising up, the Iranians said to themselves (and perhaps this is the soul of uprisings): "we must change, certainly, the regime. . . . But above all, we *must change ourselves*. Our way of being, our relation to others, to things, to eternity, to God, etc., all must be completely changed, and *there won't be any real revolution save on the condition of this radical change in our experience*."
>
> (Foucault, 1979, cited from Paras, 2006, p. 155, emphasis in original)

This statement reveals striking parallels between Iran and China. Seen through Foucault's eyes, the Iranians' craving for personal freedom and revolutionary change was firmly connected with their desire to effect their own self-transformation rooted in new experiences. Based on my own experiences living in China during much of the 2000's, the same appears to be true for Chinese: instead of an immanent totality-producing individual subject as a result of some functional principles, *it is the individual consciousness of autonomous Chinese rooted in everyday life experiences that reconfigure the mechanisms of power, autonomy, and reflexivity*. This reconfiguration can ultimately lead to an aspiration for active self-transformation and the transformation of their surroundings (cf. Marolt, 2008).

Many Chinese netizens hold the opinion that the best way they can make a difference in the physical world is by doing a good job at writing in the blogosphere (Marolt, 2008), including Weibo-style microblogs and other social media. In other words, they are 'going public' because they think that they have something meaningful to say. Altering one's everyday surroundings means taking charge of one's life. Any such endeavor requires and enhances the capacity for free and critical counter-hegemonic thinking. Either implicit or explicit, the chapters in this volume show that China's Internet provides the public space where this capacity can be nurtured, in an environment permeated with heterogeneous diversity that fosters engagement with ones' everyday surroundings. After all, articulating one's thoughts – what George Konrad and I. Szelenyi (1979) call "the art of communicating words" – has always been conducive to critical thinking. Yet only if individuals realize the concreteness of their mental grounding in cyberurban place-worlds, and their capacity for real agency and action, can they set out to actively alter place and alter themselves through the vehicle of an altered place. After all, "[s]ocial relations of production have a social as well as a spatial existence, thus space is a medium from which we can interpret how a change of spatial existence is a change of social existence" (Lefebvre, 1991, p. 129).

In this sense, a critical 'citizen' or 'netizen' becomes more than a mere transmitter of knowledge. She is first of all an individual whose abilities and talents go beyond the reflection, refraction, or diffraction of prior learning. Thus "[k]nowledge will not become a collective concern on all levels (from that of pupils and students to that of the entire society) if individuality is stifled" (Lefebvre, 1969, p. 156). *If we undervalue the individual agency upon which such knowledge is based, then we simplify and stifle the critical apparatus necessary to assess in what ways individual expression turns into collective political action*; which transforms a given society based on creative thoughts and ideas, rather than on empirical-rationalist, that is (scientifically) measurable observations. In the context of Chinese Internet studies, I thus argue that it is necessary to further extend scholarly emphases from the technocratic toward the critical, and toward internally – as well as externally – accountable political agency.

What is happening in Online China is not so much an organized political event or movement in any traditional (Western) sense; it is rather a new form of collective disturbance that defies conventional categorizations. Unlike 'disturbances' in the past, its avant-garde is not a close-knit group of 'disestablishment intellectuals', dissidents or revolutionaries; it is not even political in any narrowly restrictive sense of the word. The online spaces that make netizens' thoughts and ideas visible are not so much shared efforts towards a common revolutionary cause; instead, they should be interpreted as principled ethical expressions of alternative meanings that are rooted in, and express discontent with, the language of modernization as a dominant political project and schema of social transformation.

Of course, whether China's netizens will effectively challenge party dominance is too early to determine. The vibrancy and engagement of active online writing and discussion, as well as the avant-garde physical networks and new forms of online phenomena and institutions that are forming in the urban cultural scene, suggest this possibility. However, I second Zhou's sentiment that "[a]ny rush to make sweeping predictions will only produce more of the superficial and political fortune-telling type of research that we often encounter in contemporary China studies" (Zhou, 2005, p. 801). Yet we should also not dismiss this possibility while we conduct more in-depth research that enables informed judgment about the potential and actual influence of individual or groups (cf. Zhou, 2005).

The chapters in this volume

The value of the overall narrative presented by the chapters in this volume lies in the revelation that the personal can be political and that society can be transformed through individual action without the need of coordination and deliberation in an old-fashioned way. The chapters indicate that the concept of Chinese politics is changing and that we need to examine the online and offline as mutually constitutive spaces to grasp the ways in which new spaces create shared meanings that are different from traditional politics. The new politics is not less place-based or a-historical, but rather the opposite. It consists of richer hybrid places, permeated with meanings created by knowledgeable individual agents who find themselves in specific places and times that provide the context for their own authorial idiosyncrasies. These agents also grasp the importance of individual and shared meanings directed toward individual and societal transformation. Large parts of China's Internet reflect a substantial disaffection towards politics. However, whatever is happening in China's online spaces may nonetheless allow us to better grasp the smaller but crucial part that is actually creating new political meanings, and to assess how the political is changing alongside Chinese society – both online and offline.

The volume at hand comprises five sections, each containing two 'paired' chapters that 'speak' to each other in different ways.

Section one ("Deliberating online spaces") outlines the state of affairs of Chinese Internet studies and provides alternative ways of seeing and conceptual guidance. Marolt renders the Internet as fountain of ideas imbued with the capacity to augment individual and shared autonomy and highlights the crucial interdependencies between the online and the offline from a geographical perspective and indicates how all change is rooted in individual agency. Herold provides an in-depth analysis of how much published research on the Chinese Internet intricately promotes democracy in China and calls for research into the actual practices and attitudes of China's Internet users and how they construct their own hybrid spaces. In their own respective ways, both introductory chapters encourage transcending conceptually the artificial dichotomies between the online and offline, virtual and physical, cyber, and urban. Taken together, the two chapters remind us that the process of knowledge-production should not be an end in itself and that, as scholars, we ought to maintain a balance between mutually informative praxis and theory, using empirical insights to open up the imaginaries of conceptual ideas whose intentional elaboration may alter our understanding of empirical phenomena.

Section two ("Defining online spaces") is dedicated to augmenting our definitions of online spaces. Focusing on novel methods of control that go beyond usual interpretations of censorship, Benney argues that political communication on the Internet makes space for increased public awareness and agency, by providing an in-depth account of novel linguistic forms through which the discourse and formal apparatus of "stability maintenance" (*weiwen* 维稳) are identified and subverted. Cockain's chapter provides a welcome complication of simplistic notions of China's trajectory toward inevitable democratization. Drawing on university students' articulations of their opinions of the internet, Cockain argues that microblogging (*weibo* 微博) platforms have changed the ways in which netizens confront and reflect upon social issues, but that online representations of social realities can stimulate disempowerment and disengagement just as well as empowerment and engagement. The Internet might therefore "be a catalyst for control rather than a mechanism for democratization." Taken together, the two chapters serve as reminders that the online and the offline are intricately linked and that the complexity of state-society relations does not diminish once we focus our attention on the virtual sphere. In terms of agency, repression breeds docility but also opens up new avenues of engagement. Interactions between the Chinese party-state and Chinese people ought thus to be viewed in all their empirical complexity, without imposing judgment that puts blinders on our ontological and epistemological ways of seeing.

The third section ("Claiming online spaces") examines how new online media are used strategically to claim the space that lies between online and offline controls. Liu and Yang show how independent candidates for local people's congresses maneuver within and negotiate the cyburban spaces of autonomy that lie between online and offline controls, and how this process helps them sharpen their rhetorical strategies to successfully express and propagate their political views. Drawing on the case of the Wenzhou train crash, Schucher and Bondes use their chapter to point out that even short-lived online debate indicates Chinese people's growing reluctance to accept specific features of China's political system. The two chapters remind us that geography matters when it comes to the rise and decline of online events, and how online discussions are rooted in specific offline spaces (and people).

Section four ("Enjoying online spaces") is zooming in on the entertainment and community-building aspects of Online China. Jin and Herold re-evaluate the new labor practices of 'gold-farming' and the 'water army'. Often rendered as exploited by globalizing processes, skilled individuals are actually using China's cyberspace as locus for entrepreneurial aspirations and community building. Spheres that are often associated with physical labor are extended into virtual space, and practitioners create new meanings and practices through applying their skills and connections to create communities and living spaces of their own, both online and offline. Liu and de Seta examine the international world of 'fansub' groups in which the popularity of foreign language learning leads to mutual engagement and cooperation, thus fostering solidaristic civic engagement across virtual-physical and cultural boundaries.

The last section ("Shaping online spaces") is focused around the relationship between individuals and communities, serving each other's needs in mutual reciprocity. In her chapter, Pang explicates how cyber-communities manage political discussion while constantly negotiating their individual and collective goals. Xia and Kennedy's chapter adopts a novel approach to look at how professional producers of the Chinese Internet, that is people who work in China's Internet industry, using cyberspace to create new forms of agency alongside meaningful, expressive and resistant online spaces. Taken together, the two chapters emphasize how the online spaces are shaped, and how the shape of online spaces allows us to investigate the varied interdependences of individual and collective agency, and remind us that both the creation and population of alternative hybrid spaces and projects transcend the online-offline dichotomy.

I hope that a re-conceptualization of both online and offline China and their networks of relationships as attempted in this volume will allow for a deeper understanding of the importance of the Internet in today's China (and beyond).

References

Arendt, H. (1977). *Between past and future*. New York, NY: Penguin Books.

Arendt, H. (2001). *The human condition*. Albany, NY: State University of New York Press.

Casey, E. S. (2001). Between geography and philosophy: What does it mean to be in the place-world? *Annals of the Association of American Geographers, 91*(4), 683–693.

Castells, M. (1996). *The rise of the network society (The information age, vol. 1)* (2nd ed.). New York, NY: Blackwell.

Castells, M. (1997). *The power of identity (The information age, vol. 2)* (2nd ed.). New York, NY: Blackwell.

Castells, M. (1998). *End of millennium (The information age, vol. 3)* (2nd ed.). New York, NY: Blackwell.

Castells, M. (2012). *Networks of outrage and hope*. Place, ST: Polity Press.

Charmaz, K. (2004). Premises, principle, and practices in qualitative research: Revisiting the foundations. *Qualitative Health Research, 14*(7), 976–993.

Cherot, N., & Murray, M. J. (2002). Postmodern urbanism – Reality or fantasy? *Urban Affairs Review, 37*(3), 432–438.

Debord, G. (1967). *Comments on the society of the spectacle*. New York, NY: Verso.

Entrikin, J. N. (2001). Hiding places. *Annals of the Association of American Geographers, 91*(4), 694–697.

Esarey, A., & Xiao, Q. (2008). Under the radar: Political expression in the Chinese blogosphere. *Asian Survey 38*(5), 752–772.

Foucault, M. (1980). *Power/knowledge: Selected interviews & other writings 1972–1977*. New York, NY: Pantheon Books.

Gardiner, M. E. (2000). *Critiques of everyday life*. New York, NY: Routledge.

Giddens, A. (1991). *Modernity and self-identity: Self and society in the late modern age*. Stanford, CA: Stanford University Press.

Giese, K. (2006). *Challenging party hegemony: Identity work in China's emerging virreal places*. GIGA German Institute for Global and Area Studies, Working Paper 14.

Goffman, E. (1989). On fieldwork. *Journal of Contemporary Ethnography, 18*, 123–132.

Goldfarb, J. C. (1998). *Civility & subversion: The intellectual in democratic society.* Cambridge, UK: Cambridge University Press.

Goldman, M. (2005). *From comrade to citizen: The struggle for political rights in China.* Cambridge, MA: Harvard University Press.

Habermas, J. (1985). *Theory of communicative action, vols. I & II.* Boston, MA: Beacon Press.

Haraway, D. (1991). A cyborg manifesto: Science, technology, and socialist-feminism in the late twentieth century. In D. Haraway (Ed.), *Simians, cyborgs and women: The reinvention of nature* (pp. 149–181). New York, NY: Routledge.

Herold, D. K., & Marolt, P. (2011). *Online society in China: Creating, celebrating, and instrumentalising the online carnival.* New York, NY: Routledge.

Hil, R., & Bessant, J. (1999). SPACED-OUT? Young people's agency, resistance and public space. *Urban Policy and Research, 17*(1), 41–49.

Kluitenberg, E. (2006). The network of waves: Living and acting in a hybrid space. In E. Kluitenberg (Ed.), *Hybrid space: How wireless media mobilize public space* (pp. 7–16). Rotterdam, The Netherlands: NAI Publishers.

Kluver, R. (2008). *The logics of new media and the information society: Finding a theoretical base for understanding the impact of new media on the harmonious society and international relations.* Paper presented at the Beijing Forum: Cultural Diversity, Harmonious Society, and Alternative Modernity: New Media and Social Development, Beijing, China.

Konrad, G., & Szelenyi, I. (1979). *The intellectuals on the road to class power: A sociological study of the role of the intelligentsia in socialism.* New York, NY: Harcourt Brace Jovanovich.

Lachmann, R., Eshelman, R., & Davis, M. (1988). Bakhtin and carnival: Culture as counter-culture. *Cultural Critique, (11)*, 115–152.

Lefebvre, H. (1969). *The explosion: Marxism and the French upheaval.* New York and London: Monthly Review Press.

Lefebvre, H. (1991). *The production of space.* Malden, MA: Blackwell.

MacKinnon, R. (2008). Flatter world and thicker walls? Blogs, censorship and civic discourse in China. *Public Choice, 134*(1–2), 31–46.

Marolt, P. (2008). *Blogging in China: Individual agency, the production of cyburban 'spaces of dissent' in Beijing, and societal transformation in China.* Unpublished dissertation, University of Southern California.

Michael, J. (2000). *Anxious intellects: Academic professionals, public intellectuals, and enlightenment values.* Durham, NC: Duke University Press.

Paras, E. (2006). *Foucault 2.0: Beyond power and knowledge.* New York, NY: Other Press.

Poster, M. (1999). Databases as discourse, or electronic interpellations. In K. Racevskis (Ed.), *Critical essays on Michel Foucault* (pp. 271–285). New York, NY: G. K. Hall & Co.

Qiu, J. L. (2004). The Internet in China: Technologies of freedom in a statist society. In M. Castells (Ed.), *The network society: A Cross-cultural perspective* (pp. 99–124). Northampton, MA: Edward Elgar Publishing.

Tai, Z. (2006). *The Internet in China: Cyberspace and civil society.* New York, NY: Routledge.

Van Dijk, J. A. G. M. (1999). The one-dimensional network society of Manuel Castells. *New media & society, 1*(1), 127–138.

Yu, H. (2006). From active audience to media citizenship: The case of post-Mao China. *Social Semiotics, 16*(2), 303–326.

Yu, H. (2007). Blogging everyday life in Chinese Internet culture. *Asian Studies Review, 31*, 423–433.

Zhao, Y. (2008). *Communication in China: Political economy, power, and conflict*. Lanham, MD: Rowman & Littlefield.

Zhou, Y. (2005). Living on the cyber border: Minjian political writers in Chinese cyberspace. *Current Anthropology, 46*(5), 779–803.

Zhou, Y. (2006). *Historicizing online politics: Telegraphy, the Internet, and political participation in China*. Stanford, CA: Stanford University Press.

2 Users, not netizens

Spaces and practices on the Chinese Internet

David Kurt Herold

In September 2013, the Internet in China appeared to come to a crashing halt following "a stepped up campaign to rein in a forum that's challenged China's censorship regime" (Sanderson & Chen, 2013), during which "Beijing launched a roundup of Chinese bloggers" that "delighted some military hawks" (Yu, 2013). The Chinese government brought in "new legislation that in effect criminalizes online dissent" with a "vague and broad definition of online criminality" (Anderlini, 2013) that "has led to increased self-censorship by some of China's most influential bloggers, chilling political discourse in the country" as it created "an atmosphere of fear" aimed at "making people speak less" (Hancock, 2013).

"Websites and social media have become an essential forum for discussion and the spread of information . . . but authorities have signalled [sic] they are increasing controls and targeting popular users" (Branigan, 2013). Among the Internet users facing increased persecution are "influential rights activists, freelance anticorruption sleuths and even a billionaire entrepreneur" in a "devious attempt to crush normal online expression" (Jacobs, 2013) in "an Online Cultural Revolution" that is "scraping away at our brains" (Bao, 2013). Quite obviously, the Internet in China was in great danger, and Internet users were being silenced *en masse* emptying online spaces of all the voices critical of the Chinese authorities.

Yet,

> even as the Communist Party wages its most forceful crackdown to date against popular and outspoken liberal micro-bloggers, the businesses that provide these microblogging services continue to flourish.
>
> (Larson, 2013)

And

> the mobile client for the Taobao online shopping service has gained 100 million new users in the first half, bringing the total mobile client user base to around 400 million. Meanwhile, the daily active user base on the mobile client jumped by 300 percent year-on-year.
>
> (Mobile & Wireless, 2013)

And China's

> e-commerce market is expected to grow at a breakneck pace of 30 per cent in the next three to five years. . . . Online commerce is an unstoppable tide . . . [as] an estimated 240 million people on the mainland shopped on the internet [and] mainland consumers are much more likely to indulge in online shopping compared with their global peers.
>
> (Ap, 2013)

How to describe the Internet in China and how to discuss the practices of its users? As the examples above demonstrate, much of what is reported about the Internet in China is highly contradictory such as the flourishing of Sina's business despite a crackdown against Sina's Weibo microblogging service, which led Sinocism's Bill Bishop to state that understanding the Internet in China required "cognitive dissonance" (as quoted in Larson, 2013). It is interesting to note, though, that this statement conflates the Internet in China with the *reporting about* the Internet in China and carries with it assumptions about the definition and the meaning of the Internet within society. If a "cognitive dissonance" exists between a crackdown on *political* contents and the growth of *economic* opportunities online then the underlying assumptions must be that much if not most online content is political in nature, that Internet users are primarily (politically oriented) *netizens* (Internet + citizens), and that online spaces serve the function of a public sphere making the emergence of a civil society in China possible.

Based on a recent research project conducted by myself (Herold, 2013b), and supported by a similar project by Qiu and Bu (2013), I argue that most academic research conducted on the Internet in China has been based on similar assumptions and as a result focused on the *political* features and impacts of the Internet as a new technology. As Qiu and Bu (2013, p.147) put it: "Why do overseas researchers care so much about the political consequences?" From the start, the Internet in China has been discussed as a technology whose adoption would inevitably lead to an 'opening up' of China and to its eventual democratization. When a telecommunications team visited China in the early 1990s to discuss the development of China's telco technologies, they concluded that politics was the main problem for technological development in China and that the political situation would change with the introduction of the Internet (Zheng, 1994, p. 241f). This was echoed in a study by Hao, Zhang, and Yu (1996) who argued that there was "the most fundamental conflict . . . between the outlook of the established authorities . . . and media demands for unrestricted freedom of expression".

During the years that followed, politics and the Internet's influence on the Chinese state proved to be a popular topic, with publications every year that asserted that the Internet would definitely change China. Despite the lack of hard evidence, and despite the continuing success of the Chinese Communist Party to arrange itself with the Internet in China and to control the actions of China's Internet users, academic studies continued to study the impact the Internet *had to have* on China's politics (see e.g. Taubman, 1998; Tan, Foster, & Goodman, 1999; Qiu,

2000; Harwit & Clark, 2001; Chase & Mulvenon, 2002; Yang, 2003; Shie, 2004; Lagerkvist, 2005; Tai, 2006; Weber & Jia, 2007; Ernkvist & Strom, 2008; Ma, Webber, & Finlayson, 2009; Gong & Yang, 2010; Esarey & Qiang, 2011; Jiang, 2012; Link & Qiang, 2013).

Academic research on the Internet in China appears determined to assign the Internet the role of promoting democracy in China, or as James Leibold (2011) phrased it, "mainstream analysis in the West continues to stress its revolutionary potential in China. . . . A perverse kind of 'digital Orientalism' . . . prevents us in the West from asking the same sort of difficult questions about the internet's impact in China that we have long asked ourselves" (p. 1036). While nobody would seriously argue that the main purpose of the Internet in Europe or America is the provision of support for democracy, this appears to be the consensus among researchers of the Chinese Internet, which may be based more on wishful thinking than on data about Internet use in China.

> The defining fact about the Internet is that it is a network, a collection of nodes connected by ties. Any node on the Internet is accessible from any other node, and there are no differences between the ties that connect the nodes: all hyperlinks are equal. In liberal democracies, this many-to-many structure and the informality of online social relations are taken to mean that cyberspace allows people to freely engage in social and political exchanges with others who share common interests.
>
> (O'Neil, 2009, p. 1)

In the previous volume edited by Peter Marolt and myself (Herold & Marolt, 2011) the different chapters already demonstrated that the Chinese Internet contained a wealth of sites and a diversity of users that made political interpretations difficult without recourse to broad explanatory models such as the Bakhtinian carnival in all its wildness (Herold, 2011; see also Herold, 2012). In the current volume, the different chapters illustrate even better how individual Internet users largely live their online lives by working *around* government strictures, not by fighting them, thus *creating their own hybrid spaces* out of a mix of online and offline settings that are largely free from government interference – not as sites of protest, but as sites for amusement that allow people to ignore (and forget) the government and its power over offline spaces.

While Leibold's conclusion is – in my opinion – unnecessarily pessimistic about the value of non-political content of the Internet, I do agree with his assessment of the relative importance of political and non-political contents:

> The internet has certainly created new spaces for individual self-expression and interest-group mobilization. But more empirical, comparative, and cross-disciplinary research is required to determine whether Chinese netizens are employing these new platforms in fundamentally different ways from their global counterparts, and the precise implications of these changes. Might the passage of time reveal that the digital activism required to ignite a prairie fire

of revolutionary, democratic change in China is being snuffed out by the dull flicker and gentle tapping of millions of isolated, individual computers and their smiley-faced bloggers?

(Leibold, 2011, p. 14)

The Chinese Internet is filled with content produced by its users in attempts to create spaces for themselves in which to express their ideas, wishes, hopes. Politics are largely irrelevant to these spaces and their creators – just as most non-Chinese Internet users do not seem to care much for politics, but this does not render these spaces unimportant – quite the reverse. Chinese Internet users appear to be blending online and offline sites to create highly individual, hybrid spaces in which to live their lives and to explore practices outside the strict regulation of ordinary life in China. Their primary driver is not political motivations, but appears to be the wish to become *apolitical* and live beneath the notice of state authorities, exploring the freedom the Internet grants them. The techno-utopian perspective of non-Chinese academics is thus confronted with the escapist perspective of Chinese Internet users. What might be important for an understanding of contemporary China and its relationship with the Internet is not Postman's (1993) vision of society ruled by technology, but his description of humans being distracted from politics and other important issues affecting their lives by an over-abundance of mediated messages (2006), something Walter Benjamin discussed in his essay on the function and uses of works of art in the 1920s (1969, see also Herold, 2013a). While the former book by Postman has been applied exhaustively, the latter has largely been ignored, as it does not fit the prevailing discourses celebrating the liberating effects of the Internet on autocratic systems.

We need more studies that look at how people in China are using the Internet to do what they want to do, that is in what *practices* are Internet user in China engaging and how are they constructing their own hybrid spaces out of offline and online lives in relation to these practices (Hobart, 2000, p. 41f). To ask leading questions: Is politics and the pursuit of democracy *really* the most important issue for Chinese Internet users, or are they also engaging in other practices online? Are Internet users in China *really* focused on politics, or on having fun online? As Qiu and Bu conclude:

> Overseas and domestic publications are fundamentally similar in their tendency to stress macro (national and global) units of analysis and pay insufficient attention to the micro and meso. We suspect that this persistent structural imbalance might have caused a deeper problem in China ICT studies, namely the lack of diversity, especially in using social development perspectives.
>
> (2013, p.148)

Young Chinese who constitute the majority of Internet users in China (CNNIC, 2013, p. 16) are not going online to make political statements or to fight for their political rights. Instead, they often go online, because "there's nowhere else to go. . . . They are excited about the Web . . . because it gives them a wide variety of social and entertainment options" (Barboza, 2010). The Internet offers cheap entertainment in a country where the ticket prices for cinemas or the entrance fees for night clubs have sky-rocketed, while also allowing young people to engage in fun activities at the same time as they are socializing with their friends. As Fong (2009) put it, "for the vast majority of Chinese, Internet means play, not work" – or politics.

> For Chinese youth the virtual world provides a venue for expressing autonomy that is not available to them in the real world. In the virtual world, Chinese youth can do as they choose without concern about the impact of their behavior on others.
>
> (Jackson et al., 2008, p. 285)

Chinese Internet users appear to see the Internet as an escape of sorts from their offline lives (Herold, 2012), a place in which to be 'free', or at least less constricted than in offline China – even though this may only be a fiction promoted by the Chinese authorities, as many young Chinese appear to have contradictory emotions regarding the Internet and their relationship with it (Herold, 2013a). The actual attitudes of Chinese people towards the Internet and the practices resulting from those attitudes are something to which research has so far paid far too little attention. As a brief example discussion of Chinese practices on the auction site Taobao can demonstrate, the practices and beliefs of Chinese Internet users are worth looking into in greater depth.

Practices of users: a quick look at Taobao

The Chinese auction site Taobao was founded in 2003 to challenge the entry of EBay into the Chinese market. It has often been regarded as a copycat effort, but different from other such local 'copies' of international websites, for example Renren for Facebook, Youku for YouTube, Taobao managed to be successful in direct competition with the 'original' to the extent that EBay left the Chinese market in 2006. Taobao has continued to be successful "because it really understood Chinese customers" (Wang, 2010), which means that Taobao and its customers can be studied as exemplars of Chinese cultural preferences online. A comparison of the choices made by Chinese Internet users when interacting on Taobao thus reveals many possible starting points for research into the actual practices of Internet users in China.

Even a comparison of the most basic activity on Taobao and on EBay – the purchase of an item offered for sale – shows differences in the practices of the users of these two auction sites. On EBay, the purchase of an item is very straight forward, with a minimum of interaction between buyers and sellers. The buyers search the site for items they wish to purchase, decide which of the offered items to bid for or to purchase outright. A click on a virtual button initiates the transaction, after which the buyer is asked to pay for the item, preferably using EBay's own payment system (Paypal). Once the seller has received the money, he or she will then ship the item as soon as possible to the address provided by the buyer. Once the buyer has received the item, he or she is asked to rate the seller, and be rated as a buyer, which completes the transaction. Throughout the entire transaction, there is no direct contact between buyers and sellers, unless they need to address a problem that requires cooperation between them.

On Taobao, the process is very different and requires far more direct interaction between buyers and sellers, as well as a negotiation about the actual item the buyer wants to purchase – which may or may not be the originally advertised one. Once a buyer identifies an item he or she wishes to purchase, the buyer will contact the different sellers offering the item using the built-in chat client to ask questions about the item, delivery choices, as well the possibilities for a discount. Sellers are expected to be reachable throughout the time their products are advertised, and if a seller does not reply to questions a buyer poses, he or she will lose potential buyers, as other buyers notice the unanswered question(s).

Once contact is established between buyers and sellers, the buyer will ask a number of questions to determine whether the item in question is really what the buyer is looking for, while the seller will advise the buyer which item suits his or her purposes best. For example, a woman is planning to go on a winter holiday and needs a warm down jacket for this holiday. She looks on Taobao and identifies a number of sellers who have suitable jackets. After contacting them, she decides on one of the sellers, as he appears to have the widest selection of styles, colors, and sizes, while also having received a large number of positive reviews by other buyers. At this point, the seller provides her with his mobile phone number, and the conversation continues offline. She tells the seller that she is planning to go on a winter holiday in an area with temperatures down to 25 degrees Celsius below freezing. The seller immediately points out that the original item she wished to purchase is not 'a good enough' jacket for this application, and recommends a 'better' jacket to her, which can withstand the cold better. The outward appearance of the two jackets is the same, but the down filling is apparently very different.

After the item is agreed upon, the seller and the buyer negotiate the price of the product including shipping costs, before the buyer returns to Taobao to transact the purchase online. The buyer then sends the money to an escrow service, which will hold the money until the buyer signals that the purchased item has arrived and is in good repair. If the buyer does not wish to return the item, he or she will then release the money to the seller, at which point the transaction is complete.

The entire transaction on Taobao is thus a combination of online and offline elements turning a purchase on an online auction site into a blended version of a Chinese market purchase – including the in-depth discussion of the quality of the items and the haggling over the price. Taobao itself serves as a virtual marketplace, which is not 'real' enough, however, for the purchase to be completed entirely on the site. The buyers and sellers appear to prefer the 'real' contact over the mobile phone before entering into an agreement.

To use the terminology of this volume, through their practices sellers and buyers *create* hybrid spaces in which to transact business, using both online as well as offline affordances to ensure a smooth purchase. Taobao as an auction site is almost incidental in the transaction, except that it is the largest such site in China. In stark contrast to EBay, Taobao is *not* required to ensure the trustworthiness of sellers and buyers; instead the site is merely the forum for them to meet and establish contact. Trust is based on the blending of online and offline spaces, and the mobile phone serves to provide a 'real' contact between the two parties, and a handle on the actual, offline location of both the seller and the buyer in case anything goes wrong with their deal, and it becomes necessary for one of them to track down the other – offline.

The evaluation of the relative trustworthiness of a webpage, chat messages, and mobile phone contacts raises interesting questions about trust, 'the Internet', mobile phones, and the embedding or domestication of different technologies into Chinese culture. How 'real' is the Internet and associated technologies? How 'real' are people one meets online? What constitutes a 'real' contact between people? Why is a mobile phone contact 'more real' than an online chat? Is online trading or e-commerce possible in China, or does it always require an offline connection between the concerned parties? How much of what happens online are 'true' online events, and what is the difference between such online events and offline interactions employing Information and Communication Technologies (ICTs) as mere tools of communication similar to what appears to happen on Taobao? Should 'the Internet' be studied as online 'spaces', or as components of a new form of hybrid spaces, or as an extension of offline spaces? How much can be learned about current Chinese society and culture from online sources alone? What do Chinese Internet users think about 'the Internet' and their usage of different ICTs?

What I want to suggest is currently at stake in Chinese Internet Research, is not whether or not the Internet in China can be used for political purposes, or whether or not it even has political meaning. Those particular issues have been asked, discussed, and answered abundantly by academic researchers. Instead, I would like to point to the many overlooked questions around the Chinese Internet as deserving more attention than they have so far received.

Yes, the Internet has had a measurable impact on government authorities at all levels over the past 10 years – but why do individual Internet users participate in online protests and what does their involvement mean to them? Yes, online protests have managed to get a number of corrupt officials punished – but why have some protests been successful, while others have failed to get anywhere? Yes, China's Internet users are very active in employing e.g. Human Flesh Search Engines to seek out and punish 'bad' people – but why are studies on the Chinese Internet only able to refer to the same few cases of online activism? Yes, it is well known that China has around 600 million active Internet users – but why do researchers continuously focus on the few thousands who are active politically?

What do Chinese Internet users do when they are not engaged in political activism?

Exploring hybrid spaces

The chapters collected for this volume all explore the hybrid spaces in which Chinese people live who use the Internet, and attempt to push the boundaries of research into 'the Chinese Internet' by focusing on the interactions of individual Internet users inhabiting the hybrid spaces between online and offline China. The authors explored online China from multiple new perspectives, thus opening up avenues for future research.

Jonathan Benney outlines in his chapter how Internet users in China are projecting an image of passivity towards the control mechanisms of government authorities, while being very active in the pursuit of leisure and entertainment online. They thus should be studied less as active resisters of government authority and more as passive (and cynical) evaders of government notice.

Alex Cockain also argues that the main strategy used by young Internet users in China when confronted with negative aspects of the Internet is one of retreat or evasion. Their aim appears to be not to be noticed, but to live their online lives without interference either from other Internet users or from government authorities – controlled networking without too much interaction.

Liu and Yang present a study that shows how independent political candidates in China have de-politicized their own online presences in order to avoid official notice. Their campaigns for political office thus became apolitical online activities supporting their offline engagement with local people, but not overt political threats to the existing power structures.

Schucher and Bondes' chapter demonstrates how even a straight-forward online protest about the safety of China's railway network has to be interpreted as a multi-facetted interaction within a complex network of relationships between many different actors and interest groups both inside and outside of government.

In their chapter, Jin and Herold argue that professional Internet users in China are not mere employees doing their duty, but instead people with complex skill sets enabling them to live rich, 'blended' lives of their own choosing that blur the line between work and play, online and offline.

Similarly, Liu and de Seta demonstrate that online engagement in a fansubbing site serves multiple purposes for the users who combine online and offline interests to achieve their own goals beyond those of the community they joined.

Pang's chapter offers a study of the self-regulation strategies of an online community interested in political discussions, but conscious of the need to survive the gaze of the government censors to avoid financial ruin in a fiercely competitive market.

The chapter by Xia and Kennedy discusses how Internet industry workers in China create online spaces for their own self-expression in a negotiation between the demands of the state and of their employers. Their employment in the industry allows them to become agents of their own entertainment, while avoiding to engage with outside political or economic demands.

The editors and authors hope that this volume will serve to open up alternative spaces for research into the Chinese Internet and its users beyond the dichotomies of state versus netizens, censorship versus resistance, etc. The Internet accessed and used by people living in the People's Republic of China is at least as rich and diversified as the Internet accessed by people elsewhere – and just as irreverent and apolitical. It is time research *into* the Internet in China reflects this reality.

References

Anderlini, J. (2013, September 16). China intensifies internet crackdown. *Financial Times.* Retrieved September 25, 2013, from http://www.ft.com/cms/s/0/651b7022-1eb7-11e3-b80b-00144feab7de.html#axzz2fs6Cjpdr

Ap, T. (2013, September 25). Internet shopping to soar in China. *South China Morning Post.* Retrieved September 25, 2013, from http://www.scmp.com/business/china-business/article/1317149/internet-shopping-soar-china

Bao, T. (2013, September 12). China's rumors crackdown heralding an "Online Cultural Revolution." *Radio Free Asia.* Retrieved September 25, 2013, from http://www.rfa.org/english/commentaries/baotong/cultural-revolution-09122013103217.html

Barboza, D. (2010). For Chinese, Web is way to entertainment. *The New York Times* Retrieved July 28, 2014, from http://www.nytimes.com/2010/04/19/technology/19chinaweb.html

Benjamin, W. (1969). The work of art in the age of mechanical reproduction (H. Zohn, Trans.). In H. Arendt (Ed.), *Illuminations* (pp. 217–251). New York, NY: Schocken Books.

Branigan, T. (2013, September 17). Chinese Communist party intensifies online crackdown. *The Guardian.* Retrieved September 25, 2013, from http://www.theguardian.com/world/2013/sep/17/chinese-communist-party-online-crackdown

Chase, M. S., & Mulvenon, J. C. (2002). *You've got dissent!: Chinese dissident use of the Internet and Beijing's counter-strategies.* Washington, DC: Rand Corporation.

China Internet Network Information Center (CNNIC). (2013). *The 32nd statistical survey report on Internet development in China.* Beijing, China: CNNIC.

Ernkvist, M., & Strom, P. (2008). Enmeshed in games with the government: Governmental policies and the development of the Chinese online game industry. *Games and Culture, 3*(1), 98–126.

Esarey, A., & Qiang, X. (2011). Digital communication and political change in China. *International Journal of Communication, 5,* 298–319.

Fong, C. (2009). 'Sea turtles' powering China's Internet growth. *CNN.* Retrieved July 28, 2014, from http://edition.cnn.com/2009/TECH/09/30/digitalbiz.redwired/index.html

Gong, H., & Yang, X. (2010). Digitized parody: The politics of egao in contemporary China. *China Information, 24*(1), 3–26.

Hancock, T. (2013, September 21). Blog crackdown chills China's political debate. *Fox News.* Retrieved September 25, 2013, from http://www.foxnews.com/world/2013/09/21/blog-crackdown-chills-china-political-debate/

Hao, X., Zhang, K., & Yu, H. (1996). The Internet and information control: The case of China. *The Electronic Journal of Communication, 6*(2). Retrieved July 31, 2014, from http://www.cios.org/EJCPUBLIC/006/2/00625.html

Harwit, E., & Clark, D. (2001). Shaping the Internet in China: Evolution of political control over network infrastructure and content. *Asian Survey, 41*(3), 377–408.

Herold, D. K. (2011). Noise, spectacle, politics: Carnival in Chinese cyberspace. In D. K. Herold & P. Marolt (Eds.), *Online Society in China: Creating, celebrating, and instrumentalising the online carnival* (pp. 1–19). New York, NY: Routledge.

Herold, D. K. (2012). Escaping the world: A Chinese perspective on virtual worlds. *Journal of Virtual Worlds Research, 5*(2). Retrieved July 31, 2014, from https://journals.tdl.org/jvwr/index.php/jvwr/article/view/6206

Herold, D. K. (2013a). Captive artists: Chinese university students talk about the Internet. *SSRN*. Retrieved July 31, 2014, from http://ssrn.com/abstract=2259020 doi:10.2139/ssrn.2259020

Herold, D. K. (2013b). Through the looking glass: Twenty years of research into the Chinese Internet. *SSRN*. Retrieved July 31, 2014, from http://ssrn.com/abstract=2259045. doi:http://dx.doi.org/10.2139/ssrn.2259045

Herold, D. K., & Marolt, P. (Eds.). (2011). *Online Society in China: Creating, celebrating, and instrumentalising the online carnival.* New York, NY: Routledge.

Hobart, M. (2000). *After culture: Anthropology as radical metaphysical critique.* Yogyakarta, Indonesia: Duta Wacana University Press.

Jacobs, A. (2013, September 23). China's crackdown prompts outrage over boy's arrest. *The New York Times.* Retrieved September 25, 2013, from http://www.nytimes.com/2013/09/24/world/asia/crackdown-on-dissent-in-china-meets-online-backlash-after-boys-arrest.html?_r=0

Jiang, M. (2012). Chinese Internet events. In A. Esarey & R. Kluver (Eds.), *The Internet in China: Online business, information, distribution and social connectivity.* New York, NY: Berkshire Publishing.

Lagerkvist, J. (2005). The rise of online public opinion in the People's Republic of China. *China: An International Journal, 3*(1), 119–130.

Larson, C. (2013, September 17). China's Internet companies battered by censorship – and yet thriving financially. *Businessweek.* Retrieved September 25, 2013, from http://www.businessweek.com/articles/2013-09-17/chinas-internet-companies-battered-by-censorship-and-yet-thriving-financially

Leibold, J. (2011). Blogging alone: China, the Internet, and the democratic illusion? *The Journal of Asian Studies, 70*(4), 1023–1041.

Link, P., & Qiang, X. (2013). From "fart people" to citizens. *Journal of Democracy, 24*(1), 79–85.

Ma, J., Webber, M., & Finlayson, B. L. (2009). On sealing a lakebed: Mass media and environmental democratisation in China. *Environmental Science & Policy, 12*(1), 71–83.

Mobile & Wireless. (2013, August 26). Taobao adds 100 mln mobile client users in H1. *Telecompaper.* Retrieved September 25, 2013, from http://www.telecompaper.com/news/taobao-adds-100-mln-mobile-client-users-in-h1-962875

O'Neil, M. (2009). *Cyberchiefs: Authority and autonomy in online tribes.* London and New York: Pluto Press.

Postman, N. (1993). *Technopoly.* New York, NY: Vintage Books.

Postman, N. (2006). *Amusing ourselves to death: Public discourse in the age of show business.* New York, NY: Penguin.

Qiu, J. L. (2000). Virtual censorship in China: Keeping the gate between the cyberspaces. *International Journal of Communications Law and Policy, 4*, 1–25.

Qiu, J. L., & Bu, W. (2013). China ICT studies: A review of the field, 1989–2012. *China Review, 13*(2), 123–152.

Sanderson, H., & Chen, L. Y. (2013, September 16). China reins in popular voices with new microblog controls. *Bloomberg*. Retrieved September 25, 2013, from http://www. bloomberg.com/news/2013-09-15/china-reins-in-popular-online-voices-with-new-microblog-controls.html

Shie, T. R. (2004). The tangled web: Does the internet offer promise or peril for the Chinese Communist Party? *Journal of Contemporary China, 13*(40), 523–540.

Tai, Z. (2006). *The Internet in China: Cyberspace and civil society.* London, UK: Routledge.

Tan, Z. A., Foster, W., & Goodman, S. (1999). China's State-coordinated Internet infrastructure. *Communications of the ACM, 42*(6), 44–52.

Taubman, G. (1998). A not-so World Wide Web: The Internet, China, and the challenges to nondemocratic rule. *Political Communication, 15*(2), 255–272.

Wang, H. H. (2010, September 12). How EBay failed in China. *Forbes*. Retrieved January 11, 2014, from http://www.forbes.com/sites/china/2010/09/12/how-ebay-failed-in-china/

Weber, I., & Jia, L. (2007). Internet and self-regulation in China: The cultural logic of controlled commodification. *Media, Culture & Society, 29*(5), 772–789.

Yang, G. (2003). The co-evolution of the Internet and civil society in China. *Asian Survey, 43*(3), 405–422.

Yu, M. (2013, September 19). Inside China: Internet crackdown on opinion leaders. *Washington Times*. Retrieved September 25, 2013, from http://www.washingtontimes.com/ news/2013/sep/19/inside-china-internet-crackdown-on-opinion-leaders/

Zheng, C. (1994). Opening the digital door: Computer networking in China. *Telecommunications Policy, 18*(3), 236–242.

Part II
Defining online spaces

3 "The corpses were emotionally stable"

Agency and passivity on the Chinese Internet

Jonathan Benney

The exercise of discipline over the Internet by the Chinese party-state is very well known. The state restricts access to many types of information and harshly punishes those who gain access to it. This state discipline is observable from a national level, where a "Great Firewall" blocks access to websites and Internet services, to a local level, where Internet cafes are closely monitored and supervised by police. While it is very difficult to assess, from the perspective of the party-state, what it would take for this policy to be considered successful or effective, it is undeniable that the discipline of the state shapes online life in China.

The consequences of this situation have had interesting effects on the Chinese Internet. In a complex, pluralist, internationalized medium such as the Internet, discipline has its limits. Strategies of supervision and discipline can be avoided or subverted by users who have sufficient knowledge or desire to do so. The methods of circumventing discipline can be technical, such as the use of virtual private networks (VPNs), or based in the manipulation of discourse, such as the invention of coded words to avoid censorship. The high level of circumvention of online discipline necessitates the study of methods of control other than supervision, censorship, and punishment. Børge Bakken (2000) suggests that, in China, the "disciplinary society" can be complemented with an analysis of the "exemplary society" (pp. 5–6). The disciplinary society depends on the classic Foucauldian techniques of surveillance, discipline, and punishment; the exemplary society interacts with the world of discipline by providing models of good and desirable behavior which, through sufficient education and inculcation, individuals will eventually come to emulate.

This chapter argues that, in contrast to the offline world, the Chinese party-state has been less able to develop coherent *non*-disciplinary strategies to control Internet use and users. In parallel with this, the development by citizens of distinctive methods of Internet use – symbols, images, and linguistic techniques in particular – has had the dual effect of subverting the online discipline of the state and of creating netizens' own models of behavior. This analysis is sited contextually within the ongoing debates about stability in China. The doctrine of social stability has been a lynchpin of state discourse in China since the beginning of the reform period: in Bakken's terms, stability is now a form of state exemplar, applied to individuals' emotional lives as well as to the Chinese economy and the totality of Chinese society. From the mid-2000s onwards, the development of a formal stability maintenance (*weiwen*) apparatus, which has appropriated some of the functions of the regular law enforcement structure, has turned this discourse from a much-discussed principle to a practical reality.

This chapter examines how this enhanced discourse of stability, together with the more practical threat of the stability maintenance apparatus, is affecting online life. In particular it demonstrates that the development of a subversive online argot has allowed Chinese Internet users to identify this stability discourse, to deconstruct and to satirize it, to identify that it is opposed on a conceptual level to the agency of the individual, and to form networks which have the potential to oppose it. The labeling of the so-called *bei* society (the "passive society") has allowed netizens both to pinpoint this discourse of passivity and identify that it comes from the party-state. Internet users on message boards, blogs, and social networking sites are thus making a statement about their perceived lack of agency and at the same time expressing their fundamental mistrust of the language of the state. Even so, it is worth questioning whether this culture of urbane, transgressive resistance has any real effect on Chinese political discourse or even on its own users.

Negotiating stability online

Two particularly deep problems form the core of this chapter's analysis: the rise of the Internet, and the state doctrine of stability. Both of these challenge the traditional picture of Chinese society as controlled by the party-state: the Internet through its poorly regulated and constant flow of information, and the doctrine of stability through its clash with the active, revolutionary rhetoric of traditional Maoist discourse. To consider the Internet first: it is now undeniable that websites, email, blogs, and so on have increased the diversity of information available to citizens in China. Information may now reach the user from a wide-ranging and diverse range of sources, reflecting the views of people from many different places and with many different ideologies: the microblog site Weibo is the clearest manifestation of this. What is more, the Internet has provided a vast forum for new modes of satire and parody, which are both done simply for amusement's sake and also as a means of criticizing officials and official ideologies (Li, 2011, p. 72). Compared to broadcast media, for example, official state discourse online is at risk of being ignored in favor of more exciting or realistic spectacles, or, even worse, being lampooned and mocked.

The risks of the Internet to hegemons are well established. The discourse of stability, however, provides a more complex challenge to state discourse. Elizabeth Perry (2007) makes the argument that the Chinese party-state is at root still a fundamentally revolutionary organization, one that is maintaining "both the ideological and the organizational features of its revolutionary past" (Perry, 2007, p. 22). The revolutionary society, she argues, "demands active engagement . . . by society" (Perry, 2007, p. 21), but, by definition, never moves towards substantial citizen representation, democratization, and so on. Developments in modern

China, however, complicate the questions of public engagement. Specifically, the active embrace of a language of "stability" from the mid-2000s onwards calls the label of "revolutionary authoritarianism" into question and suggests that what Perry herself anticipated is beginning to come true: that the economic and social situation has developed in such a way that the Chinese state is moving from a revolutionary outlook to "stable authoritarianism" – the paradox of this being that the deregulation that allowed for such rapid economic development is in itself one of the main factors that is harming China's stability.

Since the Deng period, stability has been used in China as a "cognitive filter" used to enhance the legitimacy of the state (Sandby-Thomas, 2011, p. 33). Peter Sandby-Thomas identifies three key categories in which stability has been used in official Chinese discourse: national stability, economic stability, and social stability (Sandby-Thomas, 2011, p. 51). National or political stability, in the sense that the government never changes, is a natural desideratum of the authoritarian state. Economic stability is *prima facie* used to signify low unemployment and stability in prices; in the Chinese context it commonly also signifies economic growth (Sandby-Thomas, 2011, p. 87), despite having been much internal debate at a policy level about the distinction between growth and stability (see Dittmer & Wu, 2006, p. 73). Social stability, in the sense that the world around the individual does not change dramatically from day to day, is a separate issue, and one which is more likely to clash with the Chinese party-state's revolutionary outlook.

But beyond social stability, there also lies emotional stability, in the sense that the individual's *experience* of, and emotional response to, life does not change dramatically. The desire for state subjects to be emotionally stable, in particular that they are not openly angry or dissatisfied, has been implicit in the post-Mao party-state project since Deng Xiaoping took power. The state discourses of stability, of being "moderately well off" (*dadao xiaokang shuiping*), of achieving human quality (*suzhi*), of the "harmonious society" (*hexie shehui*), and of the creating of a "wealthy, educated, consuming, and above all 'responsible' middle class" (Tomba, 2009, p. 596), have constantly been intertwined (Schoenhals, 1999; Tomba, 2009). Thus, the promotion of the idea of stability in government discourse is never simply restricted to one epistemological sphere. It is linked inherently to the discourse of cultivation of citizens and the development of "civilization": and in both of these desired states, the primacy and authority of the party-state is never supposed to be questioned (see, for example, Dynon, 2008).

The word "stability" (*wending*) is frequently used in official Chinese news sources, such as the *People's Daily* newspaper and Chinese Central Television (CCTV) programs. Since the beginning of the reform period, it has generally been used as a catch-all label for any states of affairs desired by the state: it "was always presented in a nominalized form that served to 'mystify' its definition and thus allowed it to be discursively flexible" (Sandby-Thomas, 2011, p. 155). Rather than having much to do with stability in an empirical sense, it signified a conscious turning away from the "movement" (*yundong*) technique character-istic of the Mao period, and support for the market economy: "the creation of a permanent and ideally self-sustaining *market-driven* momentum in the economic

36   *Jonathan Benney*

sphere constitutes the Party's main means for achieving and ensuring political stability" (Schoenhals, 1999, p. 596). Thus, while "stability" has appeared frequently in government discourse since the 1980s, it has generally been used as a signifier of state authority and the maintenance of a Dengist economic program. In Perry's terms, this strategy might be read as signifying an attempt to make the state appear as if it is moving away from the revolutionary approach, given the public's enormous level of revolutionary fatigue after the Mao period, while at the same time making no substantial change to its authoritarian nature and revolutionary approach to government.

However, there have been clear transitions in the stability discourse over the past decade, and particularly since the mid-2000s. First, the word stability is being used more and more frequently in official discourse. Figure 3.1 demonstrates a substantial increase in the use of *wending* in the text of articles in the *People's Daily* after 2005, with a 50 per cent increase in use between 2007 and 2011.

Analyses of the Chinese Academic Journal database and the China Core Newspaper database show similar trends. The most striking example is the instances of *wending* in the China Core Newspaper database, which increased over three times (from 60,639 instances to 190,374 instances) in the single year 2006.

Interestingly, a graph (Figure 3.2 below) of the instances of *wending* in the *titles* of articles during the same time period reveals no corresponding trend, in fact decreasing from 2009 to 2011, while the use of the word *wending* increased – which might suggest that, while stability is no more often a *subject* of articles in itself, it is more frequently used as a means of *describing* a situation in the news. It is possible to speculate about the underlying strategy by the state media, and the effect on readers, which eventuates from this use of stability as a descriptive label. By suggesting that stability is a descriptor for many situations, or a yardstick by which events might be evaluated, the state is evidently aiming to promote stability not just as a public good but as an epistemological framework. At the same time, readers now encounter the word *wending* in articles which are not just about

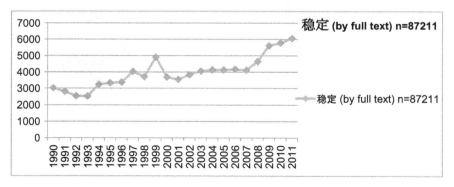

Figure 3.1 Instances of the word "*wending*" (stability) in the text of articles in the *People's Daily,* 1990–2011.

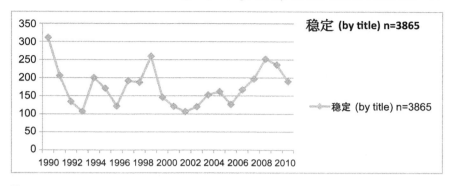

Figure 3.2. Instances of the word *wending* (stability) in the titles of articles in the *People's Daily,* 1990–2011.

stability per se but which might be about any topic; a situation which is very likely to increase public awareness of the links between stability and the party-state, but which correspondingly increases the risk that the public will become fatigued of the term and frustrated when it is used.

This empirical analysis is consistent with a second observable trend, which is that the stability discourse is increasingly used not merely on a national economic and political level, but also on a behavioral and emotional level. Thus, stability is not merely a descriptor for the ideal situation of the state as a whole; it is also becoming a descriptor for the ideal behavior of individuals. Thus the concept of stability and the strategies of state exemplars are increasingly merging. "Social stability" is now more frequently used in official discourse. Hu Jintao is reported to have said in 2007 that "*social* stability is the cherished desire of the masses and an important precondition of reform and development" (2011, p. 61), and this has been reflected in the more frequent use of the term in the official media (with 68.22 instances per month during the years 2009–2011, as compared to 52.25 instances per month during the years 2005–2007).

Emotional stability is also an increasingly significant concept on a political level as distinct from a psychological level. People involved in disasters such as earthquakes or train crashes are frequently said to be *qingxu wending* or "emotionally stable" after the disaster has occurred (see Hu & Pan, 2012, for example). This phrase has been used in the official press since the 1990s at least, but the increased emphasis on social stability and the "mass incidents" of public protest that often occur in the aftermath of disasters have given it added resonance. When juxtaposed with the awkward realities of disasters in China – namely that many people are hurt in the long-term, often because of official mismanagement, and that there tends to be a great deal of public rumor and discussion about these disasters (see Wei, Bu, & Liang, 2012, for example) – the claim that citizens are emotionally stable under difficult transitions appears to be partly a depiction of an exemplary citizen rather than being simply propaganda or a lie. "Emotional stability", however, as an extension of the other forms of stability described above, implies a passivity to the affairs of the state, and a refusal to protest or complain – an outlook consistent with the uses of state stability during the whole of the reform period, but inconsistent with the revolutionary outlook which has traditionally underpinned public discourse in China, and, furthermore, with the increasing desire for citizens to have high levels of individual agency in their lives.

Hence, I now consider how the discourse of stability is played out in the official media on an individual basis: that is, how particular media stories are used by the state to promote stability as a desirable norm, and how individual agency is treated in each case. In particular, I consider how stability is expressed in stories about Internet use. As the cases below demonstrate, the ideal online individual (from the perspective of the party-state) combines loyalty to the state (and embrace of artificial state discourse) with a passivity and lack of response to the chaos and carnival of Chinese online spaces.

It is unclear whether the people in these stories have been created or engineered by the central government or whether they are a consequence of what the state media is told to report on. They are used in articles and television programs about the Internet as interviewees, case studies, or merely as on-screen or printed images. In the examples below, I draw particularly from the *People's Daily* as a convenient source of official state discourse, and one untainted by the vagaries of public debate. However, these state models appear in the regional press, in the broadcast media, and online across China.

What characteristics do these models have? First, they are localized users of the Internet, rather than national or global users. The only six stories in the *People's Daily* containing the word *zaixian* (online) in their headline published 2012 have included the following:

- the inauguration of an anti-corruption website (Xie, 2012), which allows users to view and report matters pertaining to local corruption;
- a report about the use of the Renmin Wang online forum (run by the People's Daily) by members of the Air Force aerobatic flying squad, who were communicating with people in various cities who had viewed their displays (Huang & Wen, 2012);
- a report on the use of provincial-level websites by the Jiangxi provincial government, which were aimed at the dissemination of government information and the provision of government services, and which, it was claimed, had gradually moved from being "technically oriented" to being "content-oriented" and "service-oriented" (Wei, 2012);
- a report on the use of online voting as a means of policy consultation within the Chinese Communist Part (CCP) (*People's Daily,* 2012); and
- a discussion on the use of online government strategies – including websites and microblogs – within Guangdong province (Du & He, 2012).

Each of these Internet users uses the network aspect of the Internet to speed up communication and make it more efficient, but makes little use of its capacity to gain access to diverse global sources of information. The point of the Internet as depicted in these articles is not browsing or socializing, but targeted access to local sources of information for practical benefit. These models of Internet use are of course congruent with the "walled" nature of the Chinese Internet and the high level of discipline over content exercised by the party-state.

Second, model Internet users are highly vigilant: they navigate rather than surf the Internet, and are constantly alert, indeed paranoid, about what might be found there. The state has engineered a discourse of vigilance which is framed as an attempt to maintain the accuracy of online information and to guard against the spread of rumor, but which it is more reasonable to suggest is a means of making Internet users suspicious about any unofficial online information. "Each netizen should verify the facts before they forward information so they can stop fake news before it leaves his or her hands", suggests a lawyer in a *China Daily* article on microblog rumors, which also provides a list of cases in which online rumors were found to be untrue (Cao & An, 2011).

The *hen huang, hen baoli* case is one of the best-known examples of the public backlash to this type of modeled online vigilance. On 27 December 2007, the official daily news and current affairs program *Xinwen Lianbo* aired a segment which alerted viewers to the dangers of pornographic and violent material online, in which a high school-aged girl claimed that she had been using the Internet when a pop-up window appeared, the content of which she called *hen huang, hen baoli* ("very sexy, very violent") (Li, 2011, p. 77; Tang & Bhattacharya, 2011). Immediately, Internet users began to mock and satirize the speaker, particularly concentrating on the unlikeliness of the scenario she described (to have a web page, which was *both* pornographic and violent, pop up randomly was seen to be extremely unlikely) and the unnaturalness of her language, which seemed to be entirely orchestrated to fit the theme of the segment. Much has been made about the online response to this image, and the subsequent explosion of *hen huang, hen baoli* as a catchphrase, but less time has been devoted to the constructed image of the speaker herself, a passive consumer of online content whose response to unfamiliar material was not curiosity or engagement, but prudish shock.

In summary for this section, then, my description of these Internet phenomena is intended to convey two arguments. The first is that the Chinese party-state is straddling the conceptual divide between a revolutionary approach to the control of communication, which involves the promotion of models of Internet use characterized by incuriosity and vigilance, and a managerial approach characterized by discipline, which necessitates the striking of a balance between the individual's freedom to communicate, the state's capacity to censor, and the media's capacity to "nudge" discourse in the direction desired by the state. From a historical perspective this is consistent with Perry's suggestion that the Chinese state is gradually making the transition away from a revolutionary approach to governance, and the growth of subtler means of "passive censorship" in the deregulated Chinese media (Zhao, 2008, p. 34). It is also conceptually consistent both with the growth of the stability discourse described above and with the transition to a discourse of "social management" (Trevaskes & Nesossi, 2012).

Second, the public's reaction to state Internet discourse demonstrates an unresolved, and presumably irresolvable, ambiguity about the content and use of the Internet in China. It is obvious that the Chinese state needs the transfer of information on the Internet to be, in general, free, both because it is necessary for commercial transactions and because it is a major source of leisure and communication for individuals. In other words, the Internet in practice enhances the agency of individuals, whereas state discourse *about* the Internet aims to marginalize this agency. These commercial and social benefits now cannot simply be removed by the state, but the consequent practical freedoms are inconsistent with the party-state's unchangingly restrictive policies on political discourse. The Internet, therefore, by definition challenges *both* the revolutionary style of leadership and the subsequent style of governance by social management and its rhetoric of social stability.

The *bei* culture and online opposition to the stability movement

The Grass Mud Horse, the now exceptionally well-known character of a deliberately provocative online video satirizing state discourse while making various crude and profane puns, examined in depth by Cui (2009), Li (2011), Meng (2011), Tang and Bhattacharya (2011), Tang and Yang (2011), and Wang (2011), is the most obvious symbol of a whole range of linguistic strategies and terms which have become popular across the Chinese Internet. One particularly notable entry in this lexicon is the public use of the Chinese word *bei* (被). *Bei*, when placed in front of a verb, normally generates a syntactical compound a similar to the English passive voice. As in English, the agent may be omitted, so that "*X bei Y kanjian le*" means "X was seen by Y", and "*X bei kanjian le*" means "X was seen [by someone not stated]". It is widely, if somewhat controversially, held that the use of the passive voice, especially with the agent omitted, is a means of increasing the perceived impersonality of a text, particularly in scientific and legal writing (Martínez, 2001; Rodman, 1981) and in political situations where the writers desire to avoid blaming or targeting particular actors (Achugar, 2007, pp. 532–534).

Since about the time of the Grass Mud Horse video's publication, Chinese commentators and linguists have observed a new and unorthodox use of *bei*. *Bei* is being used as a passive marker on verbs such as "commit suicide" or "drink tea" which cannot normally be expressed in the passive (in English, for example, one cannot "be suicided" or "be drunk tea"). Table 3.1 provides some of the words characteristic of this linguistic technique.

Since 2007, a range of Chinese writers, particularly in the field of linguistics, have noted this trend (some include Cao, 2009; Hou, 2010; Shao, 2010; Shao & Liu 2010; Wang, 2011). In general, it is used to convey a sense that the actor mentioned has been forced or given no option but to do a particular thing, and – since the agent is omitted – that this compulsion is coming from an unspoken source. More concretely, it is mainly used to convey a sense of intervention in the affairs

Table 3.1 Selected list of novel phrases beginning with *bei,* sorted by number of Google hits for each phrase. Google hits are not wholly effective means of tracking the relative popularity of the different *bei* phrases, but they provide a general indication of the popularity of these phrases and of their relative commonness.

Characters	Pinyin	Standard English meaning in active voice and meaning when used in passive voice	Google hits (as of mid-2012)	Source
被和谐	*bei hexie*	harmonize ("be harmonized" refers to censorship)	20,100,000	Wang (2011)
被幸福	*bei xingfu*	be happy/blessed ("be made to be happy" refers to situations where people are forced to express a sense of satisfaction contrary to their will or their inner emotions)	4,610,000	Wang
被时代	*bei shidai*	"age of compulsion", "passive era"	4,360,000	Wang
被代表	*bei daibiao*	represent ("be represented" indicates that the state is providing forms of representation which are unrepresentative or which do not intend to represent the needs of stakeholders)	3,220,000	Wang
被精神病	*bei jingshenbing*	be mentally ill ("be made to be mentally ill" refers to situations where it is claimed that people are mentally ill for political reasons, or where they are driven to mental illness by pressure from the state)	2,710,000	Wang
被喝茶	*bei hecha*	drink tea ("be made to drink tea" refers to being interviewed by police)	2,480,000	China Digital Times (2012)
被慈善	*bei cishan*	be benevolent ("be made to be benevolent" refers to forced donations from members of a particular enterprise or organization) (see Lin, 2012)	1,630,000	Wang
被就业	*bei jiuye*	find employment ("be made to find employment" generally refers to people employed temporarily on spurious grounds in order to manipulate statistics, for example of the percentage of university graduates who are employed on graduation)	1,580,000	Wang
被结婚	*bei jiehun*	marry ("be made to be married")	1,580,000	Wang
被××	*bei XX*	"whatever" (place-filler)	1,560,000	Wang
被自杀	*bei zisha*	commit suicide ("be made to commit suicide" as a result of pressure from police or the state)	1,520,000	Wang

(Continued)

Table 3.1 (Continued)

Characters	Pinyin	Standard English meaning in active voice and meaning when used in passive voice	Google hits (as of mid-2012)	Source
被自愿	*bei ziyuan*	volunteer ("be made to volunteer" or "be volunteered" for political or economic reasons)	1,440,000	Wang
被失踪	*bei shizong*	be missing ("be disappeared", referring to circumstances where people disappear mysteriously, presumably for political reasons)	1,390,000	Wang
被跳楼	*bei tiaolou*	kill oneself by jumping from a building (be made to do so)	1,350,000	Wang
被怀孕	*bei huaiyun*	be pregnant (be made pregnant)	1,290,000	CDT
被小康	*bei xiaokang*	be well-off or comfortable ("be made well-off", without the consent of the individual)	945,000	Wang
被捐款	*bei juankuan*	donate ("be made to donate") (see Lin, 2012)	853,000	Wang
被开心	*bei kaixin*	be happy ("be made to be happy" or to appear happy)	598,000	Wang
被稳定	*bei wending*	be stable ("be stabilized" in the sense of being forced to appear stable or being censured)	455,000	CDT
被富裕	*bei fuyu*	be rich ("be made to be rich", presumably through illicit means)	308,000	Wang
被退休	*bei tuixiu*	retire ("be made to retire" for economic reasons)	274,000	Wang
被艾滋	*bei Aizi*	have AIDS (be given AIDS)	197,000	Wang
被满意	*bei manyi*	be satisfied ("be made to be satisfied" or to appear satisfied)	170,000	Wang
被情绪稳定	*bei qingxu wending*	be emotionally stable ("be emotionally stabilized" or be made to appear emotionally stable, for example in response to a crisis)	53,600	CDT

of individuals; further, it is intended to convey that, while the acts are intended to be perceived as being performed under the agency of the actor themselves, the actors are actually being coerced by others. Examples of this include *bei juankuan* ("be donated") and *bei tuixiu/bei cizhi* ("be retired"), which are used in situations where individuals are forced to donate money or to retire under the coercion of their employers or the state (Shao & Liu, 2010, p. 107).

People involved in contentious politics, such as the netizens who have contributed to the spread of the Grass Mud Horse symbol, have used this language to facilitate the communication of even more politically controversial ideas. For example, *bei zisha* ("be suicided") or *bei tiaolou* ("be made to jump from a building") are used to describe cases described as suicides but in which it seems more likely that the dead person was murdered or was compelled to commit suicide, for example in the case of workers at the Foxconn factory ("Jiashu cheng", 2010). *Bei daibiao* ("be represented"), although grammatically conventional, is often used to indicate cases where individuals who are nominally supposed to represent the interests of the people provide only the appearance of representation without actually doing so (Liang, 2009). *Hecha* (or "drink tea") is used to describe the situation where individuals are informally detained without arrest by police or security forces, as if they have been invited to meet casually for a cup of tea; *bei hecha* (which would mean something like "be made to drink tea") refers to situations where people are seized for this purpose. The year after she wrote an essay supporting the Grass Mud Horse movement (Cui, 2009), author Cui Weiping was detained after writing an essay about the Tian'anmen incident; her description of this event was published as *Wo weishenme bei hecha* ("Why I was made to drink tea") (Cui, 2010). *Bei hexie* ("be harmonized") is used to describe cases where contentious material disappears from the Internet, the implication being that the state has deleted it as a means of creating the impression of a "harmonious society".

These various novel and popular uses of *bei* have been abstracted in various ways: the two most significant ones are the term "*bei XX*" meaning "to be [whatever]ed", and the idea of the "*'bei' shehui*" (the "*bei*" society, or the passive society). Although linguists, rather than sociologists or political scientists, have made much of the Chinese-language analysis of this trend, various authors have identified some salient features of the *bei* society.

> The users of this language are netizens. What the bei language is metaphorically describing is a passive situation where people are ordered about and do not have freedom, where the rights of the weak are toyed with arbitrarily by the rights of the strong, so that the weak feel wronged without recourse.
>
> (Shao & Liu, 2010, p. 111)

In other words, the use of *bei* language, together with the construction of the idea of the *bei* society, is used to express resentment both at individuals' lack of personal agency and of the overwhelming power of the state. This, then, is a form of protest against authoritarianism, but it is also a protest against emotional superficiality and the idea of passivity: many of the *bei* terms express implied resentment at being made to appear well-off, happy, satisfied, comfortable and emotionally stable, when the real emotional palette of citizens is far more complicated and far more weighted towards forms of negativity and criticism which cannot be expressed in state media.

It is also important to keep in mind that the *bei* discourse, like most linguistic innovation in China, is spreading largely through the Internet. The "prosumer" generation who facilitated the spread of the Grass Mud Horse and other similar ideas are engaging in a constant process of incremental creation: basic sources, whether they are government exemplars, objects of popular culture, or even features of the language itself, are constantly being appropriated, adapted to new purposes, changed into different media, tinkered with, and discussed. The whole process of creating a *bei* discourse is diametrically opposed to the style of Internet usage embodied by the *hen huang, hen baoli* girl – and indeed to the whole idea of a harmonious, bordered, state-approved Internet.

This *bei* discourse has also been used to attack the state's stability discourse. The most telling example of this has been the use of the satirical catchphrase *sizhe qingxu wending* ("the dead were emotionally stable"), used together with the phrase *bei wending* ("to be stabilized"). The best-known case of this discourse occurred in January 2010, after a disaster at the Lisheng coal mine in Xiangtan county in Hunan province, where 25 miners were killed and others trapped. The county government published a press release in which it was claimed that "the operation had achieved very good results" and that "relatives of the dead were very emotionally stable" – without stating exactly what had happened or who had been killed (Wang, 2010). Immediately, users of microblogs such as Weibo and online forums began to attack the press release and to satirize its content. The specific arguments made by the Internet users were first, that the authorities were withholding information about the disaster and preventing journalists from gaining access to information, and second, that the authorities were prioritizing the protection of leaders over the welfare of the miners and their families (Wang, 2010).

This linguistic strategy is symptomatic of a characteristic of modern Chinese society which can be labeled in multiple ways: as struggles for individual or "grassroots agency" (Marolt, 2011), as resistance to the "subjectification" of young people in China (Cockain, 2012, pp. 10–12), or as a manifestation of the "abstract anger", anomie, or sheer unhappiness felt by Chinese citizens as their society develops in rapid and unpredictable ways (Brockmann et al., 2009; Yu, 2009; Zheng, 2012, pp. 30–33). All of these analyses are valid, but for the purposes of this chapter it is necessary to highlight a different angle: the way in which the discourse of *bei*, with its emphasis on the conflict between the passive citizen and the active state, is reflecting and exploiting the gap between the revolutionary, the authoritarian, and the consultative strategies of the Chinese party-state, as they are expressed through the media. At some level, whether conscious or subconscious, users of *bei* understand that citizens of China are being portrayed as passive subjects in the state media, and that the state is promoting a discourse of stability – and that this state framing strategy is inconsistent with their experience of life, both in the sense that the experiences of modern Chinese citizens tend to be plural and complex, and in the sense that the discourse of passivity and stability does not account for the emotional side of the human experience. As such, while it is perfectly conceivable that the users of *bei* or of the Grass Mud Horse meme or of anything similar may support the actions of the party-state in some or most circumstances, it is far less likely that such a user would have no personal experience of the state's official public discourse, both in its revolutionary, nationalist mode, and its passive discourse of stability, and would not appreciate some of the inconsistencies between them.

This brings me to the limitations of the *bei* discourse, and, more broadly speaking, of citizens' attacks on exemplars. It is a mistake to regard online phenomena such as the Grass Mud Horse as being fundamentally teleological. The fact that the Grass Mud Horse song rails against *hexie* and that the term *bei hexie* refers to censorship does not prove that the song is designed as a criticism of Chinese censorship policies. The *bei* discourse is even more incoherent. Its advantage is its linguistic subtlety and flexibility, which means that it can be adapted to any situation, and that it is far harder to censor than particular Internet buzzwords (like *caonima* or Grass Mud Horse). Furthermore, this very strategy of appropriation and slight distortion of state language indicates that many Internet users are aware of the means by which the state is attempting to control discourse, through the use of language and the creation of exemplars as well as through censorship. This transparency would not have been possible before the popularization of the Internet.

It is therefore impossible to ignore the problem that the *bei* discourse does not convey any particular message. Whether it is an attack on stability or an attack on state exemplars, or both, it conveys a sense of dissatisfaction with individuals' lack of agency – but little else. An attack on symbols, as embodied by the Grass Mud Horse, or on state discourse, as in the satire of *hen huang, hen baoli*, has a tendency to become symbolic in and of itself. The symbols, like the horse, become fetishized and commodified rather than being intellectually engaged with or discussed. This has some value in facilitating the spread of new ideas, but is likely to reduce the epistemic or the intellectual value of the ideas behind the symbolism. Whereas the symbols or models created by the state can be linked to government campaigns which have practical effect, there is little evidence that the symbols or the terminology of resistance can do so effectively; nor that the existence of online resources implies the ability to create or mobilize offline resources.

Furthermore, if we rely on the argument that the *bei* discourse is a manifestation of anger, subjectification, lack of agency, and so on, and that it is specifically directed against the Chinese state (or at least local authorities), the question arises whether the state should in fact be concerned about this attack on its authority. Arguably it should not be, at least from the perspective of the higher levels of government. An angry populace may on occasion riot or be provocative, but that may – say, in the case of anti-Japanese demonstrations – be used to reinforce the authority of the state; a disenfranchised group of individuals may be able to target problematic local officials and replace them, as happened in the village of Wukan, without any threat to the state or to officials. But, even in this case, perhaps the *bei* discourse is too abstract and too symbolic to address the local – localized activism necessitates empirical and personal arguments as well as slogans and symbols.

All this having been said, it is still important to note both the enormous spread of this attach on state discourse, and, furthermore the far-reaching potential consequences of the manipulation of discourse by citizens. This chapter has concentrated on the official state media as a means of demonstrating the increasing flimsiness of its new exemplars and the ease with which its statements can be criticized in public. Communication is only one facet of political and social change, but, in the battle to control and promote ideas to the population of China, the state is losing ground – even if citizens are not necessarily gaining much ground.

Conclusion

By suggesting an analysis of online state-society relations which concentrates on the means of control other than the disciplinary society, this chapter has aimed to make some new observations about Chinese state control of the Internet. Individuals' perceived lack of agency, combined with the sheer diversity and plurality of the Internet, have led to a complicated struggle between the state and the public, in which the state's discourse of stability has been appropriated and mocked, and where new forms of citizen communication – functioning on a very basic linguistic level – have been set up in their place.

This struggle regarding the language of stability has taken place in a China which is gradually abandoning its revolutionary roots in favor of other forms of authoritarianism. Internet authoritarianism in China is only increasing as time goes on, with the state promising even more stringent restrictions on flows of data, anonymity, and Internet governance (Bandurski, 2012). But both the transition from revolution to stability and the deregulation and increased pluralism of the media have jeopardized the state's attempt to create a model online individual, a stable, passive consumer of approved content. The construction of public forms of discourse which explicitly acknowledge and attack the state's discourse of stability and its attempt to construct models, such as the *hen huang, hen baoli* incident and the development of the *bei* discourse, demonstrate a change both in the style of online communication and in China's treatment of exemplars which will be difficult to reverse.

Note

I would like to acknowledge the research assistance of Mr Andrew Yeo in preparing this chapter. Translations from Chinese are my own.

References

Achugar, M. (2007). Between remembering and forgetting: Uruguayan military discourse about human rights (1976–2004). *Discourse & Society, 18*(5), 521–547.

Be represented, be suicided, be increased, be GFWed, be XXed. (2012). *China Digital Times*. Retrieved September 20, 2012, from http://chinadigitaltimes.net/space/Be_represented,_be_suicided,_be_increased,_be_GFWed,_be_XXed.

Bakken, B. (2000). *The exemplary society: Human improvement, social control, and the dangers of modernity in China*. Oxford, UK: Oxford University Press.

Bandurski, D. (2012). Rule of law: A ring to bind China's Internet. *China Media Project* (2012). Retrieved December 28, 2012, from http://cmp.hku.hk/2012/12/27/29924/

Brockmann, H., Delhey, J., Welzel, C., & Yuan, H. (2009). The China puzzle: Falling happiness in a rising economy. *Journal of Happiness Studies, 10*(4), 387–405.

Cao, D. (2009). "Bei" zi xin yongfa jiedu. *Xiandai yuwen, 11*, 56.

Cao, Y., & An, B. (2011). Weibo gives rumors no time to thrive. *China Daily.* Retrieved September 13, 2012, from http://usa.chinadaily.com.cn/china/2011-11/04/content_14035477.htm.

Cockain, A. (2012). *Young Chinese in urban China.* Oxford, UK: Routledge.

Cui, W. (2009). Wo shi yi zhi caonima. Retrieved September 19, 2012, from http://www.bullogger.com/blogs/cuiweiping/archives/281821.aspx.

Cui, W. (2010). Wo weishenme bei hecha. *Radio France Internationale.* Retrieved September 21, 2012, from http://www.chinese.rfi.fr/%E9%A6%96%E9%A1%B5/20100603-%E5%B4%94%E5%8D%AB%E5%B9%B3%EF%BC%9A%E6%88%91%E4%B8%BA%E4%BB%80%E4%B9%88%E8%A2%AB%E5%96%9D%E8%8C%B6

Dittmer, L., & Wu, Y-s. (2006). Leadership coalitions and economic transformation in reform China: Revisiting the political business cycle. In L. Dittmer & Liu G. (Eds.), *China's deep reform: Domestic politics in transition* (pp. 49–80). Lanham, MD: Rowman & Littlefield.

Du, R., & He, L. (2012, May 15). Guangdong shengwei xin banzi zaixian "hui" wangmin. *Renmin Ribao*, p.11.

Dynon, N. (2008). "Four civilizations" and the evolution of post-Mao Chinese socialist ideology. *The China Journal, 60*, 83–109.

Hou, Y. (2010). "Bei shidai" de yuyanxue jiedu. *Xiandai yuwen, 2*, 136–138. 64.

Hu, R., & Pan, Y. (2012, March 10). Xinjiang luopu xian fasheng 6.0 ji dizhen. *Renmin Ribao*, p. 4.

Huang, Z., & Wen, S. (2012, February 23). Ba yi feixing biaoyan dui yu wangyou zaixian jiaoliu. *Renmin Ribao*, p. 15.

Jiashu cheng liang chao "bei zisha". (2010, May 18). *Xin'an Wanbao.* Retrieved September 21, 2012, from http://ah.anhuinews.com/system/2010/05/18/002947875.shtml

Li, H. (2011). Parody and resistance on the Chinese Internet. In D. K. Herold & P. Marolt (Eds.), *Online society in China* (pp. 71–88). Oxford, UK: Routledge.

Liang, L. (2009). Gedi shuijie tingzheng pin xian "bei daibiao" zhengfu bei pi wu chengxin. *Zhongguo Xinwen Wang.* Retrieved September 21, 2012, from http://finance.people.com.cn/GB/10640854.html.

Lin, Y. (2012, July 18). Guangzhou yi yinhang zongjian bingshi qian yaofei yuangong "bei juankuan" 500 yuan yishang. *Yangcheng Wanbao.* Retrieved September 20, 2012, from http://finance.gucheng.com/201207/2015006.shtml

Marolt, P. (2011). Grassroots agency in a civil sphere? Rethinking Internet control in China. In D. K. Herold & P. Marolt (Eds.), *Online society in China* (pp. 53–68). London, UK: Routledge.

Martínez, I. A. (2001). Impersonality in the research article as revealed by analysis of the transitivity structure. *English for Specific Purposes, 20*(3), 227–47.

Meng, B. (2011). From steamed bun to grass mud horse: E Gao as alternative political discourse on the Chinese Internet. *Global Media and Communication, 7*(1), 33–51.

Perry, E. J. (2007). Studying Chinese politics: Farewell to revolution? *The China Journal, 57*, 1–22.

Rodman, L. (1981). The passive in technical and scientific writing. *Journal of Advanced Composition, 2*(1–2), 165–172.

Sandby-Thomas, P. (2011). *Legitimating the Chinese Communist Party since Tiananmen: A critical analysis of the stability discourse.* London, UK: Routledge.

Schoenhals, M. (1999). Political movements, change and stability: The Chinese Communist Party in power. *The China Quarterly, 159*, 595–605.

Shao, P. (2010). "Bei shidai" de "bei" zi xin yongfa jiedu. *Zibo shi zhuanxue bao, 21*, 56–60.

Shao, P., & Liu, C. (2010). Wangluo yujing xia "bei" zi de xin yongfa yanjiu. *Jinan zhiye xueyuan bao, 3*, 107–111.

Tang, L., & Bhattacharya, S. (2011, May 31). Power and resistance: A case study of satire on the Internet. *Sociological Research Online, 16*(2). Retrieved September 13, 2012, from http://www.socresonline.org.uk/16/2/11.html.

Tang, L., & Yang, P. (2011). Symbolic power and the Internet: The power of a "horse". *Media, Culture & Society, 33*(5), 675–691.

Tomba, L. (2009). Civilization and the middle class in urban China. *Positions, 17*(3), 591–616.

Trevaskes, S., & Nesossi, E. (2012). Human rights. Retrieved September 18, 2012, from http://www.thechinastory.org/lexicon/human-rights/

Wang, C. (2011). "Bei" zi xin yongfa qianxi. *Yanjiusheng luntan, 4*, 121–122.

Wang, P. (2010). Cong "sizhe qingxu wending" dao "kuangnan xiaoguo hen hao". *Epoch Times, 9*. Retrieved September, 21, 2012, from http://www.epochtimes.com/gb/10/1/9/n2781620.htm

Wang, S. S. (2012, January 2). China's Internet lexicon: Symbolic meaning and commoditization of grass mud horse in the harmonious society. *First Monday, 17*(1). Retrieved September 19, 2012, from http://firstmonday.org/htbin/cgiwrap/bin/ojs/index.php/fm/article/view/3758/3134

Wei, B. (2012, April 9). Jiangxi xianji yishang zhengfu wangzhan zaixian fuwu nengli tisheng. *Renmin Ribao*, p. 20.

Wei, J., Bu, B. & Liang, L. (2012). Estimating the diffusion models of crisis information in micro blog. *Journal of Informatics, 6*(4), 600–610.

Xie, L. (2012, January 17). Renmin wang: Fanfu changlian zaixian fangtan kaibo. *Renmin Ribao*, p. 6.

Yu, J. (2009). You yi zhong "chouxiang fennu". Retrieved July 28, 2012, from http://opinion.hexun.com/2009-08-31/120881647.html

Zhao, Y. (2008). *Communication in China: Political economy, power, and conflict.* Plymouth, MA: Rowman & Littlefield.

Zheng, Y. (2012). China in 2011. *Asian Survey, 52*(1), 28–41.

4 Regarding subjectivities and social life on the screen

The ambivalences of spectatorship in the People's Republic of China

Alex Cockain

In recent years, micromessaging services such as *Xinlang Weibo* (新浪微波, hereafter *weibo*), a Twitter-like social networking service launched in August 2009 soon after the Chinese government blocked its citizens from accessing both Facebook and Twitter, have come to constitute key lenses through which netizens see the social world, used by almost half of the Chinese Internet population (48.7%), or approximately 250 million users (see CNNIC, 2012, cited in Chan, Wu, Hao, Xi, & Jin, 2012, p. 345). Generally speaking, it has been argued that access to such technologies has had a transformative impact, and recognition of this has, in turn, led to dramatic revisions in perceptions of not only the Chinese public but also the government that, in conjunction with various other state-owned organizations, rents out bandwidth to private enterprises and individuals (see Herold, 2011, p. 1). Gone are those images from the not-too-distant past of not only politically apathetic and passive citizens (Zheng, 2012, p. 28) but also the government which, depicted as a real-life manifestation of a fictional Orwellian Big Brother, had *complete* control of all public media (Link et al., 2002, p. 2). Now the more common picture is of technologically competent netizens with tendencies, as Zheng (2012) notes, "to be active, even proactive, participants" who are not only making "greater endeavors to articulate their interests in public forums" but also emblematic of a Chinese society that is "full of anger" (p. 28). The central government, meanwhile, now appears out-of-touch and slightly inept, being constructed as a "net-nanny" (Goldkorn, 2008) operating a firewall that most netizens are more than capable, metaphorically speaking, of finding ways of climbing over (翻墙, *fanqiang*), thus gaining access to information deemed by censors as being inappropriate. Seen together, netizens and the government are seen as participating in a kind of cat-and-mouse game (Martinsons et al., 2005) bearing some resemblance to the kind of tactical dance that Livingstone and Bober (2006) evoke when writing about the dynamics that exist between children and parents regarding Internet usage in a UK context (p. 106). In order to further illustrate the capacity of the Internet as a powerful tool toward democratization, commentators point to sharp increases in the amount of "collective actions", – from 8,700 in 1993 to 90,000 in 2006, before doubling to 180,000 in 2010 (Liu & Chen, 2012, p. 49).

It is in such a context that this chapter contends that although changes in media, most notably the emergence of images, discussion and debate on micromessaging sites such as *weibo*, have dramatically altered the ways in which netizens confront and reflect upon social issues, this does not necessarily have an empowering and democratizing impact upon Chinese society. My central argument is that the Chinese Internet in general and micromessaging services such as *weibo* in particular have become fetishized, becoming ascribed with romantic qualities and constructed within discourses of power and resistance, as well as a utopian and one-sided strand of technological determinism or cyberlibertarianism that depicts the Chinese Internet in general, and micromessaging services in particular, as having the capacity to fundamentally alter, in specific ways, various aspects of Chinese social and cultural life. Drawing largely upon Western discourses, such views tend to celebrate new forms of media as "means for individuals to be freed from the oppression of their governments" (Bell, Loader, Pleace, & Schuler, 2004, p. 30). This chapter seeks to insert ethnographic detail into these technologically deterministic views by showing that "technology *is* social; that it emerges in particular contexts . . . and has a social and cultural life" (Bell et al., 2004, p. 135). More specifically, this chapter first explores how positive and negative views of the Internet coexist, resulting in considerable ambivalence, before providing a description of the doubt, fear, and powerlessness that tend to emerge as a consequence of spectators' exposure to social issues through the frame of computer monitors and mobile phones. Then, the chapter focuses upon how the Internet is implicated in the construction of a dystopian social world that ultimately induces spectators to retreat, as a defense mechanism, since this has the capacity, to apply Simmel's (2002) words, to bring about, albeit in uneven ways, "the sort of distanciation and deflection without which . . . life could not be carried on at all" (p. 15).

Such arguments are based primarily on reflection upon data generated through a series of focus groups conducted with, and elicited written responses from, students studying at Shanghai Normal University during the late Spring of 2012. I have used a pseudonym for each informant in order to maintain confidentiality. Before inviting participation in my research, I introduced the nature and scope of my enquiries, explaining that the results were intended for publication in due course, emphasizing that I would like to quote specifically from their communications. Consent was given in each case. In addition to these techniques, there is a more traditionally ethnographic "flow of life" component to this research, given that this chapter draws upon participant observation, or what Guobin Yang (2003) refers to as "guerilla ethnography" (p. 471), most notably through my own spectatorship of social issues through the frame of *weibo* and my albeit extremely limited participation in discussions online relating to issues appearing, and being discussed, there. In order to highlight these differences in data collection, this chapter uses terms such as young Chinese, students or informants to refer to those people with whom I conducted face-to-face ethnographic research, whilst the term netizen is used to indicate those whom I did not encounter in physical locations.

Ambivalent views toward subjectivities and social life on the screen

The paragraphs below highlight how views toward both subjectivities and social issues online are characterized by extreme ambivalence, encompassing not only profound beliefs in the authenticity and truth of the online world but also, sometimes almost simultaneously, extreme doubts regarding the accuracy of people and events depicted there.

Faith in authenticity online

Discussions regarding the Internet typically began with informants expressing relatively positive views, whilst also stressing their quotidian, practical and "calculated use of media" (Olsson, 2006, p. 123); opinions that have much in common with utopian and cyberlibertarian discourses regarding the Internet (see Damm, 2009, cited in Chu & Cheng, 2011, p. 24). Informants believed that more genuine, less inhibited, expressions of subjectivity were possible on the Internet, emphasizing how when online they felt less constrained by those rules they were subject to in much of their offline lives. This led informants to articulate views of the Internet as a freer space in which, amongst other things, they could partake in more lighthearted and trivial activities than those typically endorsed and permitted in offline contexts. Wang Yao, a female informant, talked about how she believed the Internet not only enabled her to attain a wider perspective on the social world, but also heightened feelings of proximity to others. "The Internet allows us to know more about the world", she said, "we can easily find out about things that happen far away from us. It gives us the option to know about other people's ideas. It brings us closer".

Informants also accredited the Internet with being able to improve not only the social world but also the subjectivities of those netizens who were witness to certain events online. Informants reflected, for example, upon how the Internet was implicated in the creation of a more caring social environment, as was the case when informants reflected on how, during a rainstorm, a young woman had held an umbrella for a beggar. One male informant felt this was an incident that showed the existence of a compassionate social environment, and led him to revel in the romantic capabilities of the Internet:

> Through the spreading of the Internet, countless people have learned about this beautiful and kind-hearted action and have given her lots of praise. This helps to create a caring social atmosphere. Maybe next time people see beggars in the rain, they will follow the example of this behavior. This shows that the Internet has the power to change society.

Informants explained how the Internet enabled them to feel informed and, by virtue of this, empowered. As one student put it: "Freedom of expression was limited in the past, but the Internet gives people a safe and free place in which to express their own opinions. We can learn many views that are different from our own".

Such access to media led informants to compare themselves favorably both to people in other countries in which media was tightly controlled and to their own parents and grandparents who had grown up amidst a vastly more regulated, controlled and restricted mediated environment. "I think the old China is like the North Korea of today", said one informant, before proceeding to say, "if we look at the North Korean people, we will say 'Oh, that's ridiculous, it's very childish'. The way they love their leader is just like the way our parents loved Mao Zedong before".

As well as perceiving the existence of more authentic, and less inhibited, subjectivities online, informants suggested that the social world they were able to gaze at through their computer monitors and mobile phones was less mediated and in fundamental ways more "real" than that which they were able to encounter through other forms of mediation. Such a closer engagement with reality meant that informants felt able to see power in a more direct, and less mediated, way. This had the effect of increasing informants' engagement with the Internet. "We just want to know the truth", said one female informant, with an almost desperate tone to her voice, yet nonetheless implying in some significant way that the Internet enabled her to discover the seemingly fleeting and elusive commodity. Another female commented in a rather more matter-of-fact manner about how she and her classmates sought out opinions online which were not constructed by those official agencies to which they were typically subject in almost every offline aspect of their lives. "Sometimes we are forced to believe the things we are told by our teachers, by the government and by the authorities", she said, "but we want to find something that is not written by the government but by others so we can build up our own opinion by reading the story from different sides". Informants were particularly interested in finding out whether or not some of the negative press relating to China, often appearing in Western media, was in fact true. This led some students to discover events from the past, amongst which were, as one female student commented, "Mao liking to sleep around and the 1989 June 4th massacre".

Such beliefs expressed by informants about being able to see realities in less mediated and censored ways are echoed not only by netizens but the wider Chinese public. As Lasseter observes, when observer estimates relating to the number of people who died in the 2012 Beijing floods were significantly higher than official figures, the Internet enabled "fact" as well as rumour to circulate, creating counter-narratives to those constructed within official discourses (2012). There are an abundance of examples of how official untruths were exposed as such by virtue of the presentation and circulation of contrary information online. Consider, for example, when a municipal government in southwestern China suspended the construction of a metals factory after bloody street protests. The police issued a warning that they would severely punish anyone involved in further protests, yet postings on Chinese social media claimed that thousands had gathered outside local government offices the following night demanding the release of students detained in the previous day's protests (Bradsher, 2012).

Out of such alternate versions of events emerge poignant questions such as those posted on *weibo* that, beside photographs of the aftermath of floods in Beijing, questioned whether or not the government pursued growth at the cost of safety, and whether or not common Chinese people were being sidelined by the ambitions of the rich (Lasseter, 2012). Such views are cynical in the sense that they perceive there to be a fundamental conflict between society's stated motives and its real objectives, and the emergence of these alternate depictions of reality online conspire, in profound ways, to expand those "limits of acceptable speech" (Butler, 1997, p. 34) or, to use a language associated with Foucault (1973), to extend those "conditions of possibility" (p. 168) through and in which netizens, informants and the wider Chinese public can attain information relating to social issues. Accordingly, the view of the Internet and *weibo* as influential tools that have the capacity to impact upon, shaping and altering, the ways in which citizens can gaze at mechanisms of power in Chinese society as well as empower informants and netizens should neither be ignored nor understated.

Even when informants knew that their access to reality was restricted, this did not always diminish, but sometimes even enhanced, the social satisfaction that could be gained from the Internet. As Bakhtin (1984) has observed, "Forbidden Fruit is [often] sweetest" (p. 189), with the "rules of the 'game'" existing "only to be broken, the referee only to be ignored" (Fiske, 1987, p. 245). Students spoke, for example, excitedly of wishing to *fanqiang*, believing that this provided them with a more accurate means of viewing the social world and one that, crucially, was not censored by persons such as government officials or, as was typically the case in classrooms, teachers. It seemed, in short, that some informants had an intense, almost insatiable, desire to find out the truth, and that such desires were only accentuated by the need to devise ways to circumvent the so-called firewall of China. Zhang Wei, a bright and confident male student, spoke of how he would *fanqiang* for half an hour each day in order to read about politics and, as he put it, to "find out about the affairs and scandals of senior government officials such as Hu Jintao". Zhang Wei claimed that each and every day he was able to find something out, often by using *dongtaiwang*, a kind of virtual private network software available as a download.

Nonetheless, whilst it appears that informants, and netizens, gain some satisfaction from participation in such games, it seems that pleasure is temporary and positive views about the Internet, even within the course of one discussion, give way to more dystopian attitudes, resulting in considerable ambivalence. Part of the reason for the emergence of these more negative sensibilities is because demystification leaves a void. Having shown, if not quite argued, the falseness of ideologies (Halsall, 2005), there is not necessarily anything to replace them with, and this causes anxieties of an altogether different kind. Under such circumstances, the views of the social world that netizens gain becomes clouded, distorted making online spectatorship akin to, as one informant in her mid-thirties commented with irony, making reference to the Chinese idiom *wu li kan hua shui zhong wang yue* (雾里看花水中望月), "looking at flowers in a fog".

Doubt and cynicism

Though initially expressing beliefs that the Internet enabled them to gain an unmediated, and more "real", view onto the social world, informants quickly, sometimes almost simultaneously, expressed doubts about not only the nature of those subjectivities they saw online but also the nature of the mediated window that they peered through onto the social world. Informants reflected upon how people could put on masks online, becoming, as they often put it, "completely different people" (see also Cockain, 2012, p. 136f). Students referred to a classmate who had, as they saw it, become someone else online and this had damaging repercussions on her classmates' offline lives. Though my conversations with students regarding this issue could not, such was the rawness of their feelings regarding this matter, get to the heart of the events that had happened, there was a tangible sense of fear and resentment regarding the incidents which had occurred, as they perceived it as a direct consequence of their classmate's Internet usage. "She is really quiet, kind, nice and soft off line", said one female informant regarding the aforementioned classmate, "you can use beautiful words to describe her. But online she said something really terrible, not about us, but about our friends, something not so good. We changed our views about her afterwards".

Informants sought to rationalize these seemingly vast disparities between offline and online personas:

> Maybe people will just be different in their real life and on the Internet. Because some sites don't need your true information, you don't really need to worry about what you are saying. You can say something you would not say in real life.

It was clear, however, that such attempts to rationalize were not successful. "It is like having a split personality (*rengefenlie*, 人格分裂)", said one female social work major student, albeit with a degree of irony. "People may put their anger into words and post them on the Internet, but say nothing in reality", she said, "and sometimes it's really frightening because maybe when you see some of his or her words online you don't feel it's the same person that you meet in reality".

As the image of authentic online representations of subjectivity tended to fragment so did faith in the accurate picture of "reality" that informants had initially described as being conjured into existence online. Informants were aware that on *weibo*, self-censorship was pervasive with politically sensitive search words being blacklisted and postings being regularly deleted (Chan et al., 2012, p. 345). Those "technical strategies" (Livingstone and Bober, 2006, p. 102) such as blocks on search items that exist even in ordinary circumstances only become intensified when something perceived to be extraordinary happens. This was the case when, in the summer of 2012, serious flooding occurred in Beijing. At this time, *weibo* mysteriously shut down. Similarly, as Hewitt observes, with regard to the Bo Xilai affair, after several days the government blocked the names of the main protagonists (Hewitt, 2012).

Of even greater impact on informants' and netizens' trust in the authenticity of those realities constructed online was the tendency for events, especially those that stimulated extreme emotional responses such as grief and sadness, to be constructed within official ancillary texts and discourses. Netizens are aware of how emotions can become "pivotal sites for the renewal of political stability and social control", with practices of representation being central to this process (Hutchison, 2008). Representations that "provide individual experiences of trauma with a collective . . . dimension" are often constructed in such a way that feelings of shock and terror are smoothed over leaving a salient message that carries the potential to "unite individuals in a spirit of shared experience and mutual understanding" (Hutchison, 2008). Netizens cynically reacted against the ways that suffering was used, by powerful groups, as a mechanism to not only foster togetherness but also distract, divert and distort. Li Chengpeng, for example, on a swiftly deleted *weibo* post relating to the floods in Beijing, predicted how the floods would be constructed within official media (see Barefoot, 2012):

> Just like in the past, the story will have to develop along the narratives of how love knows no boundaries, of singing praises for great deeds, and of how disasters bring us together. If my guess is correct, headlines like "Rainstorm Washes out True Love between the People" will yet again appear. These kind of headlines make me sick, because it isn't that a rainstorm washed out the love between the people, but rather that a rainstorm has washed out the truth, and the truth is: a city that can't even build a working drainage system can never be ranked an international city, and when the entire nation can't build a working drainage system, it should know why the nation is always waterlogged with public opinion.

Such observations show how netizens are capable of reflecting upon how they are implicated within systems of power, being aware that grief is a site of disciplinary power. Informants were no different in this regard, though they tended to express rather more frustration at how social issues were constructed online and offline, not only by official agencies, but also by other netizens. Informants implied that the complexity of issues was often drained when they were constructed online, as was the case when Gan Lulu became discussed online after her mother filmed her naked whilst taking a shower, purportedly in order to attract suitors for her soon-to-be 26-year-old daughter who had been unable to find a boyfriend due to being busy at work. Issues such as difficulties in finding a relationship, contemporary dating habits, the continued involvement of parents in their adult children's love lives, the appropriate age to marry and how to balance work with desires to find a relationship were essentially absent, whilst the overwhelming amount of commentary comprised speculation that this was a publicity stunt and comments on Gan's physical appearance (Fauna, 2011).

Consider also events occurring in October 2011 in the southern Chinese city of Foshan when a Chinese toddler was run over by a van driver. The driver, seemingly realizing that he had hit a young infant, drove on, crushing the young girl again. The body of the girl, Yueyue, was ignored by a number of passersby who either walked or wheeled past. After some time, Yueyue was hit again. Seven minutes later, a woman finally stopped to help the young girl. Yueyue died later in hospital. The entire incident was filmed on surveillance cameras, and has been watched 1.5 million times on Youku, a popular Chinese file-sharing Internet platform. Whilst this event was of such a harrowing nature to netizens that the event could not be drained of its poignancy, even here there was a reduction of events to something much more simplistic, with the Internet implicated in the construction of heroes and villains, sometimes endorsed either by official agencies or by netizens. Chen Xianmei, the street cleaner who helped Yueyue, was constructed within official discourses as a hero because she helped the young girl as she lay dying. As testament to her altruism she was awarded about 25,000 yuan by the local government. The unnamed passersby, meanwhile, were constructed as the polar opposite, being constructed as villains. The issue is, however, complicated by netizens who, in great numbers, questioned Chen, suggesting that her act might have been motivated by desires to win fame and money rather than represent any pure form of altruism (see Joe, 2011).

A similar reduction occurred when Ma Nuo rejected a man on a famous Chinese dating television programme, saying that she would rather cry in the back of a BMW than laugh on the backseat of a bicycle. The televised incident swept the Internet and made an instant celebrity of Ma, who left the show without a match but has since entertained numerous television offers, becoming one of the most talked-about women in the country (see Bergman, 2010). Though Bergman suggests that Ma had become an object of attraction, the rather more dominant impression of her was negative. As Wu Mian (2010), writing in the Global Times, observed, netizens "condemned her for the undisguised worship of money and her sexy online portfolio", all of which only conspired to make her more famous. Ma was labeled as a shameless materialist, whilst many netizens suggested, as they did with regard to Gan Lulu, that her comments were not genuine but borne out of a desire to attract publicity. Social commentators, meanwhile, stated that Ma was illustrative of a "youth problem" (Lin, 2010). Whilst the incident undoubtedly attracted some meaningful and constructive debate, Ma's utterance was framed in such a way that it diluted the extent to which the incident could be made to speak to other issues. In short, when characters such as Ma Nuo appear online, they are constructed in such a way that they bear much resemblance to those "folk devils" described by Stanley Cohen, being portrayed in two-dimensional terms and simply blamed for social problems (1972).

Demarcations of good and bad people become entrenched in a "network of writing", engaging them "in a whole mass of documents that capture and fix them" (Foucault, 1977, p. 189), creating a virtual mediated version of the "parade" that Foucault outlines (p. 188), functioning as "a procedure of objectification and subjection" (p. 192). Such polarized constructions of "good" and "bad", in conjunction with skepticism and cynicism, limit the extent to which issues depicted and constructed online can be meaningfully engaged with.

Informants also realized that sometimes they were not altogether different from those that they saw roundly depicted as villains. With regard to the Yueyue incident, though they were shocked and frightened by the coldness displayed by those passers-by who saw Yueyue dying yet failed to intervene, they were not able to state that they were looking at people who were fundamentally different to themselves. Informants were also unable to state that they would have intervened:

> I would feel scared. But I think I would call the police
>
> I think the atmosphere is contagious, someone in the back will see the former passersby did not save her, then the second one will say "Ok, you didn't save her, I will not save her either".
>
> Actually I think it depends on who is around you. If my friend was him [referring to the previous comment made by her classmate] we would probably save Yueyue, but if my friend was someone else it would be difficult to say. It's like, sometimes, we see a beggar and we will give him or her money, but some people won't. They think he or she is cheating.

Informants were also often suspicious about the motives of others, even when they reflected upon seemingly altruistic actions, as was the case when pictures of a young female holding an umbrella over a beggar, protecting him during a rainstorm, were posted online. Tan Mei, a female student, was perhaps most extreme in this regard. With exasperation, she observed that she had seen the photograph many times because people had forwarded the image to her on numerous occasions:

> At first I felt really moved when I first saw this story. I also felt this story was really true. I also thought that this girl's heart was really good and that in spite of everybody's view – because many people now feel strange about people coming from humble origins – if . . . Later I even began to think that maybe the beggar is a relative of the girl. As for when the photographer said that he or she thought the girl was crying, I thought it was really funny. "Hello, it was raining, how do you know if she was crying or whether it was the rain?"

Although Wang Yao, a female informant, noted that the image was moving, she went on to assert that the issue would soon be forgotten, failing to have any lasting impact on spectators:

> People seldom care about others and everyone seems to be isolated, so when this girl comes into our eyes she makes us feel warm. She makes us feel apologetic for our own indifference. Maybe she touches some people's hearts, but how many people will really change their minds? How many people will actually do something for the poor? I don't know. People are so forgetful that they usually only remember the things that have a direct and close connection with them.

Informants' reactions to this image, as well as their general tendencies toward apathy, are illustrative of Sontag's assertion that there are limits to shock (2003, p. 73). Not only are netizens confronted with a steady flow of events relating to different events but they are also subject to repeated exposure – as Tan Mei had found with the image of the girl holding the umbrella – to the same image and story, such is the high degree of intertextuality in the world of *weibo*.

Informants' also expressed misgivings regarding the capacity of netizens to reach reasonable ethical decisions, as became clear when students reflected upon how public opinion had influenced a homicide case involving Yao Jiaxin. After a traffic accident in which Yao's car had struck a young woman, he stabbed her to death when, as reports suggested, he found her memorizing his license plate, presumably so as to be able to seek compensation for the accident (BBC, 2011). Yao was put on trial and sentenced to death. Informants reflected upon how extreme emotional reactions emerged, becoming enflamed in ways that were not, according to their own moral definitions, necessarily correct. In contrast to the almost unanimous view emerging online, namely that Yao's behaviour was such that he should pay with his own life, students' views were far more ambivalent, and complex. "I think that Yao Jiaxin would have been spared the death penalty if it was not for the Internet", said one female informant, before going on to explain "the power of the Internet is so strong. People said that he must die. The course of this event was influenced by 'public opinion' (*yulun* 舆论). On the Internet a lot of people said that he must die, because he is harmful to the society. Because of this they executed his death penalty immediately. Otherwise he could have got a suspension."

Of significant concern to students was how one mood could emerge, often then influencing how an event was acted upon, before public opinion shifted, throwing into question the appropriateness of the action – in this case irreversible – that was taken, with reference to the initial, and later usurped, public emotion. This was the case when students reflected upon how the public mood with regard to Yao Jiaxin shifted from absolute condemnation to something rather more ambivalent. As one student put it:

> At first, everyone was very angry and thought Yao should die. Even all the media thought in this way. So there was a lot of pressure on the courts about how to handle this case. But then, after Yao had died, the victim's family went to Yao's family and asked for 200,000 yuan in compensation. After this, much of the media, as well as many people, changed their views. The Internet has stimulated this extreme ending. People came to realize that this is a tragedy, not only for the dead, but also for others. Because ideas come too fast, people did not have enough time to think about the truth of this issue.

Students' anxieties about the extreme nature of netizens' emotional responses were to some extent a consequence of their spectatorship over the years of the type of "Internet vigilantism" to which Herold (2008) refers. Such fears about extreme emotional responses were also a consequence of the discrepancy between those messages that informants had been typically subject to within their homes and schools – which stipulated that one should not stand out and that one should, wherever possible, avoid confrontation, and keep one's true feelings hidden and go with the flow – and those more extreme online voices issuing rather more extreme challenges.

> "People on the Internet are always very emotional", said Wang Yingxia, "they share messages, but sometimes the information is not even true".
> "That's right", said Zhang Yue, "I think some people are anti-social, and because they do not like the Communist Party, they publish some fake news, and they will stir up people's anger with this news. But actually many of them are spreading lies and rumors. This is why when we read some news, we do not write our opinion immediately. We must think about it again".
> "We do not know if this is true or not", agreed Feng Xiaoyun.
> "I do not express my ideas immediately", said Wang Yingxia, "because . . . I do not believe".

Profound doubts about not only the capacities of the people they viewed online to make informed decisions but also the picture of reality they gazed at demand to be seen in a broader context because informants' misgivings appear to be echoed, even amplified, in the wider context of not only online but also offline Chinese society. Such doubts are so intense that they are suggestive of a pervasive, systemic, epidemic like mood. Chinese society has, in short, fallen into profound uncertainty. Everything and anything – the quality of baby's milk powder, the genuineness of food products, the authenticity of educational certificates, the words of politicians, and much more besides – becomes subject to skepticism. If the government were to say the Sun rises in the East, as Sun Liping (2012) notes, people would not believe it, leading him to observe that Chinese "society's ability to present truth to itself is gradually disappearing" (see Hewitt, 2012).

Such doubts ultimately envelop informants themselves. As with many other aspects of their lives, when talking about their own abilities to judge the information they saw online, informants typically lacked confidence. Like those colonial subjects described by Fanon, informants subjectivities are sites of occupation, typically revealing symptoms of an "inferiority complex" (Fanon, 1967, p. 18). Wang Yao, for example, whose utterances regarding the Internet were cited above, began by reflecting on how the Internet enabled her to learn more about the world, before proceeding to explain how this was, in her experience, a catalyst for doubt:

> The Internet also makes us confused. When you are surrounded by so much information, it's hard to identify what is right or wrong. So we have to read more and watch more before we form our own opinions. We need to have the ability to discriminate between truth and untruth.

Fears about the mean social world on (and off) the screen

In recent years, micromessaging software such as *weibo* has constituted a key lens through which Chinese netizens have gazed upon a whole range of disasters, both naturally caused as well as those that have either been exacerbated or directly caused by some form of human intervention or lack thereof. Such events, from train crashes and floods to the "evil deeds of princes" (see Baudelaire, cited in Sontag, 2003, p. 96) or CCP officials such as Yang Decai, Bo Xilai and Fang Daguo, constitute a contemporary version of that metaphorical "tissue of horrors" that Baudelaire, writing some 200 years ago, applied with reference to a newspaper (see Sontag, 2003, p. 96). Put another way, these stories that the Internet is implicated in circulating construct a contemporary Chinese version of the "Mean World" that Gerbner (1998) wrote about in the 1970s (p. 185). Such dystopian pictures are not, crucially, confined to the Internet but quickly filter into other forms of media, such as television, before entering into real spaces such as homes and schools and thus constituting much talked about topics: spinning together a series of violent and frightening images that reinforce a sense that the social world is a place of constant threat and danger.

Admittedly, witnessing this mean world sometimes stimulated positive feelings regarding informants' own lives, enabling them to experience a vivid visceral catharsis through the suffering of others. Such feelings emerged through netizens' tendencies to compare their own lives with those of others that they saw upon the mediated screen. When informants spoke of glimpsing the suffering of others, they often appeared to derive an almost guilty pleasure by virtue of seeing someone whose life was markedly worse than their own. Social Comparison Theory provides a language with which to explain this, explaining how people evaluate their own abilities by comparing themselves to others in order to reduce uncertainty (Festinger, 1954). In order to understand informants' appetites for, as Sontag (2003) puts it, "sights of degradation and pain and mutilation" (p. 86), it is also useful to invoke Hannah Arendt's (1990) notion of the "spectacle of suffering". Arendt distinguishes between those who suffer and those who do not, writing that "seeing" and "looking" are inherently different concepts because sufferer and observer are physically distant, despite the closeness that modern media brings (Beckett, 2008). This creates a spectacle of suffering with a politics of pity that is not, as Boltanski (1999) notes, based upon action but on observation of the unfortunate by those who do not share their suffering, who do not experience it directly "and who, as such, may be regarded as fortunate or *lucky* people" (p. 3). When Shao She, who had recently become a mother, saw stories about parents in Guangdong who did such things as hit their child with a clothes hanger, later burying him. "This horrific act"', as Shao She put it, that made her visibly upset nevertheless provided a foundation that enabled her to view her own, as she acknowledged herself, far from perfect performances as a mother in a better light, allowing her to derive positive feelings about her own abilities vis-à-vis those parents she encountered online and the fact that her daughter was physically secure. A female student expressed a similar sense of security when she reflected upon her own life comparing it to those who experienced demolition. "Although a lot of negative news has been reported by the media", she said, "we have a relatively comfortable life. I have never had any experience of demolition (*chaiqian*) . . . so I feel, physically, I am kind of safe".

Positive feelings as expressed by Shao She and my younger female student informant were, however, temporary and tended to become subsumed by the knowledge that they too were part of the same social environment and that they too could also become impacted upon by the issues depicted online and that the very appearance of these images confirmed the existence of a dark social environment beyond the frame of the particular story they were confronted with. The aforementioned horrific story intermingled with other narratives of pain, relating to almost every aspect of the parenting experience, had left Shao She feeling a great deal of fear about the social world that she was bringing her child into. These stories, such as one in October 2012 relating to a man offering a 5-year-old girl to a foreign man for sex in a bar in the Jingan district of Shanghai, become discussed by families coming, for a time at least, to form a "constituent part of what a society chooses to think about" (Sontag, 2003, p. 76) spinning together the impression of a dystopian social space. With regard to the story occurring in Jingan, the foreign man was said to have taken the girl to the police only to be told that there was nothing he or anyone could or would do about it. Shao She explained how the post had been removed, but ripples of fear that coalesce with those doubts explored earlier in this chapter – netizens accused the man of lying, or saying that he did not understand Chinese therefore probably misunderstood the man who was said to have offered the girl to him for sex – had already been activated, and the expression on Shao She's mother's face as she heard the story, in silence, suggested that she too, in an instance, had become implicated in this "Mean World".

Further frightening informants was the realization that in contrast to what Boltanski defines as a "pure spectator" (1999, p. 27) who "is completely independent of the scene he views" (1999, p. 27) being, by virtue of this, "detached" and not figuring "at all in the action shown" (1999, p. 27) they were a great deal more involved in the scenes they gazed upon. When they looked in the mediated mirror, the environment confronting them was one they were part of and affected by. When Shao She talked about the stories occurring just down the road in Shanghai, this made her realize that the geographical and symbolic distance between her, her baby and the dystopian social world was closer than she had wanted to believe. "I never thought these things could happen in Shanghai", she said, "the girl must have been kidnapped. It could be a girl like my daughter". Like Shao She, the female student who had initially felt safe when viewing the suffering of others also came to feel more fearful:

> When I read about this negative news, I feel really unhappy. It makes me wonder why China is like this. I have a brother and sometimes when I read about some news about kids, like just recently when in Guangdong province there was a report about a psychopath killing kids in a kindergarten. He killed a lot of kids outside their kindergarten by stabbing them. When I read about

that I called my mother to tell her to be careful about my brother and that she must send my brother into the kindergarten by herself. Now, at university, I start to think that in future, if I have a child, I do not want him or her to grow up in China. I hope to take him or her to a safe place, to a place where we can feel a sense of security. I think the Internet gives me a sense of insecurity. Although it's a tool for me to kill time, I still feel it gives me this sense of insecurity.

Whilst the Internet undoubtedly magnifies a lack of interpersonal trust and doubt, informants nonetheless "integrate and absorb a sense of danger, of mistrust, of meanness in the world" (see Gerbner, cited in Media Education Foundation, 2010) and such feelings tend to be accompanied by powerlessness, with their commentary echoing Sontag's (2003) observations that the misfortunes of others are often "too vast, too irrevocable, too epic to be much changed" (p. 70). As one informant put it:

What I say or think will not change anything anyway, so I think it is not necessary to say anything. Although I get online a lot, I sometimes feel that the Internet gives me a feeling of "powerlessness". I don't know what to do. So I just watch movies online or do some online shopping

Such powerlessness was not, however, purely because of either mediation per se or the sheer volume of images and texts (see Sontag 2003, pp. 90–94) but was partly a consequence of how the Internet is implicated in designating a hell, yet fails to tell netizens "anything about how to extract people from that hell, how to moderate hell's flames" (p. 102). Gerbner suggests that there are three types of story, namely one that is about how things work, one that refers to how things are and, finally, one that provides information as to what recipients to the story should *do about them* (1999, p. 9 italics added for emphasis). Whilst the former two are relatively passive, the third type of story compels forms of action, and though informants and netizens encounter an abundance of texts pertaining to the first two types of story, there were far fewer texts that told informants what they should do about the issues they saw depicted. Because of this, informants were, in effect, caught in a perpetual moral panic yet one in which, in contrast to those described by Stanley Cohen (1972) that ultimately deliver feelings of comfort given that the panic is generally concluded by some form of social control, no such closure is provided, leading witnesses to feel to be in a perpetual state of fear. Whilst Fanon (1967), utilizing the term of "collective catharsis" (p. 124), notes that in "every society . . . there exists, must exist a channel, an outlet whereby the energy accumulated in the form of aggressiveness can be released" (p. 124), the problem for informants such as Shao She was that there was no moment in which she could purge or expunge her fearful emotions fully because being propelled into her, as well as the general public, were further stories that, like the others stirred up sympathy and outrage: from Yueyue to close-circuit television footage of a 4-year-old girl with autism being beaten by a female assistant at a children's rehabilitation center in Guangzhou (FlorCruz, 2012), compounding a sense of fear, panic and mistrust, yet failing to provide resolution.

Chouliaraki (2006) presents spectators with three options when faced with distant suffering, namely to "switch off, shed a tear, [or] get angry and protest" (p. 1). Whilst Zhang Wei, described earlier in this chapter, appeared to have an insatiable desire to discover "the truth", most students appeared to be more than content not to discover the realities of situations. Part of the reason many informants did not seek out the truth was because often the truth, when discovered, was frightening. Commenting on *dongtaiwang* in general and the types of story that her classmate Zhang Wei searched for, one female student observed that "when I see such stories, I just turn away. They are too horrible". Like those Germans, described by Primo Levi, informants preferred to close their mouths, eyes and ears, building for themselves the illusion of not knowing and hence not being an accomplice to the things taking place in front of them (1987, cited in Boltanski, 1999, n.p.). This was certainly the case when informants reflected upon the Yueyue incident. "She died. So many cars drove over her, I couldn't keep watching the video online." "I have seen the video. No one touched her body. But it was too sad. I couldn't keep watching."

Simmel (2002) provides a means through which such tendencies toward detachment and disengagement might be understood, though it is necessary that the context of the city be replaced with that of the Internet. In both cases, participants are subject to a "swift and continuous shift" of stimuli (Simmel, 2002, p. 11), that arouses needs to create "a protective organ for itself against the profound disruption with which the fluctuations and discontinuities of the external milieu threaten it" (p. 12): a certain distant mentality emerges to defend against the excess input. Such "distanciation and deflection" (p. 15) is needed because informants such as Shao She "respond, with some definite feeling, to almost every impression emanating from another person" (p. 15). It is precisely because, as Smith (1759) observes in *The Theory of the Moral Sentiments*, "Pain besides, whether of mind or body, is a more pungent sensation than pleasure, and our sympathy with pain, though it falls greatly short of what is naturally felt by the sufferer, is generally a more lively and distinct perception than our sympathy with pleasure" (p. 39), that Shao She and a great many other netizens find refuge in the fun, frivolity and elemental side of the Internet – gazing at pictures of animals doing funny things and the like. And it is this – though well beyond the scope of this chapter – that becomes what the Internet is primarily used for, fun and those quotidian pursuits mentioned, almost as if in passing, at the start of this chapter.

Concluding thoughts

This chapter has presented an alternative to the somewhat dominant picture of engaged, and often enraged, citizens who are empowered to change aspects of Chinese society by their ability to confront social issues online, arguing instead that the Internet, whilst altering and often enlarging netizens' notions of social realities, simultaneously empowers and disempowers, stimulating feelings of engagement and disengagement with social issues. Most pertinent, perhaps, is the Internet's involvement in the construction of a mean and dystopian world that might, in fact, be a catalyst for control rather than a mechanism for democratization. As Gerbner, Gross, Signorielli, and Morgan (1986) has suggested, "fearful people are more dependent, more easily manipulated and controlled, more susceptible to deceptively simple, strong, [and] tough measures"; they "may accept and even welcome repression if it promises to relieve their insecurities and other anxieties" (p. 15). Such a way of thinking requires that the Internet be seen as an agent that, in important ways, might reinforce the status-quo rather than act against it.

References

Arendt, H. (1990). *On revolution*. Harmondsworth, UK: Penguin Books.

Bakhtin, M. M. (1984). *Rabelais and his world*. Bloomington: Indiana University Press.

Barefoot, P. (2012, July 23). Li Chengpeng: Beijing rainstorm reveals humanity and truth. *Chinasmack*. Retrieved July 30, 2012, from http://www.chinasmack.com/2012/bloggers/li-chengpeng-beijing-rainstorm-reveals-humanity-and-truth.html

BBC. (2011). China executes student for murder of hit-and-run victim. Retrieved May 5, 2012, from http://www.bbc.co.uk/news/world-asia-pacific-13678179

Beckett, C. (2008). The politics of pity: Suffering as spectacle (guest blog). *POLIS*. Retrieved November 5, 2012, from http://blogs.lse.ac.uk/polis/2008/07/23/the-politics-of-pity-suffering-as-spectacle-guest-blog/

Bell, D., Loader, B. D., Pleace, N., & Schuler, D. (2004). *Cyberculture: The key concepts*. London and New York: Routledge.

Bergman, J. (2010, June 30). China's TV dating shows: For love or money? *Time*. Retrieved September 15, 2011, from http://www.time.com/time/world/article/0,8599,2000558,00.html

Boltanski, L. (1999). *Distant suffering: Morality, media and politics*. Cambridge, MA: Cambridge University Press.

Bradsher, K. (2012, July 3). Chinese city suspends factory construction after protests. *The New York Times*. Retrieved July 20, 2012, from http://www.nytimes.com/2012/07/04/world/asia/chinese-city-suspends-factory-construction-following-protests.html?_r=0

Butler, J. (1997). *Excitable speech: A politics of the performative*. New York, NY: Routledge.

Chan, M., Wu, X., Hao, Y., Xi, R., & Jin, T. (2012). Microblogging, online expression, and political efficacy among young Chinese citizens: The moderating role of information and entertainment needs in the use of Weibo. *Cyberpsychology, Behavior, and Social Networking, 15*(7), 345–349.

Chouliaraki, L. (2006). *The spectatorship of suffering*. London, UK: Sage.

Chu, R. W-C, & Cheng, C-T. (2011). Cultural convulsions: Examining the Chineseness of cyber China. In D. K. Herold & P. Marolt (Eds.), *Online society in China: Creating, celebrating, and instrumentalising the online carnival* (pp. 23–39). London and New York: Routledge.

CNNIC. (2012). Statistical reports on the Internet development in China. Retrieved October 20, 2012, from www.cas.cn/xw/yxdt/201201/W020120116371150443810.pdf

Cockain, A. (2012). *Young Chinese in urban China*. London and New York: Routledge.

Cohen, S. (1972). *Folk devils and moral panics*. London, UK: MacGibbon and Kee.

Damm, J. (2009). The Internet and the fragmentation of Chinese society. In R. Murphy & V. L. Fong (Eds.), *Media, identity, and struggle in 21st century China* (pp. 83–95). London and New York: Routledge.

Fanon, F. (1967). *Black skin, white masks* (C. Markmann, Trans.). New York, NY: Grove Press.

Fauna. (2011, February 16). Mother films daughter naked to help her find a boyfriend. *Chinasmack*. Retrieved October 10, 2012, from http://www.chinasmack.com/2011/videos/mother-films-daughter-naked-to-help-her-find-a-boyfriend.html

Festinger, L. (1954). A theory of social comparison processes. *Human Relations, 7*(2), 117–140.

Fiske, J. (1987). *Television culture*. London and New York: Routledge.

FlorCruz, J. A. (2012, October 5). Video of autistic child being beaten provokes Internet outrage. *CNN*. Retrieved October 12, 2012, from http://www.cnn.hk/2012/10/05/world/asia/china-autistic-child-florcruz/index.html

Foucault, M. (1973). *The order of things: An archeology of the human sciences*. New York, NY: Random House.

Foucault, M. (1977). *Discipline and punish: The birth of the prison*. New York, NY: Random House.

Gerbner, G. (1998). Cultivation analysis: An overview. *Mass Communication and Society, 1*(3/4), 175–194.

Gerbner, G. (1999). The stories we tell. *Peace Review, 11*(1), 9–15.

Gerbner, G., Gross, L., Signorielli, N., & Morgan, M. (1986). *Television's mean world: Violence profile no. 14–15 and the social role of TV violence*. Unpublished monograph, University of Pennsylvania.

Goldkorn, J. (2008). Net nanny vs. great firewall. Danwei: Chinese media, marketing, advertising, and urban life. Retrieved June 15, 2008, from http://www.danwei.org/net_nanny_follies/net_nanny_vs_great_firewall.php

Halsall, R. (2005). Sloterdijk's theory of cynicism, ressentiment and "horizontal communication". *International Journal of Media and Cultural Politics, 1*(2), 163–179.

Herold, D. K. (2008). Development of a civic society online? Internet vigilantism and state control in Chinese cyberspace. *Asia Journal of Global Studies, 2*(1), 26–37.

Herold, D. K. (2011). Introduction: Noise, spectacle, politics: Carnival in Chinese cyberspace. In D. K. Herold & P. Marolt (Eds.), *Online society in China: Creating, celebrating, and instrumentalising the online carnival* (pp. 1–19). London and New York: Routledge.

Hewitt, D. (2012, September 25). Our Society's ability to present truth to itself is gradually disappearing. *Inside Story*. Retrieved September 28, 2012, from http://inside.org.au/our-societys-ability/

Hutchison, E. (2008). The politics of post-trauma emotions: Securing community after the Bali bombing (Australian National University Working Paper). Canberra: ANU. Retrieved March 12, 2012, from http://ips.cap.anu.edu.au/ir/pubs/work_papers/08-4.pdf

Joe. (2011, October 23). Lady who helped little girl run over by van rewarded 25K. *Chinasmack*. Retrieved January 10, 2012, from http://www.chinasmack.com/2011/stories/lady-who-helped-little-girl-run-over-by-van-rewarded-25k.html

Lasseter, T. (2012, July 24). Doubts about death toll from Beijing-area rain fuel new suspicions about China's leaders. *McClatchy Newspapers*. Retrieved August 1, 2012, from http://www.mcclatchydc.com/2012/07/24/157491/doubts-about-death-toll-from-beijing.html

Levi, P. (1987). *If this is a man and the truce* (S. Woolf, Trans.). London, UK: Abacus/Sphere.

Lin, Q. (2010, April 24). The dating game by Jiangsu TV. *China Daily*. Retrieved July 10, 2012, from http://www.chinadaily.com.cn/china/2010-04/24/content_9770152.htm

Link, P., Madsen, R. P., & Pickowicz, P. G. (2002). Introduction. In P. Link, R. P. Madsen, & P. G. Pickowicz (Eds.), *Popular China unofficial culture in a globalizing society* (pp.1–8). London, UK: Rowman & Littlefield.

Liu, Y., & Chen, D. (2012). Why China will democratize. *The Washington Quarterly, 35*(1), 41–63.

Livingstone, S., & Bober, M. (2006). Regulating the Internet at home: Contrasting the perspectives of children and parents. In D. Buckingham & R. Willett (Eds.), *Digital generations: Children, young people, and new media.* Mahwah, NJ: Lawrence Erlbaum.

Martinsons, M. G., Ng, S., Wong, W., & Yuen, R. (2005). State censorship of the Internet in China. *Communications of the ACM, 48*(4), 67.

Media Education Foundation. (2010). *The mean world syndrome: Media violence and the cultivation of fear*. Retrieved May 10, 2012, from http://www.mediaed.org/assets/products/143/presskit_143.pdf

Olsson, T. (2006). Active and calculated media use among young citizens: Empirical examples from a Swedish study. In D. Buckingham & R. Willett (Eds.), *Digital generations: Children, young people, and new media.* Mahwah, NJ: Lawrence Erlbaum.

Simmel, G. (2002). The metropolis and modern life. In G. Bridge & S. Watson (Eds.), *The Blackwell city reader* (pp. 11–18). Malden, MA: Wiley-Blackwell.

Smith, A. (1759). *The theory of moral sentiments*. London, UK: A Millar.

Sontag, S. (2003). *Regarding the pain of others*. London, UK: Penguin.

Sun, L. (2012). Rebuilding trust in government (Tang X., Trans.). *The Economic Observer*, 583, 42. Retrieved November 10, 2012, from http://www.eeo.com.cn/ens/2012/0903/232975.shtml

Wu, M. (2010, May 4). No BMW, no marriage for money-grubbing young Chinese. *Global Times*. Retrieved September 24, 2012, from http://www.globaltimes.cn/opinion/commentary/2010-05/528463.html

Yang, G. (2003). The Internet and the rise of a transnational Chinese cultural sphere. *Media, Culture and Society, 25*, 469–490.

Zheng, Y. (2012). China in 2011: Anger, political consciousness, anxiety, and uncertainty. *Asian Survey, 52*(1), 28–41.

Part III
Claiming online spaces

5 A framing analysis of Chinese independent candidates' strategic use of microblogging for online campaign and political expression

Yu Liu and Qinghua Yang

According to Chinese media, 2010 marked "the first year of microblogging in China" (Sina, 2010, p. 1). Microblogging is exploding in China both because it provides a popular platform for social interaction, and it plays an essential role in the coverage of breaking news as the third largest source of information among Chinese Web users (Wang H., 2011; Wines & LaFraniere, 2011). The adoption of microblogging in China through services such as Sina Weibo is facilitating a culture of public expression and speeds a diffusion of alternative ideologies. The rise of this new medium has been followed by the emergence of a new wave of independent candidates who are using microblogging to announce their candidacies and to mount political communication campaigns. While China's constitution allows for independent candidates to run in local elections, and some have been successfully elected in the past, this is the first time that independent candidates have access to a social medium that allows for the rapid diffusion of political messages and increased visibility at national, and even international, levels (Bandurski, 2011; Branigan, 2011; LaFraniere, 2011a, 2011b; MacLeod, 2011; Moses, 2011; Richburg, 2011; Wines, 2011).

At the same time, these independent candidates make use of social media outlets like Sina Weibo and Tencent Weibo knowing that they are being constantly monitored by internal controls that can block their communication or take more severe measures whenever the government deems necessary. Being cognizant of the risks involved in challenging the system, we want to know how independent candidates are framing their independent candidacy as well as to face (and interact with) the control over China's Internet. This article attempts to partially answer this question by focusing on the microblogging posts of Chinese independent candidates and looking at the framing of their posts with a qualitative approach.

Background

The latest round of local people's congress elections in China occurred between 2011 and 2012. In the beginning stages, it did not seem to differ from the last round of elections in 2006–2007. Then one of this year's first independent candidates, Ping Liu, inspired independent candidates all over the country. Ping Liu, a

laid-off worker, tried to voice her and her colleagues' discontent over their pre-
dicament by running in a district-level election as an independent candidate. She
announced her candidacy through microblogging in April and then continued her
campaign online and offline in the belief that: "The rights of the legislator are
'huge', including the joint removal of an unqualified political leader. My rights
have been infringed as I was represented by someone I did not even know. So
I hope we can make full use of our weapon, to vote, and to defend our dignity"
(as cited in Jiang, 2011, n.p.). However, she did not get the opportunity to defend
her dignity, but attracted officials' attention and was refused the right to run for
election. Her whereabouts and phone calls were under 24-hour surveillance by
local police. She was even summoned to a local police station under suspicion of
sabotaging the election, although under the law she had the rights to run in these
elections and to vote. In the meantime, one professor of the Rural Development
Institute at the Chinese Academy of Social Science, Jianrong Yu, posted on his
microblogging site to assist Ping Liu's campaign. On May 11, 2011, he wrote:

> She tried to change society by running as a district-level legislator. Although
> she had been under surveillance and control, and although she had been
> humiliated publicly, she still insisted on giving a speech to the voters in a
> rational manner. In her own way, she is defending the Constitution and fight-
> ing for our future.

Jianrong Yu is an active opinion leader on Chinese microblogging sites with
1,152,554 followers. In a matter of only five days, his posts on Ping Liu and her
stories had been reposted 90,697 times and was commented on 29,415 times,
which sped up the media hype regarding Liu's candidacy as an independent candidate on a microblogging site. Supportive comments and reposts expressed feelings
such as, "It is better to support Ping Liu when we can instead of just crying for
democracy every day", and "To support Ping Liu is to support ourselves". In the
meantime, the traditional media covered Liu's story, and Liu's political campaign
continued being a trend topic because of traditional media coverage. The heated
discussions available on the microblogging sites, and Liu's political campaign
continued to be a trendy topic because of this coverage. This discussion on microblogging and coverage of traditional media jointly enhanced the positive influence
of Liu. More independent candidates participated in the election and announced
their independent candidacy through microblogging. Thus, the phenomenon of the
independent candidate formed through Chinese microblogging.

Those who announced their independent candidacy on microblogging employed
microblogging as a tool for their political campaign: stating their political positions, calling for attention, and attracting potential supporters. Chunliu Xu, a
journalist, advertised a T-shirt sale to raise funds for his election on microblogging. Yan Xu produced a video relating his experiences, political dreams, and his
political position once a week. He also uploaded theses online, and linked the
weekly video through his microblogging pages. Zeguang Wu wrote a diary of his
experience as an independent candidate through microblogging almost every day,

recording his thoughts on the Chinese political system, the current election system and the strategies and experience of running for election. Microblogging not only became a platform where this grass-roots political campaign developed, but also has been utilized as a tool for self-promotion by these independent candidates.

New media and control over China's Internet

There is a great body of literature on Chinese Internet control (Bandurski, 2008; Harwit & Clark, 2006; Krim, 2005; Marolt, 2011). Research found that the control ranged from devices and networks, domain-names, to localized disconnections and restrictions, surveillance, etc. (MacKinnon, 2011). Internet censorship is also practiced, which is dubbed the "Great Firewall of China" (GFW) that keeps Chinese residents not only from accessing specific foreign Web sites such as Google and Facebook (FLOSS, 2011; OpenNet Initiative, 2009; Roberts, Zucker-man, & Palfrey, 2009), but also from expressing their dissent freely (Bamman, O'Connor, & Smith, 2012). The control over China's Internet has been regarded as a double-edged sword: from the government perspective, it may help to unify ideology and stabilize society, while on the other hand, censorship has deprived Internet users of their due rights of free speech and acquisition of information online.

There are four main types of censorship in China – network filtering, search filtering, chat censorship, and blog censorship – as concluded in Bamman et al. (2012). Basically, these four types of censorship all function by censoring content based on a list of key terms or words. With the recent and rapid development of social media such as microblogging in China, more user-generated content can easily be posted online and quickly spread across users' social networks. Due to the public nature of "we-media" and the social features of users' interaction, microblogging had played an important role in disseminating information as well as organizing individuals (Wines & LaFraniere, 2011), and consequently has experienced government control in several cases (Bamman et al., 2012). Bamman et al. found that one form of censorship, the deletion of certain key terms, was used frequently in Chinese microblogging. Their study showed that any message containing politically sensitive terms, whether positively or negatively framed, were deleted because of inherent political implications.

As concluded by MacKinnon (2011), Chinese Internet control may eventu-ally lead to "an atmosphere of self-censorship" (p. 40). In journalistic practice, self-censorship can be defined in a broad sense as non-externally compelled acts aiming to avoid annoying or offending powerful figures or institutions, such as the government, major advertisers, or corporations that own news organizations, in order to avoid punishment or accrue fines (Lee, Simons, & Strovsky, 2006). How-ever, in the age of social media, every Internet user could become an information source and every personal social media site could turn into a platform or a channel of public opinion expression. Therefore, self-censorship seems to be no longer a concept limited to journalistic practice, but it has become a situation all Internet users may experience when using social media.

Framing analysis and expression of political dissent in China

Social science scholars have traced framing to the work done by sociologist Erving Goffman (Gitlin, 1980; Iyengar, 1991; Pan & Kosicki, 1993; Scheufele & Tewksbury, 2007; Snow & Benford, 1992; Tannen, 1993, among others). In *Frame Analysis: An Essay on the Organization of the Experience*, Goffman (1974) defines frames as "Schemata of interpretation" used "to locate, perceive, identify and label" events and incidences around us (p. 21). Framing has been used as a tool for the construction and deconstruction of meaning and messages across a variety of fields and disciplines, including but not limited to communication and media studies, political science, psychology, and sociology, among others (Benford & Snow, 2000). Scholars have adapted Goffman's definition to further clarify or explain the essence of the concept and to best apply it to their area of study. In media and communication domains, framing has been defined most frequently in the context of news analysis. For example, as a result of his analysis of media coverage and news frames, Robert Entman's definition (1991) of framing evolved from a mere process of "Sizing – magnifying or shrinking elements of the depicted reality to make them more or less salient" (p. 9) to a more elaborate definition specific to communication and media studies where framing means "To select some aspects of a perceived reality and make them more salient in a communicating text, in such a way as to promote a particular problem definition, causal interpretation, moral evaluation, and/or treatment recommendation for the item described" (Entman, 1993, p. 52).

Thornton (2002), in her study of political dissent in China, defined framing as "The deliberate interjection of critical and dissenting views into the public sphere – that rely upon a measure of indirection for their success" (p. 662). However, this definition is specific to the context of the study, not only in the framing task specified, but also in its strategy for success, which might be different in more liberal political contexts. In summary, while its core meaning endures, *framing* has taken on new specialized definitions as scholars from a variety of fields and disciplines have applied it to specific contexts and phenomena.

Various scholars within the discipline of sociology have built on Goffman's initial definition of *frames* as well, making theirs more context-specific. Thornton (2002) found three frames of expressing political dissent in China. Given China's political opportunity structure, she states, Chinese dissenters have attempted to express their dissent and opinions by making use of irony, ambiguity, and metonymy (p. 665). This is because, as she argues, framing in China cannot be done as overtly or explicitly as in more liberal political contexts – the political opportunity structure does not facilitate mobilization. Thornton concludes that "Under such conditions, the most viable form of dissent may well be that which masquerades as the politically irrelevant beneath a mask of compliance" (p. 666).

Research questions

Given the emergence of independent candidates who announced their participation in elections for local people's congress across China via social media, the Internet control prohibiting them, the censorship they faced, and the self-censorship they might have experienced, the research question is generated as follow:

RQ: How did independent candidates for the elections for local people's congresses employ their microblogs to negotiate the spaces between online and offline controls of the political sphere in China?

Methodology

To better understand the creation of new narratives of control, interaction, and resistance in China, this study adopted the qualitative approach. The qualitative inquiry has great value and contributions to mass media research. As Tuchman (1991) claimed, qualitative research is an ideal method for media research and studies on mass communication. Qualitative method differs from quantitative method in many respects. While quantitative research offers a generalization based on statistics, qualitative research seeks to explain a specific circumstance based on in-depth understanding (Berg, 2009; Creswell, 2006). To better understand and interpret certain situations, "Qualitative researchers typically study a relatively small number of individuals or situations and preserve the individuality of each of these in their analyses, rather than collecting data from large samples and aggregating the data across individuals or situations" (Maxwell, 1998, p. 75).

Qualitative content analysis was conducted to examine the frames used by Chinese independent candidates. The independent candidates' microblogging posts were selected for this study because microblogging allowed "independent candidates" to become a political phenomenon across China and abroad, rather than isolated instances that few people knew of. In addition, independent candidates have used microblogging as a powerful tool to announce their candidacy, advocate their political ideas, and reach their potential supporters (Richburg, 2011). Sina Weibo and Tencent Weibo, Twitter's equivalent in China, have been utilized by the independent candidates and selected for this study. These two main microblogging service providers attracted more than 140 million and 200 million users respectively when the data collection started. First, the *China Open Constituency Map* (2011) was used to identify independent candidates who announced their campaigns online. The *China Open Constituency Map* is a Google map that provides information and online links to almost all Chinese independent candidates. By following the independent candidates' microblogging sites, it helped identify more independent candidates who did not appear in the *China Open Constituency Map*. This was possible since these independent candidates usually follow each other to share news and policy opinion, as well as to support and encourage each other. Several independent candidates were also located by searching within Sina Weibo and Tencent Weibo using key words "independent candidate", "candidate", and "legislator".

To work with a manageable number of microblogging sites, we selected a sample of 20 independent candidates. The 20 independent candidates were selected based on their popularity on the microblogging sites rather than by random selection.

Popularity was determined by the number of followers of each candidate. This approach was used because one of the unique characteristics of microblogging, which is different from the other social media, is the instant posting system, whereby the microblogging users' updates will be instantly and directly delivered to the followers (subscribers). As a powerful social media, microblogging facilitates communication from opinion leaders to tens of millions of followers. The followers could either passively read, or actively repost and comment on the very microblogging message. Therefore, it is assumed that the more followers one independent candidate has, the higher their opinion leadership and the more opportunities that his or her messages will be broadcasted to a greater extent. In addition, if the messages convey information concerning independent candidacy such as criticism of government and details about the campaign, then these messages would be diffused to a bigger population and have the potential to be even more influential. In summary, the top 20 opinion leaders were chosen among 100 independent candidates because of their level of reach and influence within the network. Data collection began approximately when each selected independent candidate announced that he or she was running for election in May or June 2011 and concluded when they announced the final results of their independent candidacy on microblogging respectively.

All the microblogging posts were analyzed according to Berg's (2009) stages of model of qualitative content analysis and strategy of open coding and axial coding. Berg suggests five stages to analyze the content: identify the research question, determine analytic categories, read through data and establish grounded categories, determine systematic criteria of selection for sorting data chunks into the analytic and grounded categories, begin sorting the data into the various categories. Open coding and axial coding provided a systematic view to classify and analyze the content gained from qualitative study. During open coding and axial coding, researchers should not relate respondent's demographic information with coding. It helps researchers to better interpret the coding objectively.

Findings and discussion

Although none of the sampled independent candidates were elected to Local People's Congresses this year, it is doubtless that they made a great contribution by providing a different voice to the political sphere of today's China. To announce their intention to run for election and claim their political identity via microblogging also allowed their independent candidacy to reach potential supporters and facilitated their discussion on a variety of social and civil issues to be heard by a considerable audience. By covering topics through their microblogging sites such as health care, education, housing, economy, property rights, taxes, transportation, and socially vulnerable groups including women, rural immigrants, the disabled, the poor, and gays, these independent candidates not only held critical view towards government, but also laid out their positions on these issues. In the meantime, they shared progress about their political campaign and offline controls they encountered as independent candidates, such as being monitored by the police and national security, being persuaded to quit the race by their local neighborhood commission or the leaders in their working organizations, and being stopped from campaigning to the public in their election district. It is noticed that due to the offline controls they have experienced, the online censorship they have faced, and the self-censorship they have encountered, these independent candidates employed the following strategies to negotiate the space between online and offline controls to conduct their campaign and express their political views.

Low profile strategy and depoliticization

While these independent candidates tended to actively engage in online and offline political campaigns to a greater level to seek parliamentary seats in local congress election, which is their primary purpose of running independent candidacy, some of them would like to see their independent candidacy depoliticized. First, the term independent candidate or independent candidacy, which is believed to be not a term rigorously defined and utilized (Liang, 2011; Xu Y., 2011), can have serious politically sensitive implications. Frequent use of the term could bring more attention to them or their microblogging sites. Being fully aware of potential Internet control and online censorship, these independent candidates would rather not put too much emphasis on the embedded meaning of this term or the potential political significance of running for election at a grassroots level in today's China. Also, they preferred not to discuss the meaning of being independent candidates very excessively or see their running for election being over-interpreted by media, potential voters, and even the officials. One candidate stated that every independent should cherish and protect the current environment and not give too much political significance to their political activities (Xiong, 2011). Another independent candidate even preferred not to talk about the meaning of being an independent candidate, because it was never his goal in running for election. As a citizen who ran for election, his concerns were all about "How to run for election in accordance with law, how to visit voters, how to get to know voters' appeal, and how to eventually win the final election" (Xu Y., 2011), which is echoed by several other independent candidates' aims of "seeking welfare of the community and building better livelihood" (Xiong, 2011). The contradiction here further demonstrated how these independent candidates avoided any politically sensitive expression online to ensure the potential of the existence of independent candidates offline.

Rather than speaking loudly to discuss the political implications of independent candidacy, most of the independent candidates preferred to keep a low profile. They tend to avoid talking about running for the election as independent candidates; instead, they are more prone to express critical opinions towards social controversial issues or lay out their positions on these issues (e.g. Shi, 2011; Wang J., 2011), or even only to cite (repost) others' microblogging posts instead of writing themselves (Luo, 2011). Some independent candidates stated on their microblogging sites that they would not easily take interviews with foreign media organizations (e.g. Xiong, 2011; Xu Y., 2011) to bring in unnecessary chaos. Some of them tended to consider the election itself as nothing special and their political participation as only an exercise of the election rights they have (Yao, 2011, cited as in LaFraniere, 2011b). After all, "To the majority of Chinese people, by no means is it difficult to participate in elections as one simply needs to register for elections. In this case, it is unnecessary to imagine the process to be an extremely serious issue", as one independent candidate suggested, in order to intentionally attenuate the political overtones of the election (Xiang, 2011). In addition, another independent candidate expressed on his microblogging site, "Running for election is not a change . . . Also, candidates are neither a hero nor a warrior; they are just the most ordinary citizens and voters in China" (Xu Y., 2011). Announcing independent candidacy more or less indicated their intentions to actively engage in political activities, however, different from political candidates who usually try to attract the attention from media coverage and potential supporters to a greater extent, these independent candidates employed the low profile strategy. These aforementioned microblogging posts also seemed to be posted to cater to the official interests ("not a change", "not a hero", "ordinary citizens") and avoid offending the authority (not to "bring in unnecessary chaos"). The "atmosphere of self-censorship" concluded by MacKinnon (2011, p. 40) seemed also influenced their choices of key words and their ways of expressing political positions.

To summarize, when the idea of running for election as independent candidates was initially diffused over offline and online China, slogans like "one person one vote, to change China" or "elections change China" rapidly spread all over the Internet and seemed to have created political and social change as a national phenomenon. However, to seek more space for the ones who actually and actively run for independent candidacy, most of the sampled independent candidates would rather interpret it as an opportunity of political participation or engagement for ordinary citizens, which brings in more independent candidates, more volunteers, more ordinary citizens who heard about the elections (Xu Y., 2011), rather than take it as a potential call for collective action behind their independent candidacy (Yao, 2011, as cited in LaFraniere, 2011b). In addition, by depoliticizing independent candidacy and keeping a low profile, the microblogging candidates strategically minimize their chances of offending more relatively powerful official organizations and individuals. If they fail to depoliticize their candidacy, they are bound to challenge certain parties who hold different opinions, no matter what political views these candidates hold. After all, it is not possible to please everyone; when an opinion is voiced, there will invariably be voices of disagreement. Therefore, the best way to offend less powerful and authoritative figures and institutions is to express fewer opinions, especially regarding politically sensitive topics. This is also considered a general self-censoring strategy.

Irony

Irony, as one of the key rhetorical approaches in literature and one of the frames of expressing political dissent discussed by Thornton (2002), was widely utilized by the selected Chinese independent candidates in issuing critical opinions towards current controversial issues. Modern linguistic theorists separate irony into four categories, namely verbal irony, dramatic irony, Socratic irony, and irony of fate (Kreuz & Roberts, 1993). In this study, irony is mainly referred to as "verbal irony", by which these independent candidates' intended opinions are intentionally masked by their literal meanings. Through the incongruity between the literal and intended connotations, these Chinese independent candidates were able to utter judgmental opinions without directly offending authorities on certain social issues, such as corruption, social inequity, abuse of power, health care, education, etc. Consequentially, they are allowed more freedom to express themselves online.

As microblogging is a powerful and influential medium to communicate with electorates, the political candidates invariably made good use of it to sympathize and show alignment with voters, by putting themselves in grassroots' situations and attracting social issues that were against the general public's interests. For example, one of the candidates, Shuxin Liang, wrote in his blog joyfully as follows, "[We' can finally enjoy free death" (Liang, 2011). Although it seemed that Liang was celebrating "free death" ostensibly, he was actually referring to and celebrating the Shenzhen municipal government executive's policy passing on June 1st of "exemption from funeral service costs". Since June 15 this year, in accordance to the policy, the basic service cost of the funeral of the household and non-permanent residents of Shenzhen will be covered by the government, including the remains' shipping, storage, farewell, cremation, ashes storage or ecological burial (sea burial or tree burial). The maximum free allowance was 1,830 Yuan. This "free death" policy is of such significance because it seems that the cost of death and the funeral is beyond affordability for the majority of lower class Chinese people. Therefore, Liang responded to public concern by commenting on this provincial policy in an ironic way. By using an ironic way of expression, this independent candidate could sharply criticize serious social issues or inveterate inequity in a humorous way.

Some of them also used elements from pop culture to parody social phenomena and ridicule censors and authorities. For instance, one independent candidate who criticizes China's mainstream news media ironically stated,

> I have a dream: to live forever in CCTV news, where the children can go to school, the poor can afford medical care, people can live in low-rent housing for 77 yuan (11 dollars) per month, employees' wages increase by 11%, the employment rate reaches 99%. In the CCTV news, there are no increasing commodity prices and traffic jams, but significant environmental improvements and high criminal arrest rates. Therefore, if I ever reach old age, please bury me in CCTV news.
>
> (Luo, 2011)

By combining Martin Luther King's famous "I have a dream" speech and lyrics from one of the most popular songs – *In the Spring* – in China, Luo is satirizing the propaganda function of China's mainstream news media pretending that everything is going well without disclosing any problems with the country or the society, and the audience will only be influenced by its agenda setting function and can hardly learn the real "news" happening in reality through such mainstream news, such as China's Central Television (CCTV). The actual issue concerned in this post is the trustworthiness of the mainstream media, and the official media's role as the "mouthpiece" of China's government. However, both "media trustworthiness" and "mouthpiece" are politically sensitive keywords to some extent due to their relevance to the freedom of press and expression. This may result in the deletion of the entire post by the blog administrator. If the posts made use of these terms in such a direct manner, the independent candidates will not be allowed to have their voice heard or express dissent at all.

The same approach was also used by other independent candidates in expressing dissent on other social issues. The writer and journalist Chengpeng Li, for example, wrote in his microblogging page the following humorous but thought-provoking passage:

> I steadfastly refuse to emigrate even if I had a billion dollars: with one billion, I could lead a better life than the President of the United States, construct an office building more luxurious than the White House, have relationships with a number of young ladies even more coquettish than the "bunny girls", hire policemen more ruthless than CIA officers, and recruit a band of bodyguards stronger than Tyson; I could have military vehicles clearing the way for my Mercedes-Benz motorcade. It would not be a big deal if I hit and killed pedestrians. I only need to tell him that my dad is Li Gang. Oh, no, tell him that "I just killed Li Gang" instead.
>
> (Li, 2011)

The "Li Gang scandal", mentioned in this microblogging post, is a typical case highlighting the social inequity in China. His son Qiming Li was drunk and drove a black Volkswagen Magotan into two university students. A female student was killed and the other suffered from a fractured left leg. However, instead of sending these two victims to the hospital immediately, Qiming continued driving and intended to shirk his due responsibilities. When caught by security guards, he shouted out, "Go ahead, sue me if you dare. My dad is Li Gang!" Such arrogance triggered public outrage across the Chinese Internet. Through the "human flesh search engine", Chinese netizens found out that Li Gang was the deputy director of the local public security bureau, which deluded Qiming into thinking that his father's position could give him immunity to punishment. Behind this seemingly comedic microblogging post was a non-comic social issue of inequity, which disclosed that people from the privileged class, mainly the people with power and wealth, completely override the general public by enjoying exclusive rights and doing whatever they want. In comparison, the general public is vulnerable and powerless in front of the privileged class and is deprived of the equality, in terms of economic status, political latitude, and even survival rights. By imagining the luxurious life of a wealthy Chinese citizen with a billion dollars, Li is clearly referring to the corruption of the government officials and the problem of social inequity in this microblogging post. Similar to the previous example, the key words "corruption" and "inequity" are of even greater sensitivity and might be filtered automatically by the microblogging detection system, which would render the post unpublishable. However, by strategically using irony in their microblogging posts, these independent candidates could enjoy a higher possibility of avoiding microblogging's key-term deletion system's detection.

The creative and strategic use of irony employed by these independent candidates had not only allowed them to negotiate for more online space for political expression on certain social issues, but it had also been utilized by them to describe what difficulties they had encountered in their real lives. They felt the need to avoid more potential offline control and be cautious of having offline control transferred to online control, as occurred in the case of Chengpeng Li, who ironically depicted how he experienced the offline monitoring:

> Given that you have been monitored for a long time and are aware of the monitoring on the other side, and the person on the other side also knows your awareness, the people on both sides become so familiar with each other and consequently develop a tacit mutual understanding. In addition, since both the people monitoring and being monitored are lonely, there are times you really want to share something with the person on the other side. What a fascinating relationship it is! Imagine there is an attractive lady on the other side, who is as dedicated as a monitor as well as curious as a female, and finally she couldn't help starting such a date. . . . This is an idea for a novel I made up recently.

Obviously, it is Li himself who romanticized such monitoring behavior in an ironical way, which is too ideal to be true. Although, monitoring telephones is actually technically illegal as an invasion of privacy, Li did not label it in this manner. Moreover, Li ended the description of the whole process as an idea for his creative writing, which might help deter blog censorship and the key-term deletion mechanism. Therefore, being conscious of the potential censorship he may encounter, Li chose to not cross the "line", ensuring more online space for his independent candidacy through rhetorical tools in his microblogging posts.

Irony in political communication is comparable with the ironic comedies in theatre; the audience may laugh to tears at the hilarious and silly behaviors of the comedians at the beginning. After a while, however, they would ponder deeply the comedians' miserable lives and the social injustice, probably, also with tears.

Ambiguity

In order to construct a "harmonious society" and control public ideology, Chinese media framework is under the supervision of the government and Internet users are constrained from voicing dissents freely. Against this backdrop, ambiguity is popularly applied to give certain words more than one interpretation, disguising the writer's real intention. Similar to irony, these independent candidates use ambiguous description in their microblogging sites to avoid expressing them-selves in a straightforward manner. Expressed in such a way, the posts may be censored and not be published if the content is offensive to the government, which is always the case. Since the readers cannot directly penetrate the true intentions of literal words, they are encouraged to discover the writer's thought process. On the other hand, to avoid the extreme expressions and being "harmonized (deleted/blocked)" by Internet censorship, the independent candidates frequently resort to ambiguity to secure more room to speak, especially in commenting on certain sensitive social issues. For instance, Luo (2011) put forward in his microblog that "Those who lose brightness are not only the blind", which could be interpreted in several ways because of his ambiguous manner of expression. It is quite rea-sonable to interpret this post as a reference to the sensitive case of Guangcheng Chen, a blind Chinese activist of human rights issues in rural China before fleeing to the United States. Only in this way can Luo express his opinions on this issue, which was the hottest topic during that time, for the reason that any post including Chen's name will be "harmonized" (deleted) online due to censorship. Another plausible interpretation could be that the masses lose their brightness, which could be conscience, sense of justice, or hope, due to the censorship and inability to be informed of the social reality.

Compared with Liang and Li, another candidate, Shang Xia, is a "moderate commentator" who criticized the corruptive government ambiguously by writing "If given a chance to rewrite one of the four masterpieces, I would choose 'water margin' (also known as 'Shuihu Zhuan') without hesitation" (Xia, 2011). This sentence could be simply interpreted that Xia is talking about his personal pref-erences in Chinese literature; however, when uncovering the significance of the words "water margin" and giving it thoughtful consideration, the readers would discover another interpretation and find the hidden meaning behind this remark. The "water margin" story was set in the Song Dynasty, which depicts a group of 108 heroes gathered at Mount Liang (or Liangshan Marsh) to rise up against cor-ruption in the government. By mirroring the history of the Song Dynasty, when greedy officials corrupted the government, Xia insinuated that the corruption was similarly severe in contemporary China and arms should be taken up against it. As explained in the previous section, mentioning corruption directly, or even rebel-lion in this case, will not only reduce the possibility of having this post published and reaching his potential supporters, but it would also expose him to more poten-tial offline controls.

Other than voice their opinions on social issues, ambiguous expressions could also be used to depict these candidates' political vision for China. Different from the historical allusion of Xia, Shuxin Liang poetically stated, "The haze of the sky will one day be dispersed, and the birds will bring us the new branches to nest" (Liang, 2011). This sentence could be interpreted by some readers simply as a lyric line to express his beautiful wishes for the future. However, in the back-ground of the political election, readers would also have reasons to understand this microblogging post in a way that Liang was expecting the election to be a new starting point which would bring positive changes to society.

There are also independent candidates who conveyed ambiguity just by avoiding posting comments on the controversial social issues and just focusing on his or her own election campaign activities, such as Hong Liu (2011). Her microblogging site during the selected period was more an election diary recording the details of every day's campaign, than a discussion forum where candidates could participate in. No matter which way they chose to construct their expression, ambiguity provided them with a circuitous way of expression and an approach to avoid confrontation with the government, the dissenters, and the public, and to negotiate more space for the freedom of speech in a controlled online system.

Metonymy

Thornton (2002) suggested that metonymy is another approach of political expression. By using metonymy, independent candidates could avoid directly talking about intended issues, topics, or concepts, which may be sensitive within the political framework, but refer to another concept instead, which would be inherently associated with the core concept. Through adopting metaphors, independent candidates could give out opinions rhetorically, and avoid offending the other stakeholders. When recalling his experience as an independent candidate, Chunliu Xu (2011) used an analogy for the election by discussing football games:

> For the game I participated, I knew that the rules were set up by them, the venues were constructed by them, and all the ticket inspectors and security guards were on their side. But I still didn't anticipate that competing with the opponents was not the only thing I need to be concerned about. What's more, my teammates might be injured or quit; the audiences might all cheer for my opponents; and my understanding of the rules might even result in boos. When I finally got the ball and was about to shoot, a referee ran over and took the ball away. It turned out to be that the referee was also on their side.

In this case, "them" referred to the Chinese government, which, in Xu's opinion, controlled the election by setting up the rules, staging the event, supervising the procedures, and even factitiously altering the result if it is not what "they" expected. By referring to an imaginary football game, Xu metaphorically conveyed his dissatisfaction with the lack of freedom in local congress elections and called for a more unrestrained stage for people to exercise their entitled political rights. This very metonymy was also utilized by another independent candidate, Yan Xu (2011), who stated that it is impossible to defeat an opponent with a whistle in a game, particularly when there was not a referee on the court. Through these posts, the candidates exposed the offline control they were confronted with through the senior government officials' pre-determining the election results. Feeling that their deserved political rights as Chinese citizen were not being protected, both candidates were making an attempt to make complaints and appeal for change. Such voices, not in line with the government's ideology, can only be heard through rhetorical strategies due to keyword deletion and online censorship.

In these two examples we can also see that the independent candidates were quite familiar with the potential consequences of the offline controls and where to draw the line in fighting for their due rights in such a controlling system. Instead of combating government officials directly and arguing about the election results, which would do nothing but escalate the conflict, they addressed offline controls through mitigated and more peaceful means by expressing dissent in a rhetorical way. Only in this manner can these independent candidates avoid becoming entangled with potential trouble and continue to express themselves.

While expressing dissent in a relatively moderate way, independent candidates also resorted to metonymy to materialize and visualize abstract terms. One example came from one of Chengpeng Li's (2011) microblogging posts, in which he analogized China to the "largest community in the world", the People's Congress to the "Homeowners' Association", and the general public to the "homeowners". In this community, as Li stated:

> The sewer was blocked for a long time but no one repaired it and the elevator was also left unrepaired until someone was killed inside. The members of the Homeowners' Association were not publicly elected by the homeowners, but enjoyed autocratic power in making decisions and refused rights of dissent.

This post conveyed the author's dissatisfaction with the current political system, which obviously opposed the government and could not pass the censorship filter. Only through the use of rhetorical tools, masking the true intention of the post, can the author avoid keyword deletion under the supervision system and allow his voice of dissatisfaction to be heard.

This figure of speech can be also found in many other cases, such as one of Luo's (2011) posts:

> It is the Internet users that form the ridge of China: in addition to completing their arduous daily job, they are also taking many other institutions into account, such as the Ministry of Railways, the Red Cross, and the Office of Urban Management, to take care of the issues including unfair demolitions, law and justice, news media, food security, and to expose corruption and all other social injustice. Not only are they doing these for free, but they are also fighting for the ideal society from the bottom of their hearts.

By "ridge of China", Luo attached significance to the netizens of China, who are crucial in exposing most of the negative news coverage concerning social issues, which would otherwise be filtered by China's mainstream news media. In this regard, it is the netizens who shoulder the responsibility of uncovering these issues and informing the public, owing to the dysfunction of China's political and media systems.

In summary, these independent candidates employed several tactics – low profile strategy, depoliticization, irony, ambiguity, and metonymy – to comment on a variety of social issues, express their dissent and political beliefs, and eventually to negotiate more space for their independent candidacy. However, it is also necessary to note that although analyzed separately, the aforementioned strategies are by no means mutually exclusive, and the independent candidates usually applied these frames of expressing political messages in a combined way. On the other hand, it is also found that the independent candidates weaved rhetorical expressions into plain narration in airing opinions and their attitudes. For instance, when discussing the offline controls, Jian Wang (2011) posted on his microblog:

> (I feel that) our Communist Party branch is marginalized as the leaders of the Party organization haven't called me for a talk yet. (Under such circumstances) I would like to take the initiative, rather than wait passively to be summoned, to bridge the communication gap between the common people and the government, in the hope that everyone's voice can be heard and respected.

The methods of the government's offline control of Chinese people concerned in this post are of particular importance in light of abundant Internet use, which makes online control possible. By calling these independent candidates to have a talk, the officials could execute top-down supervision. A warning might be issued if these candidates still had strong will to continue their campaigns. Although this post shared many characteristics in common with the other posts, such as being dissatisfied with offline controls, giving vent to pent-up feelings via social media, and applying rhetorical strategies, it stood out from the other posts as Wang did not just conclude with the difficulties brought by offline controls. He also provided promising solutions. In other words, through rhetoric and narration, this independent candidate skillfully converted a negative issue of control into a rosy prospect of mutual understanding in his microblogging post to seek more space between online and offline controls he may encounter.

Conclusion

The current study contributes to the understanding of social media's role in political communication within China's social and political system characterized by few political opportunities and greater freedom empowered by social media. Along with the rapid explosion of social media like microblogging, this year's Chinese local people's congress elections witnessed the emergence of a group of independent candidates who announced their will to participate in the elections and campaigned online to complement their offline campaign activities.

Microblogging, as a powerful new medium, has not only facilitated their online campaign to create more awareness of independent candidacy in the online community, but also helped reach out to potential supporters in the offline one, because these independent candidates might otherwise not be able to utter their dissatisfaction and criticism or carry out their campaigning activities due to the limited political opportunities in China. However, like a double-edged sword, microblogging acted as a platform where the government played an upgraded controlling role and where the independent candidates needed to depend on rhetorical tools to bypass such controls and secure space for relatively free political expression. Moreover, new media enabled every independent candidate to be both an information source and a gate-keeper simultaneously. Under this framework, self-censorship became an increasingly important strategy that the candidates frequently resorted to, protected them from stepping over the line, and avoided unnecessary trouble in both their political identity and independent candidacy.

Facing censorship, self-censorship, other types of control over China's Internet, and potential obstacles caused by offline controls, these independent candidates need to be strategic to circumnavigate Internet control through key word deletion and negotiate the boundaries of their independent candidacy online and offline. The present study indicates that these independent candidates had made creative use of the rhetorical strategies such as irony, ambiguity, and metonymy, as well as resorted to self-censorship, in order to give voice to their views on a variety of social issues ranging from health care and education to injustice and social inequity. They also utilized depoliticization and low profile strategies to state their moderate aims of independent candidacy as well as to avoid attracting officials' attention. As a result, these rhetorical strategies enabled them to play around the grey area to successfully voice their political views and beliefs.

This study also provided some suggestions for future research. Since the fall of the Berlin Wall in 1989, a third wave of democratization (Huntington, 1991) spread to Eastern Europe, Africa, and Asia. China is one of the countries which experienced a huge societal transition in the last three decades, although it has not abandoned communist rule. While political scientists heavily focused on transition studies during these years, few studies in the media studies and political communication fields have paid attention to societal transition's influence on political communication in China. This study may offer some insights into future research on online political expression or communication in the context of China's societal transition with the explosive use of social media. Also, the creative use of these strategies could shed some light on studies of how citizens seek for spaces to politically express themselves via social media within online and offline controls.

References

Bamman, D., O'Connor, B., & Smith, N. A. (2012). Censorship and deletion practices in Chinese social media. *First Monday, 17,* pp. 3–5. Retrieved December 20, 2012, from http://firstmonday.org/htbin/cgiwrap/bin/ojs/index.php/fm/article/view/3943/3169

Bandurski, D. (2008). China's guerrilla war for the Web. *Far Eastern Economic Review.* Retrieved December 20, 2012, from http://feer.com/essays/2008/august/chinas-guerrilla-war-for-the-web

Bandurski, D. (2011). Changing China: One vote, one person. The China Media Project. Retrieved December 20, 2012, from http://cmp.hku.hk/2011/06/08/13056/

Benford, R. D., & Snow, D. A. (2000). Framing process and social movements: An overview and assessment. *Annual Review of Sociology*, 26, 611–639.

Berg, B. L. (2009). *Qualitative research methods for the social sciences* (7th ed.). Boston, MA: Allyn and Bacon.

Branigan, T. (2011, September 19). China's boom in "citizen candidates" sparks backlash. *The Guardian*. Retrieved December 20, 2012, from http://www.guardian.co.uk/world/2011/sep/19/china-citizen-candidates-clampdown

China Open Constituency Map. (2011). Retrieved December 20, 2012, from http://maps.google.com/maps/ms?ie=UTF8&hl=en&lci=com.google.latitudepublicupdates&msa=0&msid=207218016920381578262.000484cad2a623d3ded44&ll=37.439974,109.423828&spn=38.660096,79.013672&z=4

Constitution of The People's Republic of China. Retrieved December 20, 2012, from http://english.peopledaily.com.cn/constitution/constitution.html

Creswell, J. W. (2006). *Qualitative inquiry and research design: Choosing among five traditions.* Thousand Oaks, CA: Sage.

Entman, R. M. (1991). Framing United-States coverage of international news – Contrasts in narratives of the KAL and Iran Air incidents. *Journal of Communication, 41*(4), 6–27.

Entman, R. M. (1993). Framing: Towards clarification of a fractured paradigm. *Journal of Communication, 43*(4), 51–58.

FLOSS. (2011). How to bypass Internet censorship. Retrieved December 20, 2012, from http://en.flossmanuals.net/bypassing-censorship/

Gitlin, T. (1980). *The whole world is watching: Mass media in the making and unmaking of the New Left.* Berkley and Los Angeles: University of California Press.

Goffman, E. (1974). Frame analysis: An essay on the organization of experience. New York, NY: Harper & Row.

Harwit, E., & Clark, D. (2006). Government policy and political control over China's Internet. In J. Damm & S. Thomas (Eds.), *Chinese cyberspaces* (pp. 12–41). New York, NY: Routledge.

Huntington, S. (1991). *The third wave. Democratization in the late twentieth century.* Norman/London: University of Oklahoma Press.

Iyengar, S. (1991). *Is anyone responsible? How television frames political issues.* Chicago, IL: University of Chicago Press.

Jiang, X. (2011). China's boom in citizen candidates for local people's congress election. *The Asia Weekly*. Retrieved December 20, 2012, from http://www.yzzk.com/cfm/Content_Archive.cfm?Channel=kk&Path=2409380812/23kk2a.cfm

Kreuz, R. J., & Roberts, R. M. (1993). On satire and parody: The importance of being ironic. *Metaphor & Symbolic Activity, 8*(2), 97– 109.

Krim, J. (2005, April 14). Web censors in China find success: Falun Gong, Dalai Lama among blocked topics. *The Washington Post*. Retrieved December 20, 2012, from http://www.washingtonpost.com/wp-dyn/articles/A51712-2005Apr13.html

LaFraniere, S. (2011a, December 4). Alarmed by independent candidates, Chinese authorities crack down. *The New York Times*. Retrieved December 20, 2012, from http://www.nytimes.com/2011/12/05/world/asia/china-clamps-down-on-even-a-by-the-book-campaign.html?pagewanted=all&_r=0

LaFraniere, S. (2011b, October 31). In China, political outsiders turn to microblog campaigns. *The New York Times*. Retrieved December 20, 2012, from http://www.nytimes.com/2011/11/01/world/asia/political-outsiders-turn-to-microblog-campaigns-in-china.html?pagewanted=all

Lee, C., Simons, G., & Strovsky, D. (2006). Censorship in contemporary Russian journalism in the age of the war against terrorism: A historical perspective. *European Journal of Communication, 21*(2), 189–211.

Li, C. (2011). Chengpeng Li's personal microblogging site. Retrieved December 20, 2012, from http://www.weibo.com/lichengpeng

Liang, S. (2011). Shuxin Liang's personal microblogging site. Retrieved December 20, 2012, from http://www.weibo.com/liangcha

Liu, H. (2011). Hong Liu's personal microblogging site. Retrieved December 20, 2012, from http://www.weibo.com/beijingliuhong

Luo, Z. (2011). Zhiyuan Luo's personal microblogging site. Retrieved December 20, 2012, from http://weibo.com/luozhiyuan

MacKinnon, R. (2011). China's networked authoritarianism. *Journal of Democracy, 22*(2), 32–46.

MacLeod, C. (2011, June 1). Independents enter China's political arena. *The USA Today.* Retrieved December 20, 2012, from http://www.usatoday.com/news/world/2011-06-02-china-independent-politics_n.htm

Marolt, P. (2011). Grassroots agency in a civil sphere? Rethinking Internet control in China. In D. K. Herold & P. Marolt (Eds.), *Online society in China* (pp. 53–67). New York, NY: Routledge.

Maxwell, J. A. (1998). Designing a qualitative study. In L. Bickman & D. J. Rog (Eds.), *Handbook of applied social research methods* (pp. 69–100). Thousand Oaks, CA: Sage.

Moses, R. L. (2011, June 3). Will independent candidates light a fire under Beijing? *The Wall Street Journal.* Retrieved December 20, 2012, from http://blogs.wsj.com/chinarealtime/2011/06/03/can-chinas-new-peoples-representatives-light-a-fire-under-beijing/

OpenNet Initiative. (2009). Internet filtering in China. Retrieved December 20, 2012 from http://opennet.net/research/profiles/china-including-hong-kong

Pan, Z., & Kosicki, G. M. (1993). Framing analysis: An approach to news discourse. *Political Communication, 10*(1), 55–75.

Richburg, K. B. (2011, September 9). China sees surge of independent candidates. *The Washington Post.* Retrieved December 20, 2012, from http://www.washingtonpost.com/world/asia-pacific/china-sees-surge-of-independent-candidates/2011/09/07/gIQAc7tNEK_story.html

Roberts, H., Zuckerman, E., & Palfrey, J. (2009). *Circumvention landscape report: Methods, uses, and tools.* Retrieved December 20, 2012, from Berkman Center for Internet & Society, Harvard University. http://cyber.law.harvard.edu/publications/2009/2007_Circumvention_Landscape_Report

Scheufele, D. A., & Tewksbury, D. (2007), Framing, agenda setting, and priming: The evolution of three media effects models. *Journal of Communication, 57,* 9–20.

Shi, P. (2011). Pu Shi's personal microblogging site. Retrieved December 20, 2012, from http://weibo.com/hnsp

Sina. (2010, September 9). The white book of Chinese microblogging's market. Retrieved December 20, 2012, from http://wenku.baidu.com/view/7fe75c88d0d233d4b14e6976.html

Snow, D. A., & Benford, R. D. (1992). Master frames and cycles of protest. In A. Morris & C. Mueller (Eds.), *Frontiers in social movement theory* (pp. 135–155). New Haven, CT: Yale University Press.

Tannen, D. (1993). *Framing in discourse.* New York, NY: Oxford University Press.

Thornton, P. (2002). Framing dissent in contemporary China: Irony, ambiguity and metonymy. *The China Quarterly, 171,* 661–681.

Tuchman, G. (1991). Media institutions: Qualitative methods in the study of news. In K. B. Jensen & N. W. Jankowski (Eds.), *A handbook of qualitative methodologies for mass communication research* (pp. 79–92). New York, NY: Routledge.

Wang, H. (2011, March 28). Microblog becomes netizens' 3rd largest source of information. *The People's Daily*. Retrieved December 20, 2012, from http://english.peopledaily.com.cn/90001/90776/90882/7333258.html

Wang, J. (2011). Jian Wang's personal microblogging site. Retrieved December 20, 2012, from http://weibo.com/interactivelab

Wines, M. (2011, June 10). China appears to be moving to halt grass-roots candidates. *The New York Times*. Retrieved December 20, 2012, from http://www.nytimes.com/2011/06/10/world/asia/10china.html

Wines, M., & LaFraniere, S. (2011, July 29). In baring facts of train crash, blog erode China censorship. *The New York Times*. Retrieved December 20, 2012, from http://www.nytimes.com/2011/07/29/world/asia/29china.html?pagewanted=all

Xia, S. (2011). Shang Xia's personal microblogging site. Retrieved December 20, 2012, from http://www.weibo.com/xiashang1969

Xiang, L. (2011). Ligang Xiang's personal microblogging site. Retrieved December 20, 2012, from http://www.weibo.com/xiangligang

Xiong, W. (2011). Wei Xiong's personal microblogging site. Retrieved December 20, 2012, from http://www.weibo.com/u/1927148274

Xu, C. (2011). Chunliu Xu's personal microblogging site. Retrieved December 20, 2012, from http://www.weibo.com/jpg46

Xu, Y. (2011). Yan Xu's personal microblogging site. Retrieved December 20, 2012, from http://www.weibo.com/hzxuyan

Yao, B. (2011). Bo Yao's personal microblogging site. Retrieved December 20, 2012, from http://www.weibo.com/wysr2007

6 China's dream of high-speed growth gets rear-ended

The "Wenzhou 723" microblogging incident and the erosion of public confidence

Günter Schucher and Maria Bondes

On July 23, 2011, around 8:30pm, high-speed train D3115 traveling along China's eastern coast from the city of Hangzhou to Fuzhou came to a halt over a viaduct near the city of Wenzhou. Shortly after, high-speed train D301, also traveling to Fuzhou from Beijing, crashed into its rear end. Due to the force of the collision, two of the first train's coaches and four of the second train's were derailed, and a total of four cars fell off the viaduct, killing 39 and injuring around 200 passengers, according to a detailed description of the accident's sequence of events is given by Osnos (2012) and Johnson (2012). Minutes later, a message posted on Sina Weibo by user @yangjuanquanyang started receiving a lot of attention: "Help! . . . Children are crying all over the train! Not a single attendant to be seen! Come help us fast!"(All of the English quotes of microblog posts mentioned in this chapter are the authors' own translations). Within 10 hours, the message had been reposted more than 100,000 times and received more than 18,000 comments. In the following week, there were 10 million messages, including reposts, related to the accident on Sina Weibo, and a total of 26 million posts across Chinese microblogging platforms (Shank & Wasserstrom, 2011; Wines & LaFraniere, 2011; Xinhua, 2011d).

This unprecedented flood of public outrage agitated many observers inside and outside China due to its sheer scale and the fact that these millions of microbloggers "congregated" online without being mobilized by any organization. Set only months after the uprisings in the Arab region and at a time when social media were widely hailed as "liberation technology" (cf. Diamond & Plattner, 2012) and the driving force behind the so-called Twitter revolutions both in Western media and scholarly discourse (Christensen, 2011; Lotan et al., 2011; Morozov, 2009; Shirky, 2011; Sullivan & Xie, 2009), Western media practitioners were fast to draw lines to the Arab Spring, hoping to spot a major step towards a Chinese "microblogging revolution" (Buckley & Lee, 2011; Chin, 2011; Yi, 2011). Such interpretations were rarely based on a critical assessment of what had really happened, however. In this chapter, we take a step back and critically assess the following questions: Why exactly had "Wenzhou 723," as the incident became known in China, become the largest "online mass incident" (*wangluo quntixing shijian*) since the advent of Chinese microblogs? What were all these people blogging about?

To answer these questions, we systematically analyzed the contents of more than 4,600 posts published in the aftermath of the accident on China's largest microblogging platform, Sina Weibo. Based on our analysis, we argue that the incident can be understood only by considering the crash's pre-history and the many problems that have surfaced in China over the previous years. Consequentially, the majority of microbloggers addressed issues like safety, corruption, or the opaque handling of the crash as central themes. Since the overambitious high-speed railway (HSR) program had also been elevated to an allegory of China's rise and the Chinese Communist Party's (CCP's) development strategy, the netizen community turned the crash into a metaphor of everything that has been going wrong in China's development.

The rest of the chapter is organized as follows. In the next section, we will delineate China's HSR program and the pre-history of the Wenzhou train crash, as they provide the contextual knowledge needed to understand the Wenzhou incident. In section three, we will briefly discuss our data and coding before taking a closer look at the posts in the fourth section. We will first outline the central issues tackled during the online debate and sketch its development throughout the incident and then proceed to draw a more detailed picture of the discussion and the sentiments that prompted millions of microbloggers to voice their opinion in the aftermath of the train crash, which many netizens regarded as the epitome of present-day China. In section five, we will then discuss the Wenzhou incident in the light of broader social developments. We will conclude with a brief reflection on the question whether the "Wenzhou 723" debate was only tolerated as a convenient "steam valve."

A "National dream": China's HSR program

The massive outburst of public indignation that flooded the Chinese Web in the aftermath of the Wenzhou train crash was the culmination of a long line of public doubts and anger about China's immense high-speed train program, which had built up over years of extensive public campaigns intended to portray the project as a national symbol of China's growth and the strength and innovativeness of the Chinese leadership. The program was accompanied by corruption scandals, technical failures, and safety concerns almost right from the beginning, however.

Although initially designed as a practical solution to the long-standing problems of China's railway system, the enormous HSR program – one of the world's largest single investments in the passenger rail sector to date – was soon elevated to a symbol of national pride. As an explicitly national undertaking, the Ministry of Railways (MOR) hoped to make the HSR program a lasting symbol of China's rapid ascendancy and increasing power (Wu, 2011), an evidence of China's management capabilities and technological progress. Former Minister of Railways, Liu Zhijun, celebrated a new world speed record (486 km/h) as "a major contribution that China has made to the world's high-speed railway technologies" and praised HSR as an embodiment of the "Chinese dream", "a miracle on earth created by the Chinese people". In a similar vein, MOR spokesman Wang Yongping boasted that technologies employed by China's HSR "are far superior to those used in Japan's Shinkansen [high-speed railway]" (Bandurski, 2011a).

This showcase of national achievement was also closely concatenated with the CCP to boost its legitimacy. The high-speed trains were named "Harmony" (*hexie*) – the denominator of President and Secretary-General Hu Jintao's ideological core concept of a "harmonious socialist society". The landmark line connecting China's two largest cities, Beijing and Shanghai, originally expected to be opened in 2012, was finished ahead of schedule in 2011, requiring only 38 months to complete. The rail went into service on July 1 as the "Pride of China" (Xinhua, 2011a; 2011b). The launch was seen as the embodiment of Hu Jintao's "Scientific Development" concept (his second ideological core concept) and a gift to the Party on its 90th anniversary.

However, from an early stage, the project's image was severely shaken by high-level corruption scandals, massive safety concerns, and a series of technical failures and accidents that preceded the deadly train crash in Wenzhou. The MOR and its minister Liu Zhijun (2003–2011) played the leading roles in this entanglement. Within the Chinese political system, the MOR has an exceptional grip on power due to its having 2.1 million employees, financial authority in the name of the government, its own system of police and courts, and almost exclusive decision-making power over China's railway policy. It is thus known as "Boss Rail" (*tielaoda*) among Chinese bureaucrats and is said to have been an "independent kingdom for years", which successfully obstructed various reform attempts concerning both its monopolistic power and the privatization of China's railway industry (Lam, 2011; Lan, 2012; Osnos, 2012; Wang, 2011; Wu, 2011).

The MOR under Liu Zhijun rushed ahead in the implementation of the HSR project, working at an unprecedented speed that was soon criticized as "excessive" by a research team at the Chinese Academy of Sciences (Yue, 2011), and as an authoritarian, "techno-nationalist" development model that was compared to the "Great Leap Forward" during the Mao era (*Century Weekly,* 2011; Yue, 2011). Criticism mounted that over-hasty construction and the lack of independent quality controls had not only led to high costs and ineffective investment, but also resulted in severe safety oversights (Lou et al., 2011).

These safety concerns received nationwide attention after Liu was dismissed on corruption charges in February 2011. State media reported that Liu had received RMB 800 million (USD 120 million) in kickbacks in return for granting contracts to favored suppliers. If the figures prove correct, the incident would be among the largest corruption cases to date. Liu's case is also notable as he was the highest-ranking Chinese official to be charged with corruption since 2006. Soon after his removal, evidence of poor financial control began to emerge, including over RMB 187 million (nearly USD 30 million) misappropriated during the construction of the Beijing–Shanghai high-speed railway (Yan, 2011).

Following Liu's dismissal, media speculation about the quality of China's railway construction forced the Ministry to address the public's safety concerns. In April, it launched a nationwide safety check of both HSR and regular railway tracks, which allegedly found the safety situation along railway lines to be "severe" (Xin, 2011). Shortly after the opening of the Beijing–Shanghai track at the end of June, daily malfunctions and delays together with poor public relations on the part of the MOR started to irritate passengers (Bandurski, 2011b). Throughout July, in the weeks leading up to the Wenzhou train accident, public anger started to seethe on Chinese microblogs, with passengers posting pictures of blacked-out and lopsided trains stranded in the heat without any air conditioning. By July 12, 286,000 posts concerned with the "Beijing–Shanghai high-speed rail malfunction" had appeared on Sina Weibo (Bandurski, 2011a). The number exploded after the train crash near Wenzhou on July 23.

Data and coding

We systematically analyzed more than 4,600 Chinese microblog posts published on Sina Weibo in the aftermath of the accident. Although the online debate triggered by the train crash was not restricted to Sina Weibo (Zhu et al., 2012), we concentrated on this platform as it is the leading microblogging service in China, with 140 million active users by May 2011 (ChinaNews, 2011). For our analysis, we relied on data provided by the WeiboScope Search archive, a project established by the Journalism and Media Studies Center (JMSC) at the University of Hong Kong. The project uses the information retrieval software Lucene as an indexer to conduct full-text searches on Sina Weibo, indexing every four hours and storing all the linked information in an internal database Unless censored within the time period before the initial indexing (at a maximum of four hours), our sample thus contains all the posts made, regardless of whether they were deleted after initial indexing since there is no suitable way of including posts that were generally blocked from publishing, for example via keyword-based censorship. WeiboScope's subsample, and thus also our coded sample, consist of users with more than 1,000 followers, which is a rather low threshold for the Chinese microblogging community, but excludes all first-time users.

The WeiboScope archive features a search engine that allows keyword searches. Since the netizen community did not settle on consistent hash tags during the incident, we chose the Chinese term for high-speed train (高铁 *gaotie*) as a search term since it showed the best returns in terms of numbers and relevancy. We conducted a search query for each day of the four-week period immediately following the train collision, starting on July 23, and stored all the posts in chronological order in an internal database. The downloaded posts totaled 70,255. Due to the large amount of data and the fact that the number of posts declined rapidly after July 29, we restricted our coding to the first nine days after the accident (July 23 to 31). To capture variation in time, we coded the first 20 posts after each half hour according to their publication date, amounting to a total of 4,635 posts. Due to downloading problems with the search engine, our data contain some gaps in the timeline.

In a first round of binary coding, we excluded all the posts that were unrelated to the Wenzhou incident, thus restricting the sample to 4,001 items, or approximately 85 per cent of the total number of posts. While irrelevancy ranges around 10 per cent during the first two days, it increases to around 20 per cent during the following week. All the posts related to the Wenzhou incident were then content-coded by two native Chinese speakers (inter-coder reliability tests were regularly conducted). In a third round of coding, the central issues in the debate were determined during two iterations of open coding by the authors and the two coders. The resulting coding scheme was then used for definitive coding.

Public voices: what are they blogging about?

The issues debated on Sina Weibo in the aftermath of the Wenzhou accident show that "Wenzhou 723" was far from being a "microblogging revolution". Apart from pure "information" given by microbloggers on the accident, related events, on high-speed trains in general, or their own travel plans, we identified 10 major issues discussed during the incident, which deviate in their level of abstraction. Referring to the pre-history of the crash and the development of China's HSR program, the netizen community discussed the HSR program itself, safety problems of China's railway system, and corruption within the MOR or on the part of its officials. Two further issues were directly related to the accident: first, the opaque handling of the crash and the rescue efforts by the authorities (including all kinds of doubts about the official explanations related to the cause of the accident), and second, the disappointing coverage of the accident in the official media.

The debated issues went well beyond the collision itself, however, widening their scope to the national level and linking the accident with broader debates in society: the two major issues were (a) safety concerns, particularly related to recent consumer safety scandals, and (b) corruption among Chinese officials more generally. Moreover, the netizens went one step further, taking the scope of issues to another level: by relating the accident and the above problems to China's development path and/or China's political system, they turned the crash into a metaphor reflecting the downside of China's rapid development, triggering a critical debate about China's growth model and national policies. Finally, consumer boycotts were widely discussed, and appeals for them were circulated. The results of our issue coding are presented in Figure 6.1. Since we allowed for the multiple coding of posts, the number of codes outnumbers the number of posts.

An analysis of the distribution of issues shows that the majority of posts were concerned with the rather specific issues related to the HSR and MOR (HSR program, safety of railways, corruption in the MOR) and those directly linked with the accident (critique of the media and opacity). By far the largest share of posts deals with railway safety (between 31 per cent on July 31 and 51 per cent on July 23, averaging at 39.7), followed by critique of the authorities' opacity in handling the accident (9 to 30 per cent, on average 21.6). The two other HSR- and MOR-related issues (corruption in the MOR and a general discussion of the HSR program) involve smaller shares of 6.8 and 4.8 per cent respectively. The amount of posts criticizing media coverage is minor at 1.4 per cent.

However, while the posts that extrapolate safety and corruption problems to China at large are fewer in numbers (4.0 and 1.3 per cent respectively), the discussion of China's development path is remarkably prominent (between 3.1 per cent

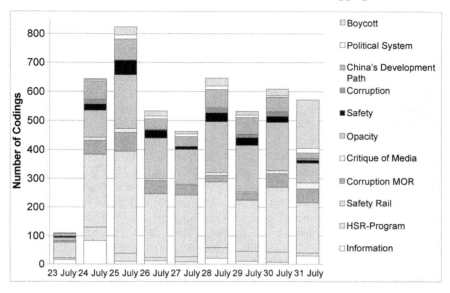

Figure 6.1 Central issues on Sina Weibo during the Wenzhou Incident, July 23 to 31, 2011.
Source: authors' own calculations.

on July 31 and 11.7 on July 29, averaging at 8.4), which demonstrates that the accident triggered a significant debate about the state of Chinese society and the downside of the country's rapid transition. The issues of safety and corruption are frequently linked with reflections on China's development path. Nevertheless, far from being a "microblogging revolution", only 1.6 per cent of the posts in our sample refer to the political system, and none directly challenge the political status quo. Finally, while calls for action and boycotts remain limited throughout the debate (5.4 per cent on average), they become the dominant issue on July 31 (29 per cent) when a call for consumer boycotts caught many readers' attention. We identified two boycotts: almost right from the start of the debate users appealed for the collective return of already bought tickets and the boycott of HSR for the next 30 days; later they called for the boycott of mineral water distributed for free in the trains.

Throughout the incident, humoresque and satirical expressions of microbloggers' opinions were a central feature of the debate and amounted to nearly one-third of the posts in our sample, confirming other studies' findings of a renaissance of humor and parody in cyberspace (Perry, 2001; Yang, 2009a). Digital media technically extend the possibilities of taking cues from official symbols of authority, appropriating them and inverting officially sanctioned rituals, rhetoric, images, and videos for subversive purposes (Esarey & Qiang, 2008; Tang & Bhattacharya, 2011). In our sample, humor and parody are often transmitted in images and less often in videos; they mainly transport the same issues and memes discussed above.

Our content analysis of the development of the debate on Sina Weibo in its half-hourly sequence shows that despite the turbulent unfolding of events in the aftermath of the crash, which was characterized by interactions between the authorities, the netizens, and the media, only two events had any significant impact on the debate: the burial of wrecked carriages on July 24 and Prime Minister Wen Jiabao's visit and press conference at the site of the accident on July 28. The major events during the incident, which were widely debated on Sina Weibo, were (1) the burial of wrecked carriages at the site of the accident on the early morning of July 24; (2) the rescue of a toddler from the wreckage around 5 PM on July 24, hours after the official rescue efforts had been concluded; (3) a late evening press conference on the same day given by MOR spokesman Wang Yongping; (4) the unearthing of the buried car on July 25, which was attributed to online public opinion in state media; (5) Prime Minister Wen Jiabao's visit to the site on July 28, arriving around 10 AM, and his subsequent press conference, at which he announced that railway safety was a top priority; Wen claimed an illness had been responsible for his late arrival in Wenzhou; and (6) the publishing of a critical editorial written by the CCP's flagship newspaper, the *People's Daily*, which called on China to say no to a "blood-smeared GDP" (*daixue de GDP*) on the same day. Figure 6.2 shows the half-hourly development of the three HSR/MOR-related issues.

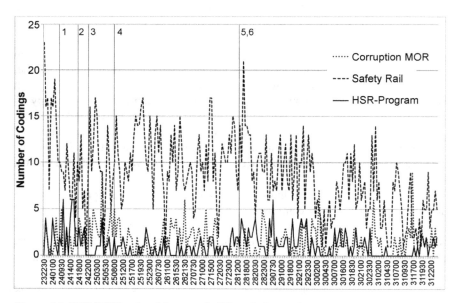

Figure 6.2 HSR/MOR-related issues at half-hourly intervals.

Source: authors' own calculations. The numerals and timelines refer to the events described in the text. The time format is ddhhmm, for example, 232230 means July 23, 22:30 o'clock.

Aside from railway-related safety concerns that peaked right after the crash and again around noon on July 28, there are no significant amplitudes. Railway safety, which was a major theme during Wen's visit to Wenzhou, remained the dominant issue throughout the debate. Reflections on China's HSR program and corruption remain at a relatively low level. As for China-related issues, the picture is similar despite displaying more, but minor peaks (see Figure 6.3). This time, however, in addition to Prime Minister Wen's visit to Wenzhou, the burial of the train carriages seems to have impacted the debate. The discussion regarding China's development path, in particular, peaked on July 28 and remained a prominent issue for two days after the visit before dropping on July 30. Corruption and safety display similar developments on a lower level. While corruption at a national level is only addressed in less than two posts for most of the time, safety issues are frequently discussed in close correlation to China's development. A closer look at the minor peaks on July 25 and 26 reveals no references to any particular event.

Strikingly, Figures 6.2 and 6.3 show that the more specific HSR/MOR-related issues and the broader reflections about safety, corruption, and China's development path display similar developments. All of the issues discussed oscillate around a certain level for a week, the broader issues showing higher amplitudes, before they markedly decline. While we do not know how many critical posts failed to appear due to censorship – posts that were not censored ex post within a

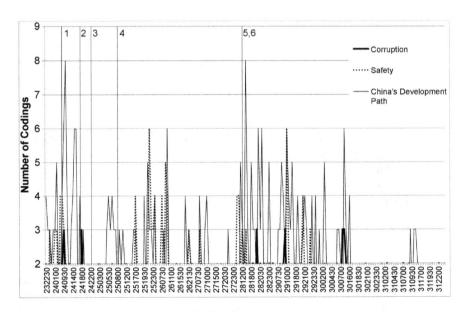

Figure 6.3 National-level issues, by half-hourly intervals.

Note: in order to enhance visual clarity and highlight the peaks, we begin the display of the number of codings (Y-axis) at two.

Source: authors' own calculations.

maximum of four hours after their publication are included in our sample – this finding suggests that specific complaints were not replaced by more general considerations during the incident; a generalization or radicalization of the debate did not take place. Or, to turn the argument around, critical views on China's growth model and its political system were expressed right from the beginning.

From HSR to China's growth model: the Wenzhou crash as the epitome of China

A better picture of the incident and the sentiments that prompted millions of netizens to voice their opinion in China's microblogs is gained if we move beyond mere numbers and take a closer look at the posts published in the aftermath of the accident.

Great plans, great disasters – HSR safety and MOR corruption

Problems regarding safety and corruption had accompanied China's HSR project at every stage of its planning and implementation. It is thus not surprising that the obvious lack of safety of China's HSR and railways was the major issue during the incident. The netizens' indignation was additionally boosted by the official assertion, still upheld after the crash, that China had overtaken the advanced capitalist countries in creating a vehicle of the very highest technological standard. Corruption at the MOR became blatantly obvious with the dismissal of the Minister of Railways, Liu Zhijun, and deputy chief engineer Zhang Shuguang in February 2011. At the time, their removal provoked an online debate involving more than half a million participants, ranking 18th among the 20 largest online incidents in 2011 (Zhu et al., 2012). Rather surprisingly, corruption at the MOR nevertheless remained a relatively minor issue during the Wenzhou incident.

Both issues – safety problems and corruption – were rapidly linked to the extremely speedy development of the HSR project and were decried as a new "Great Leap Forward." In his post, user @shishiluantan attacked "unbridled corruption" that stopped at nothing and commented laconically: "Crashed into the rear of the 'Great Leap Forward'" (July 24, 22:59). User @foxuezuojiamingyijutu scoffed: "Chinese railways have five great progressive aspects: The Great Leap Forward – great plans – great investments – great corruption – great disaster . . ." (July 23, 23:30). Many microbloggers felt that the MOR had been using mobile Chinese citizens as guinea pigs to test the new technology; user @haohaoshuijiao wrote: "Why use people's blood as a means to lubricate the new machines in the name of HSR's progress?" (July 24, 19:01).

The netizen community was appalled by the obvious safety problems, which stood in stark contrast with the official boasting about the HSR having the highest-level technology in the world. The short time that was taken for the design of the high-speed trains and the construction of the railway lines met with particularly harsh criticism. User @hunangongshigonggongruihuati, for example, commented: "The longer the line, the shorter the construction time" (July 28, 12:02). Many users reposted a link to an issue of *China Youth Daily* first published on December 14, 2010, that revealed that the driver of HSR No. 1 "struggled through 670 pages of German material in only 10 days" (@yangyixian, July 24, 15:00). In the eyes of the netizens, no one in the railway department seemed to be concerned with safety at this early planning stage. "Those officials must have fallen asleep!" (@changjing, July 24, 09:31). Many people called for the HSR project to slow down, such as user @wangzhaohui: "Slow down, high-speed rail! Better slow down and not kill anyone!" (July 24, 18:31). Other posts requested the project to be stopped completely.

"I believe it anyway" – opacity in handling the incident

A further major issue of concern was the authorities' handling of the incident. Numerous microbloggers openly expressed their resentment of the official explanations and the handling of the crash. Later in 2011, the term "high-speed rail system" (*gaotieti*) became a synonym for the concealment of truth by the government (Zhu et al. 2012). Practically nobody believed that lightning was the actual cause of the accident, as the authorities claimed early on. The burial of a wrecked railcar at the site of the accident – officially a necessity for the rescue efforts or a means to protect valuable technology – was also a hotly debated topic, although it did not cause a significant peak in our sample of posts. User @oldtony'yehang scrutinized: "Why [did this happen]? . . . //@Chencun: The accident hasn't been investigated yet, and yet the broken pieces are already buried? This is the most valuable material for tests to examine the cars' destructiveness" (July 24, 10:00). To explicate further, similar to Twitter's RT, the double slash "//" indicates a repost. Other than on Twitter, Sina Weibo users can comment on posts with all their comments displayed underneath the original post, thereby facilitating conversation. Each post contains information about the number of reposts and comments. Others asked for a public hearing and complained that officials were shirking their responsibility: "Really unbelievable – yesterday it was still China's HSR, today officials are rapidly eating their words. It's a Sino–Japanese cooperation" (@FudanMBA'laowang, July 25, 19:30).

MOR spokesman Wang Yongping particularly became the object of ridicule among microbloggers. Wang was later dismissed from his post because of his improper handling of the press conferences (Xinhua, 2011c). It was he who blamed lightning for the crash and upheld the assertion that China's HSR was "up to standard". When asked for an explanation of the sudden burial of the railcars, he was also the one who claimed that the burial was necessary in order to facilitate the rescue efforts, concluding, "As you believe it or not, I believe it anyway" (*zhiyu ni xin bu xin, fanzheng wo xin le*). Various replies were laden with sarcasm: "Aliens have occupied the world! Do you believe that? I believe it anyway! China's HSR is the safest in the world! Do you believe that? I believe it anyway!" (@meinujiaxiaohua, July 29, 07:41).

Many users explicitly expressed their disbelief and requested greater transparency, calling for officials to take responsibility, the careful investigation of evidence to increase safety, and respect for the victims of the crash who died:

> So far, they have not revealed any reasons, but just talk of lightning; 2. They send a spokesperson who obviously provokes public feeling; . . . 4. Then they hastily announce the end of the official rescue efforts, ignoring the fact that there is still human life in the ruins; 5. Then next to the skeletons of the people who died for their country, they [have the audacity to] insist that the technology of China's HSR is advanced.
>
> (@yunfeiyanhuo, July 26, 09:00)

An often reposted picture shows monsters throwing train cars off the viaduct, suggesting this version to be just as likely as lightning causing the train crash. Other microbloggers displayed a t-shirt with the logo of the MOR turned into a skull and the imprint: "July 23, 2011. As you believe it or not. I believe it anyway", or ridiculed the MOR's boasting in the drawing of a crashing train with a skull-faced engine and the headline "The world's no. 1".

Consumer safety in a 'corrupt society'

The microbloggers did not stop at the gates of the MOR, but widened the scope of issues to the broader problems of consumer safety and corruption that had been gaining increasing public attention in China. While taking a smaller share of the overall debate, a nonetheless large number of netizens thus critically reflected on the sociopolitical system behind the tragedy. Many users recalled the long list of previous scandals harmful to the lives of the Chinese population: food poisoning, undrinkable water, gutter oil for cooking, collapsing elevators, bridges, and houses, as well as other incidents due to scandalous policies: the Red Cross scandal, house-price hikes, or rising commodity prices.

The problem of corruption among Chinese officials extending well beyond the MOR was seen by many netizens as a manifestation of a profoundly "corrupt society" (@xuxiaoming, Aug. 30, 08:08). User @xianyuxingkong posted: "There are too many of those rotten officials around; it's already impossible to ferret them out one by one. We'll all die on the roads, bridges, HSR, and skyscrapers they constructed. Buried alive for a system. //@Dianyingrenchengqingsong: China, you've gone off the rails" (July 24, 09:30). Without a thorough search for responsibility, the rectification of mistakes, and supervision and restriction, user @xinliyuekanzhubianwanghui assessed, "our daily lives . . . will be a land-mined field full of corruption" (July 24, 09:31).

It was also indignation about corruption that prompted the large-scale consumer boycott against the mineral water brand distributed free of charge on the HSR, which took off on July 28 and became one of the dominant issues in our sample on July 31. Initially called into life due to ecological concerns, the call for the collective return of mineral water produced by the Tibetan company "Xizang 5100

Glacier Mineral Water" turned into large-scale indignation when netizens discovered that ex-minister Liu Zhijun's wife had been a member of the company's executive board. One often-forwarded post reads: "You can take a risk and ride the HSR, but whatever you do, . . . when you get this bottle, please don't drink it, but sign the top of it, let it be sent back to Tibet by the HSR . . . " (@chali, July 30, 07:56).

"We are all traveling on a high-speed train" – questioning China's development path

What made the Wenzhou incident remarkable apart from its sheer size, however, was the large-scale critical debate about the state of China's society, the downside of the country's rapid growth, and the direction of its development. To many people, it seemed like the Wenzhou train crash and the problems that had surfaced during the HSR's development and at the MOR revealed all of China's problems "in a microcosm" (@shidongxiangjiao-shiqiang, July 26, 07:32). "I suddenly felt that the HSR was the epitome of present-day China," wrote user @zhaotianbu'erbai (July 25, 08:31). And user @zuoheng assessed: "We all – the whole of China – are riding on a high-speed train" (July 24, 15:03).

To many observers, the MOR's approach to the HSR project seemed particularly symptomatic of a national "Great Leap Forward" attitude that had manifested itself in every single economic realm and the national growth model in the form of "Chinese speed" (*Zhongguo sudu,* @zuoheng, July 24, 15:03) at the cost of the ordinary citizens. This sentiment was expressed by user @beijingzhufuxian, who linked the speed of the HSR-project to one of the leadership's core concepts: "Development should advance gradually; development in leaps is not 'scientific development' . . . Developing in leaps is [like] acting blindly" (reposted by @VivianGuo'guoibaoliguoxiaoying, July 24, 09:31). And user @leileinancy wrote: "We are all little white mice in this experiment concerning China's Leap Forward" (July 24, 10:00).

Microbloggers harshly criticized "China's eagerness for quick success and instant benefit, its love to brag and show off!" (@tianyahaijiaoke, July 25, 09:00) and "the cadres' pursuit of personal achievements without concern for the masses" (@woshicengzhi, July 29, 23:10). Satiric posts displayed a picture of the two characters for railway and transformed them into the meaning "lost its way" by erasing the left part of the first character. Others posted a signal light with a cross concealing the red light, indicating that the train (or China) cannot come to a halt.

"Slow down!" became an oft-repeated request. A post forwarded many times across Sina Weibo reads:

China, please stop your dashing pace, wait for your people, wait for your soul, wait for your morals, and wait for your conscience! Do not let the trains derail, do not let the bridges collapse, do not let the roads become pitfalls, do not let the buildings become death traps. Go more slowly, let all lives enjoy

freedom and dignity, so that nobody is left behind by the "times" and everybody can reach his destination smoothly and safely.

(@sunxiaoningzaieryue, July 24, 10:01)

The appeals to slow down were given new impetus by an editorial in the *People's
Daily* on July 28, which asked for further development, "but without a blood-
smeared GDP" (RMRB, 2011). Many posts picked up the cue and questioned
whether GDP "is really that important" (@jiangsuqiaolaoye, July 29, 07:31). A
large number of netizens concluded that the incident had not happened by chance,
but because the country had blindly "pursued the GDP development model"
(@xiaoxixiyigezhutou, July 29, 07:39). Others took refuge in sarcasm: "Speed
up! Speed up more! Chinese speed! . . . Paradise, we are coming! Sing songs of
triumph aloud and bury all the rubbish and remnants" (@zuoheng, July 24, 15:03).

These assessments prompted quite a considerable number of users to generally
contest the government's "executive power" and the leadership's capability to
manage the country. When user @mengbishisuyanguang asked: " . . . China, oh
China . . . What can you manage??," user @lizhigang bitingly answered: "They
can manage propaganda and the factors of 'instability'" (July 29, 10:01). Some
blamed the "unscientific attitude" of power holders (a side blow at one of Hu
Jintao's ideological core concepts), the government, or the state system. "As
long as such a government is not changed, there will be no justice," posted user
@ziyouchenying (July 28, 12:00), and a frequently forwarded post by user @gator
reads: "The reform of our system is actually too slow. That is the reason why the
HSR is too fast. As long as the system does not change, all that should be slow is
not able to slow down" (@liusong – jiaguwen, July 29, 19:12).

However, criticism halted at the expression of public opinion and did not turn
into calls for further action. Appeals for action were limited to consumer boycotts. Moreover, the gist of online public opinion during the Wenzhou incident did
not turn directly against the political leadership, rendering all talk of a "Chinese
microblogging revolution" off base. When PM Wen arrived in Wenzhou on July
28, the majority of users in our sample attentively followed his visit and approv-
ingly reposted his picture and his assertions on the future importance of safety
issues. Despite some doubts about his alleged 11-day illness not allowing him
to make an earlier visit and some critical remarks regarding the earlier neglect
of safety ("If safety is the top priority now, what was the top priority before?"
(@baoxiaoxia, July 28, 18:34), Wen's visit did not cause any significant increase
in the number of posts targeting the political system.

The erosion of public confidence in China's growth path

The scale of the Wenzhou incident was unprecedented on the Chinese Internet.
The fact that the train crash prompted millions of microbloggers to voice their
opinions online even though it was far from being the worst catastrophe China
had experienced in recent years can only be understood against the backdrop of
the public doubts and anger that had swelled up during the development of the

HSR program and in view of incessant revelations of food, medical, environmental, corruption, or other scandals as "by-products" of a heedless quest for growth. Thus, the crash easily lent itself to serving as an allegory of the state of Chinese society.

In recent years, particularly the young and urban middle-class in China have become increasingly concerned about the well-being of the people and have been prepared to demonstrate their yearning for a better quality of life, as the growing number of NIMBY protests impressively shows (Johnson, 2010; Yang & Zheng, 2012). The microbloggers mirrored this development by linking the Wenzhou crash to other scandals and extending the debate to a critical reflection on China's growth model. The Wenzhou incident was largely what Pilling termed a "middle-class revolt", attesting the trend toward a growing social commitment on the part of young and middle-class people (Pilling, 2011). Since the new wealthy elites have transferred to high-speed trains, while many ordinary people still prefer the slower but cheaper alternative offered by conventional trains, the "Wenzhou 723" incident particularly caught the attention of large numbers of middle-class citizens (Zhu et al., 2012). This was reflected in the appeals to return HSR tickets and not to ride the train for 30 days. Yang and Zheng (2012) have labeled these disappointed young people "the Han Hans", which refers to well-known Chinese blogger Han Han – mainly focusing on domestic affairs, exposing social problems, and debating about the direction in which Chinese society is heading.

The Wenzhou incident can also be seen to reflect the trend of the erosion of public confidence in consumer safety, social security, social justice, and the like, and a growing concern with the overall problems associated with China's growth model, which have been flaring up ever more frequently in recent years. The *Global Times*, one of the Party's mouthpieces, meticulously listed various "crises of credibility", including "Wenzhou 723", on a "special coverage" website under the headline "Government Credibility Crisis" (*Global Times,* 2014). Although the post-reform generations seem to be more critical of the system (Wang, 2010), this erosion of confidence does not translate as a significant decline in public trust in the central government or the Communist Party's leadership (Easterlin, Morgan, Switek & Wang 2012; Saich, 2011; Wang, 2010; Yang & Tang, 2010;). While some surveys indicate slightly lowered trust levels (Edelman, 2012), they are still considerably higher than in other countries, demonstrating that the diffuse support of China's political regime is still quite high. In the case of the Wenchuan earthquake nearly all the blame for the mishandling of relief work fell on the local government (Han, Hu & Nigg, 2011). In our case, it fell on the MOR. Among the posts that asked about the cause, responsibility, or remedy, far more than 70 per cent targeted the MOR and only around 20 per cent adhered to the national level.

While the MOR and the Chinese leadership had hailed the HSR program as a "national dream," appealing to nationalist sentiments, the failure of this "dream" prompted the netizen community to demonstrate its growing concern about social well-being. By taking up the meme of a national "Great Leap Forward" attitude and by requesting a national "slowdown", the microbloggers voiced their growing skepticism about China's current growth model. That the call for slower growth was by no means a flash in the pan is demonstrated by the increasing number of NIMBY-protests when urban citizens speak out against projects that are claimed to bring economic progress. And 1 year after the "Wenzhou 723", when the National Bureau of Statistics revealed on July 13, 2012, that the GDP growth rate would "only" be 7.6 per cent in the second quarter of 2012, again many netizens endorsed slower GDP growth and assessed temporary "stagnation" as an excellent opportunity for restructuring the economy, but questioned whether the current leaders would have the courage to implement the proclaimed reforms (Zhang, 2012).

While taking the expression of public concerns to a new scale, the Wenzhou incident blends in with the discontinuous sequence of sizeable but short-lived online debates about social issues that have gained in frequency in the last years. The Wenzhou online discussion, although peaking exceptionally high in the days immediately following the train crash, rapidly trailed off and had lost its impetus after nine days. This can partly be attributed to official intervention: signs of censorship on the microblogging platform, though hard to measure, were limited during the first nine days. Also the traditional media, while receiving orders from the Department of Propaganda to give the crash little attention and adhere to the official version (Bandurski, 2011b; CDT, 2011), were able to report remarkably critical about the accident during the first week. In the second week, stricter censorship implementation became visible both on the Internet and in the traditional media. On July 29, the Department of Propaganda issued a media directive that was termed a "media blackout" by the *New York Times* (LaFraniere, 2011; cp. also Chen, 2011). On Sina Weibo, issues related to the train crash that had occupied the top three of the platform's hottest topics list for 10 days, were suddenly toppled by other trends such as Chinese Valentine's Day and basketball on August 2 (Chin, 2011; Custer, 2011), suggesting official intervention.

While censorship might have contributed to the rapid fading out of the online debate, a sharp increase and rapid decline in participation levels is typical for online incidents both in China (Jiang, 2010; Yang, 2009b) and beyond (Segerberg & Bennett, 2011), however. It is thus likely that official intervention only accelerated an intrinsic development. In the months following the train crash, the debate about the Wenzhou accident never rekindled to a considerable scale on the Chinese Web. High speed rail was not a major issue in the online discussion following a deadly subway crash in Shanghai on September 27 that was traced back to a failure of the same safety system used on the Wenzhou trains, which can be shown from the fact that the search term *gaotie* returned between 1,438 and 821 posts on WeiboScope for the days from September 27 to 30, 2011. Even the release of the official investigation report on the Wenzhou accident on December 28, 2011, which found 54 officials as well as the design of the local control center and onboard components responsible for the accident, did not prompt a significant increase in related posts, according to a WeiboScope search.

Similar developments have also been displayed by the growing offline phenomenon of so-called social venting incidents, spontaneous gatherings of participants without immediate (material) interests, which mainly serve to vent feelings of resentment and anger and form and disperse quickly (Yu, 2009). The Wenzhou incident can thus be interpreted as one in a lengthening list of public debates about social issues that point to a decline of public trust in the direction Chinese society is headed. Tackling a multitude of pressing social problems such as corruption, government opacity, consumer safety, and the dangers associated with over-rapid development, the Wenzhou train crash was a striking cause for the large-scale expression of these growing public concerns. Microblogging was a convenient channel to do so.

Nothing but venting steam?

Our analysis has shown that the majority of microbloggers held the MOR and its representatives responsible for the fatal HSR crash near Wenzhou and picked out issues related to the high-speed rail development program as central themes. However, since not only the MOR but also the government and the CCP had elevated the overambitious HSR program to an allegory of China's rise, "Wenzhou 723" easily lent itself as a metaphor of the aberrations in China's development and an epitome of all the risks the Chinese people are facing should the leadership continue the charted course of unbalanced growth.

However, neither the symbolism of the Wenzhou collision nor the growing social concerns of China's middle class can explain why the posts could accumulate quite freely to such a scale in over more than a week's time. According to Hassid, China's censors are especially prone to curtail online discussions when taken by surprise (Hassid, 2012). One possible explanation is that the government considers weibo a convenient "steam valve" for the public, particularly when the reason for annoyance seems rather unimportant. Another explanation points at intra-leadership struggles about the reform of the MOR that had long been impeded by the ministry itself. Right after the crash, critique of the MOR's concentration of power emerged anew in public and rumors arose that Prime Minister Wen had made a second push for reform. The first (failed) attempt to break up the monopolistic power of the MOR can be traced back to the setting up the so-called Super Ministry of Transportation in 2008 (Lan, 2012). The MOR itself under its new chief Sheng Guangzu leaked ideas of encouraging market forces (Gu, 2011). Seen in this light, the rather extensive coverage of the MOR's financial problems, Liu Zhijun's expulsion from the party, or his trial for corruption in state-led media might have been intended to support attempts to curtail the MOR's power. By June 2012, however, the MOR seemed to have regained power and reforms appeared further away, when the ministry denied media reports that outlined plans to reform "one of the last bastions of China's planned economy" (Guo, 2012; Wen, 2012).

While the effect of the large-scale but short-lived "Wenzhou 723" online incident remains not measurable, the year 2011 may be kept in mind for the intensification of the CCP's struggle with public opinion (*Global Times*, 2011). The introduction of stricter microblogging regulations in December 2011 signaled that the incident had not left China's leadership unfazed. Together with the technical possibilities for public expression provided by the new technologies, the people's growing reluctance to accept the social costs associated with China's growth model, and certain features of the political system such as corruption and a lack of transparency, which became visible in the Wenzhou microblogging debate, will keep putting pressure on China's leadership.

References

Bandurski, D. (2011a, March 10). Can social media push change in China? *China Media Project*. Retrieved July 7, 2011, from http://cmp.hku.hk/2011/10/03/15870/

Bandurski, D. (2011b, July 25). History of high-speed propaganda tells all. *China Media Project*. Retrieved July 28, 2011, from http://cmp.hku.hk/2011/07/25/14036/

Buckley, C., & Lee, M. (2011, August 12). Insight: China's microbloggers rattle the censor's cage. *Reuters*. Retrieved November 15, 2011, from http://www.reuters.com/assets/print?aid=USTRE77B0JH20110812

CDT. (2011, October 21). Directives from the Ministry of Truth: July 5–September 28, 2011. *China Digital Times*. Retrieved October 21, 2011, from http://chinadigitaltimes.net/2011/10/directives-from-the-ministry-of-truth-july-5-september-28-2011/

Century Weekly. (Ed.). (2011, August 26). Our bullet train lesson: Look before leaping. *A Century Weekly*. Retrieved March 9, 2012, from http://english.caixin.com/2011-08-26/100295367_all.html

Chen, S. (2011, July 31). Censors slap ban on crash coverage. *South China Morning Post*. Retrieved March 9, 2012, from http://www.scmp.com/article/974998/censors-slap-ban-crash-coverage

Chin, J. (2011, July 26). Weibo watershed? Train collision anger explodes online. *China Real Time Report. The Wall Street Journal*. Retrieved November 15, 2011, from http://blogs.wsj.com/chinarealtime/2011/07/26/weibo-watershed-train-collision-anger-explodes-online/

ChinaNews. (2011, May 13). 新浪微博用户数已逾1.4亿 (More than 140 million users on Sina Weibo). Retrieved July 25, 2012, from http://www.chinanews.com/it/2011/05-13/3038721.shtml

Christensen, C. (2011). Twitter revolutions? Addressing social media and dissent. *The Communication Review, 14*(3), 155–157.

Custer, C. (2011). Death on the high speed rail, day 2, *China Geeks*. Retrieved March 18, 2012, from http://chinageeks.org/2011/07/death-on-the-high-speed-rail-day-2/

Diamond, L., & Plattner, M. F. (Ed.). (2012). *Liberation technology: Social media and the struggle for democracy*. Baltimore, MD: Johns Hopkins University Press.

Easterlin, R. A., Morgan, R. Switek, M., & Wang, F. (2012). China's life satisfaction, 1990–2010. *Proceedings of the National Academy of Sciences of the United States of America, 109*(25), 9775–9780.

Edelman. (2012). *Edelman trust barometer executive summary* (p. 10). Retrieved July 30, 2012, from http://www.edelman.com/trust

Esarey, A., & Qiang, X. (2008). Political expression in the Chinese blogosphere: Below the radar. *Asian Survey, 48*(5), 752–772.

Global Times. (2011, December 29). Govt gets crash course on public opinion. Retrieved December 30, 2011, from www.globaltimes.cn

Global Times. (2014). Government credibility crisis. Retrieved March 24, 2014, from http://www.globaltimes.cn/SPECIALCOVERAGE/CredibilityCrisis.aspx

Gu, Y. (2011, August 10). Another sidetrack for China's railway reform. *Caixin*. Retrieved December 6, 2012, from http://english.caixin.com

Guo, K. (2012, June 25). Rail industry progress delayed after MOR denies report of ministry split. *Global Times*. Retrieved December 6, 2012, from http://www.globaltimes. cn

Han, Z., Hu, X., & Nigg, J. (2011). How does disaster relief works affect the trust in local government? A study of the Wenchuan earthquake. *Risk, Hazards & Crisis in Public Policy, 2*(4), 1–20.

Hassid, J. (2012). Safety valve or pressure cooker? Blogs in Chinese political life. *Journal of Communication, 62,* 212–230.

Jiang, M. (2010). Chinese internet events. Wang luo shi jian. In A. Esarey & R. Kluver (Eds.), *Internet in China: Online business, information, distribution, and social connectivity*. New York, NY: Berkshire Publishing. Retrieved April 26, 2011, from SSRN: http://ssrn.com/abstract=1655204

Johnson, I. (2012, October 5). China advances high-speed rail amid safety, corruption concerns. *National Geographic Daily News*. Retrieved October 25, 2012, from http://news.nation algeographic.com/news/2012/10/121005-china-high-speed-rail-trains-transportation-world/

Johnson, T. (2010). Environmentalism and NIMBYism in China: Promoting a rules-based approach to public participation. *Environmental Politics, 19*(3), 430–448.

LaFraniere, S. (2011, July 31). Media blackout in China after wreck. *New York Times*. Retrieved August 2, 2011, from http://www.nytimes.com/2011/08/01/world/asia/01crackdown. html

Lam, W. (2011). Troubled railway ministry casts doubt on Beijing's commitment to reform. *China Brief, 11*(15), 3–6.

Lan, X. (2012, April 12). Restart railway reform. *Beijing Review, 15*. Retrieved December 6, 2012, from http://www.bjreview.com.cn

Lotan, G., Graeff, E., Ananny, M., Gaffney, D., Pearce, I., & boyd, d. (2011). The revolutions were tweeted: Information flows during the 2011 Tunisian and Egyptian revolutions. *International Journal of Communication, 5,* 1375–1405.

Lou, J., Gui, A., Xu, E., Moh, A., Zhu, K., He, L., & Ching, C. (2011). China high-speed rail. On the economic fast track. *Morgan Stanley Blue Paper*. Morgan Stanley, p. 15.

Morozov, E. (2009, April 7). Moldova's twitter revolution. *Foreign Policy*. Retrieved March 14, 2012, from http://neteffect.foreignpolicy.com/posts/2009/04/07/moldovas_ twitter_revolution

Osnos, E. (2012, October 22). Boss rail. The disaster that exposed the underside of the boom. *The New Yorker*. Retrieved December 6, 2012, from http://www.newyorker.com/ reporting/2012/10/22/121022fa_fact_osnos

Perry, E. J. (2001). Challenging the mandate of heaven: Popular protest in modern China. *Critical Asian Studies*, 33(2), 163–180.

Pilling, D. (2011, August 3). China crashes into a middle class revolt. *Financial Times*. Retrieved December 6, 2012, from http://www.ft.com/cms/s/0/0558876e-be1b-11e0-bee9-00144feabdc0.html#axzz2wdJHYBEQ

RMRB. (2011, July 28). Renmin ribao: Mou fazhan xu anquan zhishang bu yao daixuede GDP (People's daily: Development needs safety, not a blood-smeared GDP). *Renmin Ribao*. Retrieved August 16, 2012, from http://news.qq.com/a/20110728/000165. htm

Saich, T. (2011). Citizen's perceptions of adequate governance. Satisfaction levels among rural and urban Chinese. In E. Zhang, A. Kleinman, & W. Tu (Eds.), *Governance of life in Chinese moral experience* (pp. 199–214). London and New York: Routledge.

Segerberg, A., & Bennett, W. L. (2011). Social media and the organization of collective action: Using twitter to explore the ecologies of two climate change protests. *The Communication Review, 14,* 197–215.

Shank, M., & Wasserstrom, J. (2011). China's high-speed crash leads to legitimacy crisis. *Miller-McCune.* Retrieved March 18, 2012, from http://www.miller-mccune.com/politics/chinas-high-speed-crash-leads-to-legitimacy-crisis-34518

Shirky, C. (2011, January February). The political power of social media. *Foreign Affairs.* Retrieved March 24, 2011, from http://www.foreignaffairs.com/print/66987

Sullivan, J., & Xie, L. (2009). Environmental activism, social networks and the Internet. *The China Quarterly, 198,* 422–432.

Tang, L., & Bhattacharya, S. (2011). Power and resistance: A case study of satire on the Internet. *Sociological Research Online,* (2). Retrieved August 2, 2012, from http://www.socresonline.org.uk/16/2/11

Wang, J. (2011, August 4). China rail ministry "kingdom" may be split up on fatal crash. *Bloomberg.* Retrieved January 31, 2012, from http://www.bloomberg.com

Wang, Z. (2010). Generational shift and its impacts on regime legitimacy in China. *Discussion Paper 64,* p. 28. Nottingham, UK: University of Nottingham, China Policy Institute.

Wen, S. (2012, June 16). Calls for railway ministry reform heating up. *Caijing.* Retrieved December 6, 2012, from http://english.caijing.com.cn

Wines, M., & LaFraniere, S. (2011, July 28). In baring facts of train crash, blogs erode China censorship. *The New York Times.* Retrieved July 29, 2011, from http://www.nytimes.com/2011/07/29/world/asia/29china.html

Wu, G. (2011). High-speed rail in China. *EAI Bulletin, 13*(2), 1–7, 13.

Xin, D. (2011, April 18). Safety check on track for rail. *China Daily Online.* Retrieved May 28, 2012, from http://europe.chinadaily.com.cn/business/2011-04/18/content_12343620.htm

Xinhua. (2011a, June 30), Chinese premier calls new bullet train "new chapter" in railway history. *Xinhua (BBC Monitoring Global Newsline Asia Pacific Political File, 20110702).*

Xinhua. (2011b, January 4). High-speed rail linking Beijing, Shanghai to open June 2 16011. *Xinhua (BBC Monitoring Global Newsline Asia Pacific Economic File, 20110104).*

Xinhua. (2011c, August 16). Railways ministry spokesman Wang Yongping dismissed from office: Ministry. *Xinhuanet.* Retrieved August 20, 2011, from http://news.xinhuanet.com/english2010/china/2011-08/16/c_131053386.htm

Xinhua. (2011d, July 24). Xinhua insight: Microblogs reveal the healing power of "we-media" in wake of deadly high-speed train crash in East China. *Xinhua.* Retrieved March 18, 2012, from http://news.xinhuanet.com/english2010/indepth/2011-07/24/c_131006431.htm

Yan, J. (2011, March 24). Audit finds $28m fraud in railway project. *China Daily.* Retrieved March 8, 2012, from http://usa.chinadaily.com.cn/epaper/2011-03/24/content_12221615.htm

Yang, G. (2009a). Online activism. *Journal of Democracy, 20*(3), 33–36.

Yang, G. (2009b). The power of the Internet in China. Citizen activism online. New York, NY: Columbia University Press.

Yang, L., & Zheng, Y. (2012). *Fen qings* (angry youth) in contemporary China. *Journal of Contemporary China, 21*(76), 637–653.

Yang, Q., & Tang, W. (2010). Exploring the sources of institutional trust in China: Culture, mobilization, or performance? *Asian Politics & Policy, 2*(3), 415–436.

Yi, Y. (2011, August 12). China's micro-blog revolution. *The Diplomat*. Retrieved February 27, 2012, from http://the-diplomat.com

Yu, J. (2009). Anger in the streets. *Caijing, 7*(7). Retrieved November 29, 2011, from http://english.caijing.com.cn/2009-07-07/110194431.html

Yue, Z. (2011). Expressways of excess. *Caixin online*. Retrieved October 31, 2011, from http://english.caixin.cn/2011-10-31/100319471.html

Zhang, Y. (2012, July 17). Slower GDP growth in China? All the better, say some netizens. *Tea Leaf Nation*. Retrieved July 20, 2012, from http://tealeafnation.com/2012/07/slower-gdp-growth-in-china-all-the-better-says-some-netizens/

Zhu, H., Shan, X., & Hu, J. (2012). 2011 nian Zhongguo hulianwang yuqing fenxi baogao (Analysis on Internet-based public opinion in China, 2011). In Ru X., Lu X., & Li P. (Eds.), *2012 nian Zhongguo shehui xingshi fenxi yu yuce (Society of China. Analysis and forecast [2012])* (pp. 194–214). Beijing, China: Shehui kexue wenxian chubanshe.

Part IV
Enjoying online spaces

7   Gold farmers and water army

Digital playbour with Chinese characteristics

Ge Jin and David Kurt Herold

The main advantage of the Chinese economy leading to its rapid rise was the importance of low-priced labour. European and North American manufacturing jobs were outsourced to developing countries like China where labour was comparatively weak and defenceless against exploitative practices, while governments emphasised economic growth and fostered a race to the bottom in an effort to better attract multi-national corporations. This coincided with the triumph of neo-liberalism in the developed world leading to a general decline of manufacturing jobs and the informatisation of labour in all sectors in advanced industrial countries. Employment in developed countries became increasingly service oriented and technology mediated, while developing countries, and in particular China, moved in the direction of intensive labour-based production.

With the rapid adoption of the Internet in China, and the fast proliferation of low-cost Internet access, a similar phenomenon began to be replicated in cyberspace. Labour-intensive activities were outsourced to Chinese Internet users, at first by non-Chinese Internet users, and later by companies inside China. The conditions for the emergence of virtual labour evolved out of the conjunction of existing offline economic practices and a developing digital infrastructure in China with its large numbers of Internet "have-less" (Cartier, Castells, & Qiu, 2005).

This chapter investigates the Chinese Internet as a site of cheap labour and of exploitation in which the exploited nevertheless manage to engage in playful leisure pursuits that they enjoy and that improve their professional standing. The paid-for "playbour" of playing online games, or posting on discussion boards, allows individual labourers to hone skills they can employ to follow personal interests during their spare time, while the spare time activities often benefit their professional standing and allow them to engage with other "playbourers" in communities of shared interest. Their work and play exist in a symbiotic relationship in which the individual playbourers live lives envied by many: they earn enough money to make a living, they have jobs that are almost identical to their hobbies, and they spend their days with close friends. Their jobs may not be to everybody's liking, but most of the cheap labourers in Chinese cyberspace appear to have found lifestyles that suit them, at least for a while.

The chapter will discuss two new professions in particular that have established themselves in Chinese cyberspace over the past few years: gold farmers and the water army. People in these two professions earn a living through their online activities, and their labour has a significant impact both on the Internet as a whole, as well as on their own offline lives, though mainstream society does not fully acknowledge their activities as employment. Due to the unconventional nature of their labour practices, people in these two professions have formed quasi-subcultural communities in which to share stories and to produce meaning out of their employment.

Gold farmers play online games in order to collect in-game goods, which they then sell to other gamers for real money. Virtual goods in MMORPGs (Massively Multiplayer Online Role Playing Games), range from in-game currency, weapons, or armour to be upgraded, to high-level avatars, which can be traded against real world currency in transactions dubbed "real money trade" (RMT) by the gaming community.

In China, gold farms began as small workshops with around a dozen computers each. By the mid-2000s, though, RMT in online games had exploded into a billion-dollar global industry (Castronova, 2005). Some of the gold farms observed by the first author had expanded into gaming factories with hundreds of young men working together for 10–12 hours a day in games like World of Warcraft and Lineage, while living together in dormitories, similar to migrant labourers in the factory cities of China's south-eastern provinces.

Soldiers of the water army are paid posters hired to generate floods of articles, comments or links with specific contents in certain web spaces, such as forums, news sites, or blogs. Public relations companies provide water army services to any corporation wanting to boost their online image or undermine the reputation of competitors. According to several interviews conducted by the first author with industry insiders, there are currently hundreds of thousands of people employed as soldiers of different water armies in China, mostly college students, unemployed migrant workers, or housewives.

Services a water army offers include: distorting the result of online polls, increasing the number of followers of microblogs, promoting posts in online forums, increasing hits of videos shared online, or even increasing download records for products on online app stores such as the Apple iTunes store. When hired, each soldier of the water army creates a small number of separate online identities and begins posting in the manner required on the targeted platforms. The success of a water army stems from the number of its soldiers and their uniformity, rather than the skill level of individual soldiers, which parallels worker efficiency measures in, for example, factory assembly lines.

The research this chapter is based on has been mostly ethnographic. The first author has held hundreds of in-depth interviews with gold farmers and soldiers of water armies, as well as conducted extensive participant observation in the sites of their work during the past 6 years. The stories and insights of these unconventional labourers in China provide an intriguing new perspective to theoretical discussions about the evolution of labour practices in online societies.

Labour and the Internet

While there is a vast amount of literature condemning different forms of capitalism for the exploitation of labourers going back to the 19th century, and an emerging literature on the exploitation of the free labour provided by prosumers (Toffler, 1980) or produsers (Bruns, 2008) in cyberspace, there is far less on the multiple ways in which digital labourers are taking advantage of the experience and skills gained in their employment and how they are using the grey areas between play and labour in their professions to create spaces in which to express themselves, and in which to enjoy their lives.

Even during a conference dedicated to "the Internet as playground and factory" the papers presented only projected "old" ideas onto the new technological sphere of the Internet and exclusively addressed the relationship between employers and employees online, and whether or not the latter were exploited by the former (Fuchs, 2009, p. 400). This privileging of the Marxist *relations of production* over the relationship of individual labourers to the *means of production* appears too narrow to be useful for an application to the Internet, but appears prevalent in academic publications (see also Scholz, 2013). Individual users do not need to *own* the Internet, or even the computers they use, to produce value, and even a playful exploration or self-interested software development using freely available tools can lead to a marketable product.

In connection with gold farming, Nardi and Kow (2010) have pointed out that discourses of exploitation have created imaginary "Chinese gold farmers" and by extension "the water army" that portrays them as "low wage, low tech, low culture", but that this *is only* an imaginary. They argue that the practices involved in playbour are far more complex and technologically sophisticated than the grinding of unskilled labourers. The data presented in this chapter, and additional data published by the first author in video format (Jin, 2006a; 2006b; 2006c), suggest that the experiences of online labour in China are less a story of exploitation and more one of creative uses of new possibilities, and of taking advantage of the unique positionality of the online labourers between and within online and offline spaces.

To a certain extent many of the playbourers of Chinese cyberspace could just as easily be presented as entrepreneurs instead of exploited cheap labor, given their ability to switch jobs if they decide to do so, or that they privately hone and individually sell their skills on a market fairly free from regulation. Despite their poor living conditions – when compared to the living standards in Europe or the United States – they are far better off in comparison to most other Chinese labourers, and their online skills offer them opportunities and spaces in which to explore their own identities, exchange opinions with others, and express themselves more forcefully than most other citizens of the People's Republic of China.

Similarly, Lindtner and Dourish (2011) argue that the playing of computer games in Chinese cyberspace should be seen in the context of economic development and its attendant improvement of the lives of individuals. They suggest looking at the "promise of play" and how "game play" has become "a site of economic and social production" (p. 454), rather than merely a new form of employment or the exploitation of disenfranchised labourers. As the data presented in this chapter demonstrate, it is important "to consider play not as distinct from but tightly interwoven with other fabrics of daily life" (Lindtner & Dourish, 2011, p. 458) – even for playbourers.

Wang, Ding, Lu, Xia, and Gu (2012) insist that "technology and sociality have a complex relationship" in the lives of Chinese gamers (p. 591). Their study shows how gamers blend online and offline experiences so as to increase their enjoyment of games, but also to satisfy their need to communicate with other gamers going through similar experiences. Such sharing of experiences, and the creation of technology based, but blended communities of gamers, can be observed among China's playbourer entrepreneurs as well, as the lines between online and offline, and between work and play become blurred in their daily practices.

In 2001, Pekka Himanen discussed how the advent of network society was changing people's relationship to their work. He argued for a "Hacker work ethic" (Himanen, 2001, p. 7) that is characterised by a "passionate relationship to work", meaning "the dedication to an activity that is intrinsically interesting, inspiring, and joyous" (p. 6). Looking at the gold farmers or water army soldiers in China, an exploration of the practices they engage in, both in their "work" as well as in their "lives" and how they utilise each in the other, suggests that these entrepreneurial playbourers should be seen as embodiments of Himanen's "Hacker work ethic" rather than be studied as poor, exploited slave-labourers. Despite all the hardships they endure, most gold farmers and water army soldiers appear to be *passionate* about their jobs and do mix work with pleasure and vice versa.

The playbourers of China's gold farms

In 2005, the first author noticed that stories were being circulated in the gaming communities of the United States about how a large portion of the virtual goods available in real money trade was mass produced by gaming sweatshops in China that hired people to play online games around the clock. At the same time, people in China talked about young people making a living by playing games. After some research into gaming workshops in Shanghai and the province of Zhejiang in China, the stories about Chinese gold farmers turned out to be very close to the truth.

The stereotype of the Chinese gold farmers stems from the frequent encounters with gold farmers from China that US gamers complain about in many MMORPGs. Taylor (2006) observed:

> Although it is certainly not only Chinese workers participating in the growing economy of RMT practices in MMOGs, as a tag the conflation of Chinese with gold farmer has seemed to come all too easy and now transcends any particular game.

(p. 320)

Most factory-style gold farms in China emerged in late 2003 with the release of global hits like Lineage II and World of Warcraft III. What the first author encountered during his field research in 2005 and 2006 was that gold farming had developed into a significant industry in China. Among the gold farms visited, several had hundreds of computers and employees. According to insiders of this industry, hundreds of thousands of gaming workers in China were working in almost every game with a virtual economy: they were killing monsters, mining gems, blacksmithing, tailoring, and power levelling (levelling up a customer's character to a desired level) on the virtual lands (regional game servers) in America, Europe, and Asia.

Typically, the gold farms provided meals and dormitories, and the workers lived on the farm and worked on 12-hour shifts with short breaks. Usually a gold farm employed twice as many farmers as it owned computers so farming could continue uninterruptedly for 24 hours each day. The salary for gaming workers ranged from 40 USD to 200 USD per month, which was an average wage for unskilled labour in China in 2006. However, there were a few in which the labourers were willing to work for free as long as they had a place to live and they could play games for free.

All the gaming workers encountered were male, usually in their early 20s. Most of them did not have better alternatives on the job market "as it is really difficult to find a job in China. It is really difficult" (quote from one gamer), though quite a few chose gaming as a profession because of their own desire to spend more time playing computer games. Former students from high schools or universities who spent much of their time playing computer games in Internet cafes often met gold farmers there and got introduced to gold farming as a career choice they could take up even if they underperformed in their studies. Their "dream" was expressed best by one of the gamers who said: "As a professional gamer, you can have an income, though not much; it's still a happy thing".

Some gold farmers are part-time labourers who do several hours or days of gold farming when they have some time, in order to improve their regular salaries. In one case the second author came across, a sailor working on ocean-going freighters worked as a gold farmer whenever he was off duty and in China between voyages. The gold farming represented a welcome addition to the meagre salary he received as sailor, while also allowing him to continue playing the newest computer games whenever he had the time to do so.

Most full-time gold farmers used to be either (high-school) students, unemployed or had worse jobs before they found this job. Many said that working on a gold farm was fun in the beginning, but gradually it became exhausting and boring as unlike regular gamers, they had to stay in the same spots and keep repeating the same set of tasks. Staring at a computer, clicking the mouse, and killing imaginary monsters for 10–12 hours a day is an exhausting job, but not more exhausting than most other forms of menial labour in China. Many of the gaming workers were already game fans before they went professional, and they continued to frequent Internet cafes after work to play the same games on their own on Chinese servers just to relax and have some fun, while interacting with other gamers *as* game-playing individuals.

During work hours, gold farmers cannot socialize with other, "normal" gamers, or go on joint adventures, partly because of language and cultural barriers on the non-Chinese game servers where the gold farming for the markets outside China takes place. The individual labourers are also afraid of being reported to the game companies by other gamers, as these tend to ban the accounts of suspected gold farmers. With one aspect of their work, namely power levelling, it is additionally part of the contract between the gold farm and their client that the labourers do not mess up the customer's online social life, which means the process has to happen in secret with as little contact with other gamers as possible.

The distinction between work and play is not clear-cut for the gold farmers, as there are many crossovers and connections between the two domains. Their (private) achievements in online games are directly related to their (professional) pay, while their hours and days of (professional) practice of gaming skills contribute to their achievements and their enjoyment when (privately) playing the games. Stories circulating among China's gold farmers tell of individual labourers who employed their professional skills during their spare time to obtain high-level equipment in a game, which they then sold (privately) for large amounts of money. This allowed them to quit their employment by starting their own gold farm and employing others to labour for them, thus blurring the line between play and labour.

Boundaries are also blurred in the personal relationships of individual gold farmers. Within the confines of the gold farm, the individual labourers bond through the proximity in which they work (online) and live (offline), as their in-game achievements are admired and celebrated by the people working alongside them. As one gold farmer put it: "When we so many people are playing together it's important to have fun. There is a sense of achievement."

In the same way, their skills and achievements when playing online games for entertainment in an Internet café bring them many admirers and friends among the regulars of the café, who often have limited financial means, and for whom Internet cafes and their gaming experiences online are means of escape from their hard lives. The professional game players are heroes to these mostly young and male game players who dream of being able to play games all day while being paid for it and regard it as a privilege rather than a "gaming sweatshop" (Thompson, 2005).

In the fluid world of gold farming, the offline friendships and contacts an individual labourer establishes, and which are strengthened through shared moments of life and death in the virtual world, acquire a high value for their personal and professional lives. Labourers in gold farms are usually young migrant workers from all over China, and they tend to travel from one city to another in search of better jobs. Often friends (and colleagues) from one gold farm disperse to different cities after a few years, but keep in contact through the games they share. One of the gold farmers interviewed told the first author that the most heartwarming moment of his entire life was when he felt very lonely on his birthday in a city to which he had just moved, only to log into his favourite game and discover that his former gold-farming colleagues and friends had organised a virtual birthday party and were waiting for him. As one gold farmer put it: "So many young guys playing together, it's really fun. I never imagined that one can play games and earn money at the same time. We had fun together and treated each other like brothers."

Another gold farmer talked about how the gold farm he worked on had failed, but that the owner of the farm had invited him and several other colleagues to move in with him and to continue playing in his home. They continued living together, playing online, until they found another way of earning a living with their playbour and managed to monetise their skills to start another gold farm. The relationship between owner and labourer at the gold farm was less one of employer and employees, but more of friends trying to earn a living by doing something they enjoyed. He stated: "Here we don't have employer or employee. If we can make money, we share it. If we can't, at least we are happy playing together."

This informal network of gold farmers also makes it possible for them to share news about better-paid jobs, better gold-farming facilities or environments, etc., which provide them with a sense of community, and empower them in their inter-actions with the owners of gold farms. As highly specialised labourers in a shifting industry this alleviates to some extent their uncertainty about the future, in which new games requiring new skills are frequently published, gaming companies regularly attempt to restrict RMT and gold farming in games, and the Chinese authorities might at any moment attempt to regulate or close down all forms of gold farms given their unclear legal status.

No national policy or regulations for gold farming exist in China, as yet, and government officials at all levels have tolerated the establishment of gold farms, as they provide employment for many young Chinese. With the growth of the industry, though, and the increase of RMT in the Chinese online games market, this situation will have to change at some point. While gold farms were effectively operating outside China on game servers located elsewhere, but bringing hard currency into the country, their activities were acceptable. However once Chinese labourers get paid by large numbers of Chinese customers to procure virtual goods for them, this business will in all likelihood not escape regulatory scrutiny. It will be interesting to discover how the playbourer entrepreneurs of China's gold farms adapt to forces intending to regulate, control, or even tax their activities.

Soldiers of the water army

The water army as an industry and cultural phenomenon did not receive a lot of publicity before 2010. Until then, the best-known group of paid Internet post-ers was the *50-cent-party* (*Wumaodang*). The term refers to Internet users who are paid by Chinese government (and Communist Party) officials to join Internet forums and argue against critics of the government or the Party. According to sto-ries circulating online, these paid posters receive RMB 0.50 (around 8 US cents) for each post they write, which is where the name originates.

Unlike the *50-cent-party*, the term *water army* refers to Internet posters hired by companies or individuals for commercial purposes. Since 2009, the first author has done ethnographic research in Internet public relations companies that recruit soldiers of the water army, QQ groups in which soldiers of the water army exchange ideas, as well as on the forums on which the water army is active.

Water armies first came to the public's attention during a dramatic "cyberwar" between the two Chinese IT companies Tencent and Qihoo 360. Tencent is the provider of the QQ set of services, the biggest social network in China, while Qihoo 360 is a software company known for its antivirus software, 360 Safeguard and the web browser, 360 Browser. In 2010, Tencent released its own antivirus software QQ doctor and bundled it for free with QQ, which had immediate and drastic effects on the marketshare of Qihoo 360's commercial antivirus software.

In September 2010, Zhou Hongyi, the founder of Qihoo 360's founder accused Tencent of secretly scanning the hard drives of QQ users whenever they launched the software, thus violating their privacy. Tencent denied the allegations and retaliated by making it impossible for users to install QQ on systems running 360 Safeguard antivirus software. The fight between the two companies forced hundreds of millions of Chinese Internet users to choose sides, and they went online to complain about being dragged into this war and to debate in different forums which side they should choose. Soon, however, the discussions were influenced in noticeable ways by special groups of Internet users.

Some posts in the online discussions appeared to go viral more easily than others, for example, a post saying, "Today I drove to the park and suddenly felt sentimental. Zhou Hongyi (the CEO of Qihoo 360) is a fabulous boss. Let's think about it, among those who worked for him, many became millionaires."

This "sentimental" post was spotted on a wide range of online platforms, repeatedly posted by different "original" posters. Some alert Internet users also noticed that those who spread this post were mostly newly registered users in their respective forums. Over time, increasing numbers of artificially instigated posts were identified, and it became obvious that many posters were not just there to express their opinions.

The cyberwar between Tencent and Qihoo 360 lasted 2 months, during which all the major forums in China, from Sina Weibo to Tianya, were flooded with exaggerated posts attacking (or defending) either Tencent or Qihoo 360. The overwhelming presence of the water armies in the conflict eventually even attracted the attention of the offline media, and *Focus On,* a popular programme on China's Central Television (CCTV) devoted an entire episode to a discussion of this new online development on November 7, 2010. The programme was mostly critical of the water armies, accusing them of polluting the online environment and of misinforming the public.

During an interview, a veteran soldier of the water army said that the cyberwar between Tencent and Qihoo 360 had involved tens of thousands of soldiers, more than any other water army campaigns he had seen or heard of since. He also reported that the CCTV coverage deeply affected the opinion individual soldiers had of their jobs. Before the programme, many young people just thought of their water army job as a temporary and simple way to make some money. They were generally not aware of the scale of the industry and of the social implications. After the broadcast of the programme, though, individual soldiers grew excited at being part of a force able to shape Internet opinion and culture and began to take their water army job more seriously. Some soldiers found their jobs so controversial that they became fearful. One teenage interviewee stated: "I am very scared. I didn't realize what I did was so serious. Was it a crime to post those things? I will not do this again ever."

The water army industry continued to grow despite, or perhaps because of the controversy. Currently, water army services have become a common offering of many Internet public relations companies. Water armies have been employed in the public relations campaign of *Mengniu*, the milk product company involved in food safety scandals, the ownership dispute over the cold-tea brand *Wang Laoji* between Jiao Duobao Ltd. and Guanzhou Medicine Group, and in the creation and promotion of Internet celebrities such as the model Gan Lulu.

Water armies are employed both to promote the products of a company as well as to criticise the products of competitors. In one famous example that backfired on its originator, Zhou Hongyi, the CEO of Qihoo 360, employed a water army in a fight with Xiaomi Mobile Phone, one of his competitors. On May 17, 2012, Zhou added a post to his own account on Sina Weibo, China's largest microblogging platform, claiming that the handsets produced by Xiaomi Mobile Phone were not worth their price and that the handsets his own company were about to bring to market were going to be much cheaper but also better. After his initial post was made, thousands of supporting comments were added to the post over a short period of time by soldiers of a water army. Zhou, however, later decided to delete this post, which also caused the deletion of all the comments attached to the post. This led to the sudden appearance of thousands of negative comments about Qihoo 360 and its business practices, as well as about Zhou Hongyi's character. A soldier of the water army involved explained during an interview that they were usually paid based on the number of comments they made, and that the public relations company employing them refused to pay after their initial comments supporting Zhou Hongyi had been deleted. The soldiers of the water army then took out their frustration on Zhou Hongyi who had caused their comments to be deleted when he took down his initial post.

The cost of hiring a water army remains low thanks to the abundant supply of cheap labour in China. As a result, a water army is a better option for many companies than spamming software, which can be blocked by anti-spam filters, while humans are able to create posts that are not tagged by them. Soldiers of water armies are usually recruited by Internet public relations companies, which retain 60 per cent of a client's payments, while the soldiers share the remaining 40 per cent. According to several sources, individual solders are typically paid around RMB 0.50 for each post, but if the identities they control on specific forums are established opinion leaders or they create original posts that are forwarded and commented on by many Internet users, they are paid a premium. In a chat group on QQ, soldiers working for water armies exchanged advice on how to improve their earnings per post. Some of the tips mentioned in the group were the following:

> To ensure your posts are not deleted by web masters you have to avoid being identified as a soldier of a water army.

You cannot repeat the same post too many times with the same online identity.

You should post normal posts to gain credibility for your identity in online forums.

Writing a new post is always more effective than just replying to or commenting on other people's posts.

Accumulate as many identities on as many different forums as possible.

These identities are the most important assets for soldiers of a water army.

Being a soldier in a water army means utilising online identities to spread a client's message. Thus, a soldier with a number of influential and "old" online identities will be in a better position than a soldier having to create new identities for each new job. This means that any Internet user wishing to earn money as a soldier in a water army needs to invest his or her own (private) time and effort in the creation and maintenance of online profiles in order to be more effective in their job, thus again blurring the line between play and labour when a person is employed online.

At times, individual soldiers see their online identities as simple masks emboldening them to post opinions they would not dare to put forward under their real names. Sometimes, they develop a relationship with their online identities, particularly on forums with more personal interactions. Often, they feel bad about job assignments leading to the notoriety of their online identities.

The time and effort spent on their online identities also create dilemmas for soldiers asked to post messages they believe to be wrong, as their reputation is tied up in the identities they create. Although soldiers of water armies are often required to just copy and paste what is assigned to them, they are concerned about what is posted using their own (virtual) identities. In one example, an interviewee mentioned that he was once assigned to post positive feedback on a drug he knew was fake and useless. He ended up fulfilling his duty but felt so bad about it that he logged into the forum later using a different identity to attack his own earlier post.

It is not uncommon for soldiers of water armies to be required to promote agendas conflicting with their own values, such as statements supporting fake products or financial scams or to spread libellous posts against an innocent person. Often they feel caught between fulfilling their job like digital robots and being normal participants in public discussions online.

Additionally, being a soldier in a water army affects their perception of the Internet as a platform for public discussions. Many of our sources told us that they had become highly sceptical of information circulating on the Internet, because they knew how many water armies were involved in shaping public opinion. One interviewee reported: "I now know how dangerous a place the Internet can be. Other people just don't know how vulnerable they are on the Internet. There are so many ways they can be misled and manipulated."

Though many soldiers of water armies become cynical about online public discussions, for some the job helps broaden their horizons. One interviewee, a young migrant worker who never went to college, stated, "before I joined the water army,

I only used the Internet for gaming and chatting. Now I realize there are so many forums online. I even joined a discussion about Chinese economy."

As part of an army, individual soldiers of a water army are not left without support. Successful water armies have established organisational structures that allow them to work more effectively. The water army in which the first author worked as an undercover soldier has a team that focuses on maintaining good relationships with leading Internet forums and that will contact forum administrators if posts by their water army's soldiers get deleted. It also has a training department providing basic training and guidance to newly recruited soldiers, a logistic department providing support on the creation and maintenance of accounts, identities, e-mail addresses, etc., a public relations department to promote their services to potential clients, a department in charge of deploying soldiers to post on various websites and forums (with sub-departments for each leading forum), and a follow-up department to evaluate the effects of an online campaign (see also Chen, Wu, Srinivasan, & Zhang, 2011, p. 3).

The organisational structures do not help individual soldiers of a water army to find meaning in what they do, and so many of the soldiers group together in online communities, typically in QQ groups. In several such online communities, soldiers shared stories from their work and planned collaborations on private "water" projects they wanted to do to support causes or products in which they believed, using their connections with other soldiers to agitate in private campaigns.

Individual soldiers often need to post several hundred posts a day, which leaves them little time for private interactions or offline relationships. Between projects, they sometimes stop by their own QQ groups for some honest and open interaction with peers who understand them and their problems. People outside their community do not usually understand or accept what they do, but within their own profession individual soldiers can find the support or the admiration they crave.

> Once I created a really popular post, it looked totally genuine and I used funny web slang to catch other users' attention. I was very proud of it but I could only tell other soldiers in my QQ group about it. Now, whenever they run out of new ideas for posts, they come to me.

Another interviewee talked about a public-interest-driven water army campaign. His QQ group once participated in a project that propelled a story onto the national news agenda of some peasants in a village in Guangdong who lost their homes to land confiscations by corrupt government officials. The soldiers of well-organised water armies sometimes decide to help the powerless to be heard, which demonstrates the difficulty in delineating the line between play and labour for this group of online labourers.

Online play, that is the creation and maintenance of online identities, and the participation in online forums, are almost requirements for a soldier in a water army to be successful. The skills and contacts made on the job can easily be employed for their own, private purposes, turning the off-duty communities of water army soldiers into powerful lobbying groups in today's China in which individual soldiers are empowered far beyond anything they could expect as ordinary Chinese citizens. Their work may be playbour, their working conditions exploitative, and their pay low, but they are neither helpless victims nor voiceless slave labour, but rather individual entrepreneurs marketing, honing, and using specialised skill sets in a competitive market.

Water armies, just like gold farms, are operating in a largely unregulated space. The authorities and traditional media in China have repeatedly warned against the spreading of rumours online (e.g. Epstein, 2013; Stewart-Smith, 2012), or even arrested people for doing so (Deng, 2011; Kaiman, 2012; Kan, 2011). However, none of the public relations companies offering water army services have been censored or penalised as yet, thus indicating an at least tacit approval of their business practices by the authorities. Judging from the arrests and the undisturbed businesses of the public relations companies, it appears as if *unorganised* rumour spreading is illegal in China, while *organised* rumour spreading is acceptable, even if further research is necessary to verify this.

Conclusion

Gold farmers and soldiers of water armies experience their online lives and the offline context in which they are embedded as a much more colourful and exciting existence than any of the other choices life in today's China has to offer them. Though their employment appears to consist of an endless repetition of similar, and largely meaningless tasks in routine and exploitative jobs, both gold farmers and soldiers of water armies have found ways to utilise their employment and the networks of other playbourers to add meaning to their lives.

Both gold farmers and soldiers of water armies have successfully managed to transform their boring employment into enriching social experiences through their own communities, thus turning their virtual achievements into richer – blended – lives within active communities of playbourers. Within the dormitories of gold farmers, Internet cafes, and gaming forums virtual adventures and even online grinding become meaningful and significant.

The communities of playbourers do not remove the difficulties facing individual gold farmers or water army soldiers who sit in front of their computer all day everyday earning low wages performing boring or even hated tasks. The commodification of computer game items, and the emergence of economic systems blending virtual enjoyment with the ugliness of RMT have created an exploitative blended environment comparable to the "real" sweatshops of factory-cities like Dongguan in southern China. While the proverbial "Westerner" who has more money than time exists, as does the desire to play online games to the fullest, there will always be a demand for labourers who are willing to "help" by selling their own online time and efforts at a low price.

Instead of focusing on such narratives of exploitation, inequality, or poverty, the gold farmers and water army soldiers of China suggest a different storyline. The empowerment of individuals through exposure to and training with technology appears to enable the playbourers of Chinese cyberspace to create and manage their own shared identities in communities of equals, with an influence on society far beyond their offline socio-economic status.

Overall, the examples of gold farmers and the water army demonstrate that although the Internet can produce new structures of inequalities and new mechanisms of commodification, it can also foster new forms of blended communities of playbourers able to extract meaning and value from their exploitative jobs. Gold farmers and soldiers of water armies create new meanings and practices out of their work by re-establishing their autonomy using skills and connections from their work to carve out their own communities both online and offline.

References

Bruns, A. (2008). Blogs, Wikipedia, Second Life, and beyond: From production to produsage. New York, NY: Peter Lang.
Cartier, C., Castells, M., & Qiu, J. L. (2005). The information-have-less: Inequality, mobility, and translocal networks in Chinese cities. *Studies in Comparative International Development (SCID), 40*(2), 9–34.
Castronova, E. (2005). *Synthetic worlds: The business and culture of online games.* Chicago, IL: University of Chicago Press.
Chen, C., Wu, K., Srinivasan, V., & Zhang, X. (2011). Battling the internet water army: Detection of hidden paid posters. *arXiv preprint arXiv*:1111.4297.
Deng, S. (2011, October 25). Three people punished for spreading rumors online. Xinhua News Agency. Retrieved April 9, 2013, from http://news.xinhuanet.com/english2010/china/2011-10/25/c_131212021.htm
Epstein, G. (2013, April 6). China's internet: A giant cage. *The Economist.* Retrieved April 9, 2013, from http://www.economist.com/news/special-report/21574628-internet-was-expected-help-democratise-china-instead-it-has-enabled
Fuchs, C. (2009). Conference report: The Internet as playground and factory (November 12–14, 2009, The New School, New York City, USA). *tripleC – Cognition, Communication, Co-operation, 7*(2), 399–400.
Himanen, P. (2001). The Hacker ethic: A radical approach to the philosophy of business. New York, NY: Random House.
Jin, G. (2006a, March 8). Chinese gold farmers preview. *YouTube.* Retrieved February 26, 2013, from http://www.youtube.com/watch?v=ho5Yxe6UVv4
Jin, G. (2006b, November 16). Chinese gold farmers preview two. *YouTube.* Retrieved February 26, 2013, from http://www.youtube.com/watch?v=JRrhpoMd88Y
Jin, G. (2006c, November 16). Chinese gold farmers preview three. *YouTube.* Retrieved February 26, 2013, from http://www.youtube.com/watch?v=KH1LGdjZUKQ
Kaiman, J. (2012, December 17). Chinese authorities arrest dozens for spreading Mayan apocalypse rumours. *The Guardian.* Retrieved April 9, 2013, from http://www.guardian.co.uk/world/2012/dec/17/chinese-arrest-mayan-apocalypse-rumours
Kan, M. (2011, October 26). China detains Internet users for spreading rumors. *PC World.* Retrieved April 9, 2013, from http://www.pcworld.com/article/242589/china_detains_internet_users_for_spreading_rumors.html
Lindtner, S., & Dourish, P. (2011). The promise of play: A new approach to productive play. *Games and Culture, 6*(5), 453–478.

Nardi, B., & Kow, Y. M. (2010). Digital imaginaries: How we know what we (think we) know about Chinese gold farming. *First Monday 15*(6–7). Retrieved March 23, 2013, from http://firstmonday.org/htbin/cgiwrap/bin/ojs/index.php/fm/article/viewArticle/3035/2566

Scholz, T. (Ed.). (2013). *Digital labor: The Internet as playground and factory*. London and New York: Routledge.

Stewart-Smith, H. (2012, April 9). China's Internet firms urged to prevent the spread of online rumors. *ZDNet*. Retrieved April 9, 2013, from http://www.zdnet.com/blog/asia/chinas-internet-firms-urged-to-prevent-the-spread-of-online-rumors/1600

Taylor, T. L. (2006). Play between worlds: Exploring online game culture. Cambridge, MA: MIT Press.

Thompson, T. (2005, March 13). They play games for 10 hours – and earn £2.80 in a "virtual sweatshop". *The Observer*. Retrieved March 23, 2013, from http://www.guardian.co.uk/technology/2005/mar/13/games.theobserver

Toffler, A. (1980). *The third wave*. New York, NY: Morrow.

Wang, Q., Ding, X., Lu, T., Xia, H., & Gu, N. (2012). Infrastructural experiences: An empirical study of an online arcade game platform in China. *Proceedings of the ACM 2012 Conference on Computer Supported Cooperative Work*, pp. 583–592.

8 Chinese fansub groups as communities of practice

An ethnography of online language learning

Xiao Liu and Gabriele de Seta

"Fansubs", a combination of "fan" and "subtitles", are movie subtitles made by amateur translators. As a verb, "fansubbing" indicates the activity of subtitling foreign movies, cartoons and television series, often with the aim of providing them as free downloads or video streamings from the Internet, without any authorization from the official producers or distributors. People that gather around this activity on the Internet often form online communities called fansub groups (Tian, 2011). Cintas and Sánchez (2006) limit the definition of fansubs to the fan-produced, subtitled versions of Japanese animation series that appeared in the United States during the 1980s, following the creation of the first Anime fan clubs, a phenomenon that the authors provide as an example of the amateur introduction of Japanese culture to the Western world (Cintas & Sánchez, 2006; Lee, 2011). However, profiting from the popularization of Internet access and the improvements of bandwidth and connection speed, fansubbing developed rapidly from the mid-1990s (Hu, 2005) and has nowadays become a worldwide practice, targeting not only Japanese animation but all kinds of mainstream and non-mainstream cultural products, from American TV dramas to Chinese documentaries and Middle-Eastern B-movies. Fans of different varieties of cultural products all throughout Asia gather in local online fansub groups to produce and upload subtitles, discuss a common passion and share it with other interested people (Hu, 2005; Jiang & Leung, 2012).

Following the rapid development and popularization of the Internet in China, fansubbing has become a common practice throughout the Chinese cyberspace as well. File-sharing websites and peer-to-peer software facilitate the retrieval, storage, playback, editing and sharing of multimedia products. Chinese netizens can easily download, watch and circulate foreign movies, animation or TV series that are not available through official distribution inside the People's Republic of China. Since many Chinese netizens are not able to enjoy foreign media products in their original languages, this Internet-based circulation is hindered by linguistic and cultural barriers. It is in this context that Chinese netizens proficient in one or more foreign languages, animated by a passion for foreign cultures or specific media products, translate movies, animation or even entire TV series and provide the subtitles for free to a growing and diversified audience. The entire process, from selection and discussion of the target variety of media products to the translation, writing and syncing of subtitles usually happens collectively, as the fansubbers organize in more or less cohesive online communities of practice.

This chapter studies the practice of fansubbing at the level of community. As a graduate student in a French-speaking university, and having studied French language for several years, the first author developed an interest in the experiences of Chinese French language learners. French language and French cultural products are not as popular in China as the American, Japanese or Korean ones. Yet, Chinese French learners tend to look for online multimedia materials that can help them improve their language competence. At the same time, they also tend to meet and interact online with other French learners or French speakers with similar interests and purposes. Despite the existence of many Chinese French learning websites that collect texts or multimedia materials, the emergence of fansubbing mirrors a very different experience of language learning and engagement with cultural products through online interaction. The main focus here in studying a fansub group is understanding the effectiveness of the learning process of the members of this kind of communities of practice.

For this study, a Chinese fansub group dedicated to French movies was chosen, and the first author participated in their subtitling projects in order to understand how cooperation takes place, what kind of knowledge is produced during the process, and the motivations that drive fansubbers to cooperate voluntarily without any kind of remuneration. Fansubbing appears to be motivated by two factors: a general interest in a foreign culture and the specific aim of improving language proficiency and translating competence. The online cooperation influences the group organization and the members' identification, resulting in specific hierarchies and negotiated workflows that in turn function as a framework to support the members' language-learning practices.

Fansub groups in China

Before presenting the specific analysis of the target Chinese-French fansub group, some general aspects of Chinese fansubbing practices and processes should be introduced. According to Baidu Baike (2013), there are more than 200 fansub groups on the Chinese Internet. In China, fansubbing as a practice is comparable with the one happening in other countries (Bruckman, 2002). First, since all communication and cooperative work take place in online spaces, Chinese fansub groups are not based in specific locations in the physical world, being an example of a community not tied to a geographical proximity (Yuan, 2012). Translating, correcting and synchronizing subtitles do not require any specialized equipment besides a personal computer with video-playback and word-processing capability and an Internet connection to interact with the community and upload the final product – be it a subtitled video or just a subtitle text file. Generally, the online interaction of a fansub group happens on dedicated discussion boards and private discussion groups organized through instant messaging software. Second, fansub group members are mostly young Chinese Internet users, usually university students and young professionals (office workers, teachers, etc.), with a consistent percentage of them living overseas. Despite their similar background, the group affiliation and the sharing of the same online space, they rarely get to know each other offline. Quite predictably, one recurring characteristic of fansub group members is their proficiency in at least one foreign language – in fact, in order to join a subtitling group and work actively on the production of subtitles, sometimes candidates have to prove their linguistic competence through an ad-hoc test.

Technical expertise, on the other hand, is not a pre-requisite, since members assigned to specialized duties (synchronizing the subtitles, rendering the subtitled video clip, uploading and sharing, etc.) usually learn how to use the relevant software with the help of more experienced group members. Third, nearly all of the Chinese fansub groups operate without financial support by individuals or organizations and do not have any commercial purpose. Subtitles and subtitled videos are publicly available online for free streaming or downloading. Some of the bigger fansub groups can even afford to rent a dedicated server, supporting the costs through spontaneous donations from the group members and the audience, while smaller groups prefer to upload their products to free online video streaming platforms or disseminate them through peer-to-peer file transfer software. Chinese fansub groups conform to the features of fansubbing in other countries: a voluntary, non-profit, online-based communal practice, disconnected from geographical proximity and revolving around a foreign language-proficient educated youth.

Fansub groups worldwide cater to specific audiences and culture-based media products, and Chinese fansub groups are no exception, as they also mirror the preference of their members and audiences, focusing on particular kinds of foreign media products. The most popular materials translated and released by Chinese fansubbers are American TV dramas and movies, Japanese *anime* as well as Japanese and Korean dramas. The popularity of these kinds of media products evidently mirrors the foreign (Western and Far Eastern) cultures most consumed and influential among the Chinese audience, a consumption that evidently influences the cultural life of Chinese netizens: watching American TV series is described as a fixture of the daily life of Chinese netizens (French, 2006; Wu, 2010), and their intense consumption might also impact on the lifestyle of young Chinese viewers (Jiang & Leung, 2012). At the same time, with increasing numbers of learners of different foreign languages, fansub groups introduce an increasingly differentiated variety of foreign media products to Chinese society, and Chinese netizens seem to regard the introduction of this kind of audiovisual products as a useful resource for foreign language learning, especially in the case of movies providing useful linguistic expressions and localized cultural information (French, 2006). Fansubbing appears to be an important practice for language learning and transcultural understanding.

According to experiences as a fansub group member by the first author, the subtitle making process is technically quite straightforward. Fansubbers begin with "raws", audiovisual products without subtitles downloaded from the Internet, recorded from television or ripped from DVDs. These are transcribed and translated, which are obviously the core elements of fansubbing, since its quality determines the quality of the final fansubbed movie. If subtitles in the product's

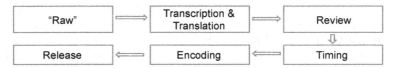

Figure 8.1 Work process of YE fansub

original language are available, they are translated directly, and no transcription is needed. The resulting script is then synched with the raw, obtaining a subtitled video that can be eventually compressed in size and uploaded online for public viewing. The workflow of Chinese fansub groups (Liu, 2011) is very similar with what González (2007) describes in the case of worldwide fansub groups, and is briefly summarised in Figure 8.1.

Fansub groups in academic discourse

Along with a growing interest in online communities, consumption of media products and copyright wars, academic research has examined different aspects of fansubbing and fansub groups. First of all, at a socioeconomic level, fansubbing has been at the center of discussions regarding the commercial threat that this practice poses to officially distributed subtitled products (Koulikov, 2010). For example, a Japanese TV station has filed complaints against the online release of amateur fansubs in Taiwan, claiming it to be a case of copyright infringement. Yet, subtitles kept being circulated on the Internet and eventually ended up appearing on pirated DVDs sold on the black market (Hu, 2005). Since fansubbing is a rather new phenomenon, only a few national governments have begun to evaluate relevant regulations; at the moment, Chinese law does not regulate it in any specific way (Xue, 2011).

A commonly voiced answer to the accusations of copyright infringement is the one arguing that amateur subtitling favors the penetration of a certain media product in a new, uncharted market without the risks of an official distribution, testing the demand and potential popularity of still unreleased audiovisual products. In fact, fansub groups usually legitimate their activities through a sort of "gentlemen's agreement" to stop the distribution of subtitled videos the moment that a determined product becomes commercially available in their country (Cintas & Sánchez, 2006). In China, some of the larger fansubs groups include in their releases declaration along the lines of "Our source videos and subtitles are all obtained from the Internet, and commercial use is forbidden. Please delete this video within 24 hours. If you do like it, please purchase the official version". Despite its questionable efficacy in improving sales of official versions and preventing pirate distributions, this sort of disclaimer evidences the fansubbers' stance on copyright issues and their distancing from filesharing communities and pirate ethics (Xue, 2011). As Lee (2011) remarks, fansubbing is noticeably different from the simple online sharing of media products since it involves, parallel to consumption, the careful, dedicated production of an added linguistic element. Moreover, as the same author argues, fansubbing (at least in the case of Japanese anime) involves a strong ethic of support to the local distribution industry.

From the point of view of linguistics and translation studies, researchers analyze the quality of fansubs and the efficacy of cultural translation. Since subtitles are translated by amateurs who often practice fansubbing as a hobby, without competent supervision and sometimes lacking the time or skill to produce a professional result, fansubs are not free of errors and misinterpretations (Cintas & Sánchez, 2006). Professionals worry that translation mistakes may mislead audiences in their approach to other cultures and hinder language learning. As Ouyang (2009) reports, also in the case of Chinese fansub groups, inaccuracies and mistakes in the translation of subtitles are attributable to the language proficiency of fansubbers and to the organizational inefficiencies of the group. Yet, fansubbing is quite a new phenomenon, and its popularization, as well as the interaction with a growing audience, could become a factor stimulating fansubbers to improve the consistency of their translations and monitor the overall quality of a group's releases (Wu, 2010). In fact, from a linguistic point of view, Chinese fansubs display a diversity of styles, as some fansub groups adopt a humorous tone, replete with Internet catchphrases familiar to most Chinese netizens, while others value formality and try to keep translation as close as possible to the original source. Despite the critical response of a part of the Chinese audience regarding the abuse of local Internet catchphrases that make subtitles seem "out of the scene", this kind of pastiche of Internet culture actually reflects on the commercial media, as some official subtitle translations echo the localized, humorous style of fansubs (Liu, 2011).

Finally, some scholars frame the practice of fansubbing as a fruitful site of intercultural exchange (French, 2006; Tian, 2011), and as a fan subculture expressing a stance of resistance towards a mass media cultural industry (Liu, 2011). Chinese audiences are no longer satisfied with the measured and cautious introduction of foreign media products on the official mass media, and thanks to the popularization of technology, they can now pursue their own personalized menu of entertainment in a self-help way (Hu, 2005). In turn, this personalized pursuit of entertainment results in the unexpected success of certain products, such as the recent case of the American television series *Prison Break*, and opens new possibility for overseas cultural industries (French, 2006; Liu, 2011).

However, besides the approaches to fansubbing from a socioeconomic, linguistic or cultural angle, little attention has been given to the role of fansubs as resources of language learning. Even if most of the cited studies argue that fansubbing as a practice is driven by the fandom for specific kinds of media products and the ethics of online file sharing, the online observations and experiences on which this chapter is based suggest that language learning is in fact a strong motivating factor for voluntary participation in the activities of a fansubbing group. This is especially the case for non-English language learners, who can rarely come across original language products on the official media, and for whom subtitled movies are a precious learning resource. In the same way, not only consuming but contributing in the production of subtitles is an equally useful way to put in practice one's studies, enlarge one's vocabulary and improve listening skills. Therefore, this paper focuses on the role that the practice of fansubbing has in the process of Chinese fansub group members' foreign language learning.

Fansubbing is a legally ambiguous (Xue, 2011), amateur-driven practice of intercultural exploration that plays a role in media globalization and resistance (Lee, 2011; Tian, 2011), and its lexicon mirrors the fleeting vernacular of Chinese Internet culture (Liu, 2011). In this chapter, an alternative understanding of fansubbing as communal practice is presented. More specifically, being organized via the Internet, fansub groups present the main features of online communities as described by Yuan (2012) such as the loose link between individuals, the fluid group boundaries and the mobility of membership. What this chapter wants to explore is the relationship between this communal aspect of fansubbing and its function in foreign language learning. In addition to their interest in foreign cultures and their related media products, people who join fansub groups are strongly motivated by the will to improve their language competence. The questions focused on are the following: How do fansub group members combine practice and learning? How do they identify with this communal practice? And how does the learning practice itself impact on the offline life of the group members?

Fansubbing groups as communities of practice

The notion of community of practice (henceforth CoP) was first used by Lave and Wenger (1991) to define groups of people who share a concern or a passion for something they do, and who learn how to do it better through regular interaction. Wenger (1998) further developed this theory and proposed clarification of the important elements of CoPs and the relation between them.

For this chapter, only one aspect of CoP will be employed, the relationship between practice and community – it is true that communities gather around all kinds of practices, but this does not mean that every community is necessarily a CoP. According to Wenger (1998), CoPs are characterized by three essential characteristics: mutual engagement, joint enterprise and shared repertoire (see also Thompson, 2005). The mutual engagement indicates the fact that members of a CoP can negotiate with one another through their actions inside the community. The primacy of actions means that membership, not linked to organizational attachment, personal relations or geographical proximity of the members, is a factor that sustains the community itself through action: members are so in virtue of their engagement in practical work. Sometimes, the heterogeneity of community members may bring difficulties or conflicts to the shared practice, straining the mutual engagement and pressing for a redefinition of its terms. Joint enterprise is another factor that holds a CoP together, and it simply indicates the purpose of the community's shared practice, as defined by the participants in the process of pursuing it. The joint enterprise is rarely defined as a stated goal, being more of a general practice that includes, as its integral components, the participants' mutual relations and accountability. Lastly, the shared repertoire is described as the collection of routines, words, tools and ways of doing things, the sort of discourse from which members draw in order to make meaningful statements about the world and to express their identity as group members.

This chapter, while acknowledging the importance of participation in the production and sharing of meaning, as well as the existence of a historical development of the community, will mostly focus on the relationship between practice and community, and its role as a catalyst for community members' language learning.

Following the proliferation of Internet access and the development of mass-scale sites of online interaction, many researchers have applied the concept of CoP to online communities. McLure Wasko and Faraj (2000) describe online communities as CoP where members never interact or even meet physically, while still managing to successfully manage and distribute knowledge. Murchu and Sorensen (2004) see online communities as complementary teaching tools that facilitate the development of relationships between members, while also making learning more interactive and thus attractive. Online communities of practice can also offer the participants a convenient platform for mutual help, since online community members tend to share their knowledge with others (Campbell & Cecez-Kecmanovic, 2011). Fang and Chiu (2010) argue that the mutual engagement of members in an online community is based on mutual trust and confidence in the community itself, which do not necessarily require face-to-face interaction or contact (Wenger, 1998).

Drawing on these theoretical debates, fansub groups can be considered as communities of practice, and evaluated as sites of language learning. Fandom researchers usually interpret fansub groups as online communities of interest built around the exploration of a particular foreign culture or specific genre of audio-visual products (Jiang & Leung, 2012). Nevertheless, language competence is a determining factor for fansub group membership, and members of fansub groups often discuss how to improve their proficiency in a foreign language as a source of motivation for their participation.

Methodology

A Chinese fansub group specialising in creating Chinese subtitles for French movies was chosen as the field site for participant observation and interviews by the first author. The particular group chosen will be referred to as *YE* throughout this chapter. The choice of a community of Chinese fansubbers of French-language movies provides ready examples of the learning aspect of fansubbing, as the limited availability of French-learning materials appears to motivate Chinese French learners to gather and create additional learning materials by themselves.

YE was founded in 2011 by fansubbers who were interested in subtitling a French animation film. Having met in the QQ group of another, bigger fansub group, they decided to create their own chatroom to coordinate the work on this specific project, proclaiming their independence from the former group, but it was only after the completion of their first project that they defined themselves as a proper fansub community and chose a group name. YE's group manager is a fan of French animation films and has past experience in subtitling. According to statistics collected, YE members are all of Chinese ethnicity, mostly learning or already with a good command of French language. Some are studying abroad or residing in different parts of the world, predominantly in French-speaking countries like France, Canada or certain African states. Nearly all members are in their 20s or 30s, and they are mostly university students and young office workers, and all have their own access to the Internet and enough spare time to dedicate to the projects of the online subtitling group. Most of the members claim to have found out about the YE group while searching for French movies with bilingual subtitles.

At the time of writing, the YE fansub group is still active, but this study is based upon observations and data collected during 10 months, from the founding of YE in late 2011 to summer 2012. During this period, the YE group completed the subtitling of nine movies, about 350 minutes worth of audiovisual materials.

The participant observation of the YE group was started with the permission of the group manager and a presentation of the research objectives to the other members. The first author had been following the larger group from which YE originated, and experienced the emergence of YE as a founding member. The data collection and participant observation on which this chapter is based was conducted online, in different sites of group activity. Besides the public interaction taking place on the group homepage and the dedicated discussion board on the Chinese social networking site Douban.com, core "backstage" interactions happened in a private chatroom hosted on Tencent's popular messaging service QQ.

Discussions were tracked using the QQ client's in-built chat logging to record entire conversations for later analysis. During direct chats with other group members, they answered questions about aspects of subtitling or related topics that helped drive the research. In addition, brief online interviews were conducted with four group members, focusing on the relation between their experiences in the group and their offline lives. The first author also took part in group activities as an ordinary member of the group and participated in the subtitling work.

As the group mainly used group emails to stay in contact with members and to save and share the documents produced during the work process, the group emails with their attached transcription drafts and corrections by other group members were also collected. Finally, in order to have an overview of the entire online environment of the group, the group's Douban discussion board, Douban ministation and Sina Weibo account were logged as the group's outward presentation of their work.

All the postings on the different websites and social networking platforms are available to the public. As Bruckman (2002) suggests, users who create content on the Internet might prefer being credited, especially when their activity produces original content useful to others and becomes freely shared. However, considering the dubious legal status of fansubbing, as well as the problematic nature of the file-sharing activities that constitutes an integral part of fansubbing, all nicknames of group members have been anonymised in this chapter, and no public content is quoted literally that might be linked back to specific identities. Quotes from interview transcripts, on the other hand, are presented with the consent of individual interviewees.

Learning through practice

A great part of the established workflow, rules and hierarchies of the YE group is the product of a continuous negotiation between group members, newcomers and audiences. Authority inside the group is negotiated through tensions in the practice, and the core positions of leadership do not entirely rely on the time spent in fansubbing or studying French, but are determined by the interactions between members. The YE group manager, motivated by a strong will to improve his French, assumed the responsibility of managing the group and coordinating the work of other members, while the group as a whole functions, thanks to a fluid organizational structure, mostly influenced by the primacy of the QQ group chatroom as platform for instant communication. In the beginning, existing members did not know much about new members' technical and language skills, nor about their willingness to participate regularly in a project. Every subtitling project was usually assigned to a small team, with two individuals responsible for it, one for proofreading and other technical matters, the other as a general coordinator. In one specific case, the initial plan was to divide the movie into three sections, assigning a transcriber and a translator to each section, with a proofreader and a synchronizer taking over the next step.

Members were asked to choose freely the work they preferred, but given the difficult and painstaking nature of transcription few users were willing to volunteer for this task – one member even tried to justify his choice lamenting that "maybe translation is the only thing I'm able to do". In order to mobilize the members and to speed up projects, the group managers changed their strategy and divided the 75-minute movie into twenty sections, then assigned two sections to each member, making them responsible for the transcription and translation of the sections. In this way, the project began to run smoothly.

To coordinate the exchange of the translated sections, the team members did not use group emails at first. Although the managers suggested this practice in the chatroom, the suggestion did not reach all members, and the use of group email was initially haphazard. Certain members preferred to send their work directly to the manager, a practice that the manager justified in terms of insecurity: "Some of them really don't have confidence in their transcription work" – most of the members chose to submit drafts to the manager because they did not want others to see a transcript full of errors or sentences marked as inaudible. As a consequence, the process and progress of the teamwork were not visible to the team members: only the managers had a sense of the status of completion, but this in fact complicated the coordination efforts.

Creation of new teams complicated the establishment of rules, but this got smoother with later projects, as the organizational structure emerged gradually from proven practices and the group learned from past shared experience. The whole fansub group started choosing movies according to the preferences of the group manager, mediated by votes of group members. Once the workflow had become accepted through trial and error, a fixed mode of task distribution was employed for subsequent projects. After having decided on a movie to be subtitled, the manager would cut the video into several sections according to the number of participating members for the French transcription. If the film already had French subtitles, the members checked and corrected the subtitles according to the actual spoken dialogues. After proofreading the transcriptions, the same members translated their section of French transcripts into Chinese. After the translation was finished, the subtitles were created, timed and encoded on the video which was then uploaded and distributed by the manager.

After more people joined the group, it became necessary to organize different teams to work at the same time on different movies. This influx of new members and the manager's reliance on group emails as main mode of project communication helped to establish this practice as a norm for all group activities. By the last project observed for this study, all project related communication happened via group emails.

Negotiations within the community often took place in the QQ chatroom, where members took advantage of the discussion space to learn about other members and to talk about both their subtitling as well as other topics. Some members complained about their lack of proficiency and of feeling overwhelmed by the transcription process. In these cases, the manager always encouraged them by reminding them how participating in the transcription was a good opportunity to improve their listening skills, and encouraged members, reassuring them about the importance of teamwork to transcribe hard-to-hear sections. Despite the heavy correction work that proofreaders had to deal with when going through the work of less skilled members, the inclusion of all members was valued more than the effectiveness of the transcription process.

Practice through conflict

The shared practices of fansubbers include the results of conflicts and tensions – agreement is not always easy to obtain, decisions are hard to arrive at and discussions can become heated arguments resulting in group divisions and desertions. However, as Wenger (1998) argues, learning is possible not only in agreement but also in disagreement. In the YE group, disagreements between members, from minor occasions to more extreme examples did not hinder the success of the fansub group as a CoP. On the contrary, disputes had a positive influence on the community, mobilizing group members around a conflict issue, opening up space for discussion and stimulating negotiation towards future shared practices.

During the very first project, the preferred style of translation became an issue, involving even the highest levels of members as the group manager and the project coordinator could not agree on what they thought was the best practice. When reviewing translations, the manager respected the style of each member and took the position that there was no right or wrong way of translating sentences, and that different versions of the same lines were equally good. The manager focused on eliminating misunderstandings and poorly constructed sentences. By contrast, the coordinator believed that the subtitles for a movie should follow a consistent style and worked hard to revise the translations to standardise expressions and overall style. This irritated the manager, who argued that the coordinator had disrespectfully altered the intellectual work of other members without consultation.

Although the coordinator insisted that she did not believe her version to be the best, and despite her willingness to negotiate individual translations, she repeatedly refused to accept proposals from other members. When the coordinator sent a group mail to all team members to solicit their opinions about this issue, only two members agreed with the manager, defending their own work, while the others remained silent without expressing their opinion.

Negotiations did not lead to a satisfactory resolution, and the disagreement ended in a rupture between the manager and coordinator. Eventually, the project was completed with two separate versions of the subtitles. Once the project was finished, the coordinator and one of her supporters left the group because of the unresolved disagreement and the resulting tensions. This contributed to the reification of the practice of proofreading as favoured by the group manager and later projects of the YE group were all characterized by a preference for maintaining the personal translation styles of individual members.

Identity and levels of membership

The first members of the YE group got together for different reasons. Most of them agreed that working together to produce subtitles was a good way to improve their language skills, but in the beginning this motivation was not strong enough to support identification with the group. Some people refused to work on the first project simply because they did not like the chosen movie or because they felt transcription work would be boring. For the second project, the YE group needed a way to make sure that members working on a project were interested in the film or were motivated enough to endure the boring but necessary transcription work.

Towards the end of the first project, several team members dropped out of the project and eventually the group. This meant the project was delayed and the finalisation of the subtitles had to be done by different group members brought in to complete the work. While this could suggest that online communities of practice have difficulties in forming stable organisational structures, it should instead be seen as a confirmation of the normal workings of a CoP. Before group members start identifying with a community, the community needs a shared history. At the time of the first project, when YE did not even have a name to support the collective imagination of its members, this shared history had yet to be written, and YE had yet to become a community of (shared) practice(s).

During the projects that followed, identification of members with the group was fostered both through shared experiences and practices, as well as through democratisation of the group, for example, in the selection of movies. The group manager suggested several movies, presenting them briefly in terms of plot, difficulty of the language and speed of the dialogue in an announcement circulated via group emails. Group members could then choose a movie that interested them, but in order to cast their vote, they had to volunteer for specific tasks such as the transcription or translation of movie sections within a specified timeframe. The organisational practices adopted after the difficulties of the first project made possible a smoother completion of later ones, and created a sense of project ownership among members who began to see their group membership as a part of their identity.

This shared repertoire of rules, practices and standards resulting from daily negotiations was an important factor for the members' identification with the group, resulting in a deeper engagement and more motivated efforts. An analysis of the chat transcripts shows that, of the eight members who participated in the first project, only the five most active participants in the group chatroom went on to join the second project. The development of a shared history had an impact on the motivation and participation of group members. This observation was confirmed by the group manager who pointed out that "older" members usually volunteered for more work than newcomers and were more regular in their submissions. They demonstrated a sense of responsibility reinforced by their experience of crucial moments in the history of the group, a history that they were often glad to share with others during discussions and leisure chats.

Over the course of several projects, three levels of users emerged in the group who differed in their levels of participation in group activities. Core members often participated in subtitling projects and interacted with other members on a regular basis, thus reinforcing the group's historical identity. Peripheral members participated sporadically, often rejecting tasks because of low language proficiency. Finally, a silent audience constituting the 'outside' of the group rarely entered in communication with other members and did not influence group activities except for occasional movie requests, suggestions or complaints.

During the duration of the research project, YE members released subtitled versions of nine movies. Twenty-six people were involved in the different projects, fifteen of whom participated in more than one project. The manager periodically cleaned up the subscription list of members who had signed up but did not participate in any group projects, so that effective members, even peripheral ones, had to at least take part in one project.

After its first release, the YE group began to attract the attention of French cinema fans and new members starting joining the group. An internal survey conducted in July 2012 by the group manager showed, though, that 14 of the 38 responding group members joined the group because of their interest in movies, while only 21 of the 38 were willing to participate in actual subtitling work. The manager reacted to this by dividing new members into two kinds: Beginning French learners without sufficient language skills to participate in subtitling but desiring to acquire more French audiovisual materials, and proficient workers able to contribute to subsequent projects. In this way, members could remain in the group even without participating in projects, but they had to fill in a simple census form and participate in the life of the community, offering their help or just their presence to members working on projects. The manager's attempts at regularizing group membership and maintaining a census of the members were not completely successful, though, as some members, especially "older" members did not respond to registration requests. Additionally, existing relationships between members complicated the managing efforts: "the ones who participated in previous projects or joined the group after being introduced by older members . . . kicking them out would have created a lot of problems with the old guard".

These tensions reveal an implicit hierarchy in the group that reinforced the shared repertoire of group members helping them to achieve their collective goals. Even when members of the audience encroached upon the group from an outside region (Goffman, 1990, p. 136) and expressed the desire to become members, they were not immediately given the same privileges as older members. Only when newcomers joined their first project were they considered peripheral members, and as long as they completed at least one project, they were not expelled even if they did not appear on the site regularly, chat with others or join another project. The group hierarchy thus became codified, outlining the way in which a peripheral member could become a core member through significant contributions, competence, participation in different projects and a regular presence in the QQ group chatroom. These hierarchical tiers with their rules and the possibility of moving into or out of the community were never explicitly stated, but they developed through the shared practice of the community. The implicit hierarchy was constantly reinforced through the reciprocal evaluation of members and their effective participation in team projects.

Group boundary and offline practice

A fansub group is included by informal affiliation in a bigger fan culture, and sometimes different groups can compete in order to complete the subtitles for the same product. Cooperation is also possible: since most fansub groups are without rigid membership restrictions, group members often take part in other groups' projects out of personal friendship or goodwill. YE's manager, for example, proofread two pending projects of the LE group, the bigger group from which YE originated, because of remaining personal ties to the other group manager:

> I chatted with Marc, one of the managers of LE fansub. He is a nice guy and loves fansubbing . . . he wanted to complete these unfinished projects, but the members of LE were too busy to resume the subtitling work. I decided to help him also because one of the projects was a movie l really like.

Besides the interaction with other groups, the fansub group was also embedded in offline spaces, as different layers of the members' personal lives influenced their daily interactions online. One layer was that of language learning: members discussed their translations but also shared their daily experiences with the French language, their learning progress and their doubts, both about their translations as members of the YE group, as well as about their levels of competence in French in general.

Another layer is that of the circulation of general information between group members, most often related to their studies or their career. Nancy, a third-year university student, was planning to go to France for an exchange program. Through the YE group, she met Zoe, a graduate student who was also planning to go to France for her Master program, and this was an opportunity for Nancy to discuss aspects of studying abroad with a student in a similar situation, feeling "comforted and encouraged", and possibly forging a new friendship. Most of the YE group members seemed to have a positive attitude towards the idea of meeting each other in real life.

Conclusion

The YE group is an example of a small, functional online community of practice that operates in a grey area just outside the global cultural industry, and in parallel with Chinese commercial media. This study of the YE group demonstrates this in different ways: the group was created as a subsection of a bigger, established group, and throughout interacts with other Chinese fansub groups with which it shares a culture of fandom and a vocabulary of amateur dedication to the practice of subtitling that make collaboration and cross-membership easier.

At a more global level, YE is an example of practices that are empowered by the widespread availability of Internet access and the popularity of foreign language learning, which have become fairly common in Chinese cyberspace. Fansubbing groups in China are organizationally and demographically similar to the ones active worldwide in translating all kinds of content into many different languages. In the specific case of China, YE mirrors the needs of a specific group of people (young, educated language learners, some of whom reside abroad) who are discontent with the commercially available media products and therefore strive to obtain their own personal choices of foreign movies, animation or television series.

In becoming members of a fansubbing group, they also demonstrate a willingness to follow their personal interests in foreign movies and in improving their language proficiency, while providing a free service to others by translating and releasing subtitles online. Their small-scale efforts to promote the Internet-based circulation of Chinese-subtitled French movies contribute to a process of cross-cultural translation, to richer choices for media consumption, to the improvement of entertainment materials available for language learners, as well as to the cross-pollination of Chinese vernacular expressions of distant lexicons. Internet culture developed on specific social networks and discussion boards mixes with a growing audience in search of foreign movies, and mainstream commercial media that looks at amateur translations as sources of successful cultural mediation.

This study of the YE group has highlighted features that have turned the fansub group into a successful community of practice. The engagement of YE members to form and maintain a functional community, their joint interest in improving their language proficiency, and their shared repertoire of fandom and identity all promote a community of practice as a viable and productive component of foreign language learning. This analysis has shown how everything in the history of the fansub group, from its formation and identity negotiation to conflicts and idle chatting, has contributed to the formation and fine-tuning of the shared practices of this community that is not limited to the online activities of the group but extends into the members' offline life, travel experiences and interpersonal relationships.

Fansubbing appears as a viable way of integrating the process of language learning with the practice of translation supporting personal interests and communal engagement. In a Chinese context, given the scarcity of foreign language media products, fansubbing is particularly useful for non-English language learners' limited access to original language products. Where the distribution of media products is unable to satisfy the needs of a diversified audience looking for learning materials, fansub groups, as effective communities of practice, demonstrate how the union of community and practice, facilitated by online platforms and digital technologies produces engagement, motivation and participation that promote learning, cross-cultural understanding, and a positive and productive environment for small-scale fandom.

References

Baidu Baike. (2013). Zimo Zu. Baidu Baike. Retrieved March 25, 2013, from http://baike.baidu.com/view/352809.htm

Bruckman, A. (2002). Studying the amateur artist: A perspective on disguising data collected in human subjects research on the Internet. *Ethics and Information Technology, 4*(3), 217–231. doi: 10.1023/a:1021316409277

Campbell, J., & Cecez-Kecmanovic, D. (2011). Communicative practices in an online financial forum during abnormal stock market behavior. *Information & Management, 48*(1), 37–52.

Cintas, J. D., & Sánchez, P. M. (2006). Fansubs: Audiovisual translation in an amateur environment. *The Journal of Specialised Translation,* (6).

Fang, Y. H., & Chiu, C. M. (2010). In justice we trust: Exploring knowledge-sharing continuance intentions in virtual communities of practice. *Computers in Human Behavior, 26*(2), 235–246.

French, H. W. (2006). Chinese tech buffs slake thirst for U.S. TV shows. Retrieved April 5, 2012, from http://www.nytimes.com/2006/08/09/world/asia/09china.html

Goffman, E. (1990 [1959]). *The presentation of self in everyday life*. London, UK: Penguin Books.

González, L. P. (2007). Fansubbing anime: Insights into the "butterfly effect" of globalisation on audiovisual translation. *Perspectives, 14*(4), 260–277. doi: 10.1080/09076760708669043

Hu, K. (2005). The power of circulation: Digital technologies and the online Chinese fans of Japanese TV drama. *Inter-Asia Cultural Studies, 6*(2), 171–186.

Jiang, Q., & Leung, L. (2012). Lifestyles, gratifications sought, and narrative appeal: American and Korean TV drama viewing among Internet users in urban China. *International Communication Gazette, 74*(2), 159–180. doi: 10.1177/1748048511432601

Koulikov, M. (2010). Fighting the fan sub war: Conflicts between media rights holders and unauthorized creator/distributor networks. *Transformative Works and Cultures*, 5.

Lave, J., & Wenger, E. (1991). *Situated learning: Legitimate peripheral participation.* Cambridge, UK/New York, NY: Cambridge University Press.

Lee, H. K. (2011). Participatory media fandom: A case study of anime fansubbing. *Media Cult. Soc. Media, Culture and Society*, *33*(8), 1131–1147.

Liu, X. (2011). *Daolie de youxi: Guonei yingshi zimozu wenhua yanjiu* (Illegal games: Research on the culture of subtitling groups in China). (Master's thesis, Northwest University, Shaanxi, China).

McLure Wasko, M., & Faraj, S. (2000). "It is what one does": Why people participate and help others in electronic communities of practice. *The Journal of Strategic Information Systems*, *9*(2), 155–173.

Murchu, D. O., & Sorensen, E. K. (2004). Online master communities of practice: Collaborative learning in an intercultural perspective. *European Journal of Open and Distance Learning, 2004/1.*

Ouyang, L. (2009). *Research on the current fansubbing in China* (Master's thesis, Hunan University, Hunan, China).

Thompson, M. (2005). Structural and epistemic parameters in communities of practice. *Organization Science, 16*(2), 151–164. doi: 10.1287/orsc.1050.0120

Tian, Y. (2011). Fansub cyber culture in China (Master's thesis). Retrieved March 25, 2013, from http://gradworks.umi.com/1491553.pdf

Wenger, E. (1998). *Communities of practice: Learning, meaning, and identity.* Cambridge, UK/New York, NY: Cambridge University Press.

Wu, Y. (2010). Zhuanboxue shijiaoxia de guonei riben donghua zimozu yanjiu (Research on subtitling groups of Japanese animation in China from the perspective of Communication Studies). (Master's thesis, Central South University, Hunan, China).

Xue, W. (2011). Waiwen yingshi zimozu qinquan wenti yanjiu (Research on the problem of legal violations of subtitling groups for foreign films). *Wangluo falü pinglun, 1.*

Yuan, E. J. (2012). A culturalist critique of "online community" in new media studies. *New Media & Society.* doi: 10.1177/1461444812462847

Part V

Shaping online spaces

9 Balancing market and politics

The logic of organizing cyber communities in China

Cuiming Pang

With the wide adoption of the Internet in China, numerous online collectives have been formed by Chinese people for various purposes. Participation in cyber communities – interest-based online collectives with a relatively stable structure, established rules and norms, and opportunities for long-term social interaction – has become part of many people's daily lives. Cyber communities provide platforms for members to express themselves while, at the same time, constrain their self-expression under the demand of the state. How do communities motivate members to remain, despite the fact that their right to free speech is restrained? Through an ethnographic observation of one Chinese cyber community, this chapter aims to make a contribution to an understanding of the prosperity of cyber communities in a context where Internet use is strictly censored.

The chosen community, which I call Tan Street (the name of this community has been altered to protect its anonymity, as was for the name of the participants' home county) was established in November 2005; by November 2010, it had more than 18,000 registered members. Most members grew up in the same county, which I call Wen County, but currently live throughout China and even overseas. Tan Street's founder created the site in order to provide a platform for the county's emigrants to communicate with each other. As the website's members began to use its discussion forum and other tools for communication and interaction, a community was gradually formed. Rules and norms, a hierarchical structure, the beginnings of long-term social interaction, and various collective activities all came into being.

I carried out participant observation on Tan Street over a period of 3 years. My observation was conducted in online field sites, where I read posts and joined in online chatting, as well as in offline sites, where I attended various activities. In-depth interviews with both managers and members were also conducted, to explore participant opinions that are not presented to the public. Tan Street is only one of numerous cyber communities in China, and it is certainly not representative of all the communities. Nevertheless, Tan Street faces issues – such as governmental censorship – that are common to all such communities in China, and is involved in various social connections, as are other communities. My detailed examination of the case of Tan Street provides insight into an understanding of the relations between communities, individual members, other social actors, and the connections between internal community practices and the external socio-political context.

This chapter specifically focuses on how political discussion is managed in communities. Evidence from Tan Street shows that community participants choose to stay in one community on the basis of their own interests and needs, and opt for another if their needs are not met. The ease with which members can move from one community to another is largely due to the abundance of alternatives and the loose barriers to community membership, a situation that is a result of the introduction of a market economy in China. This high mobility also sets limitations on managers' behavior, requiring them to take members' demands into consideration for the sake of community growth. When dealing with daily political discussion on Tan Street, managers obey governmental demands to censor members' discussions in order to be politically safe. At the same time, they take advantage of a self-censorship policy and loose supervision in order to retain members in their community. The way managers deal with political conversations reflects the organizing logic of cyber communities in China. Organizing logic specifically refers to a type of individual-collective relationship, where individuals favor their personal needs above community membership, and communities acknowledge the individual as a basic unit rather than expect members to serve the community. I argue that this type of individual-collective relationship, which is institutionalized by the marketization process in China, plays a crucial role in impelling participants to contribute to community building, in spite of community control.

In the following, I first discuss institutional forces that drive people to build cyber communities. I argue that individuals build communities in order to deal with risks and insecurities that are placed by modern institutions on their own shoulders. I then examine characteristics of political discussion on Tan Street. I argue that political discussion is an everyday reality in Chinese cyberspace, largely due to the interference of the state in all areas of the life of the individual. In the last section, I discuss the ways through which Tan Street managers supervise political conversations. I do not merely introduce how they adhere to governmental requirements, but also examine their tactics to loosen supervision, and approaches for dealing with members' questions concerning control. In studies that mention the behavior of Chinese cyber communities with regard to censorship, communities are often blamed for cooperating with the state and for their active instigation of self-censorship. The case of Tan Street, however, shows the agency of communities in balancing the conflict between market and politics, maximizing their own interests, and creating space for their members to express themselves as freely as possible.

The impetus for the rise of cyber communities

Cyber communities in China emerged in the mid-1990s in the form of newsgroups and have been popular since the end of the 1990s, concomitant with the establishment of Xici Hutong (created in 1998), the Tianya community (created in 1999), and other communities hosted by commercial websites. There are comprehensive communities with a wide spectrum of sub-topics, specialized communities with one specific theme, such as education and sports, and local communities with a focus on local culture, customs, and social issues, etc. The abundance of communities provides a variety of options for Chinese netizens to choose. What are their criteria for choosing a community? What do these criteria tell about the rise of cyber communities in China?

According to my informants, one of the main criteria for choosing a community was "common interest" with other participants. They normally had had the experience of trying out many different communities or groups in the beginning before settling on one or on a few in the end. I do not mean that they will be in a chosen community permanently. They will possibly leave a chosen community after a period of time. However, compared to the initial stage of trying out different communities and groups, the way they behave in a chosen community is more stable. The community – or sub-group within a community – they chose was based on common interest, such as music, games, raising children, finding jobs, etc. "Useful" was another main criterion. According to my informants' descriptions, "useful" is a concrete reference to "getting information", "getting rid of a feeling of loneliness", "enlarging a social network", "improving social ability", and even "clarifying career and life direction" and "making sure what we really want in our lives".

One main reason why Tan Street was attractive to my informants was their common interest in discussing their home county and in establishing contact with home county fellows. They showed great enthusiasm for discussing diverse topics in reference to their home county, including its economic development, travel industry, religion, education, dialect, food, etc. They also exhibited interest in joining offline activities, such as dinner gatherings and badminton sessions, through which they could meet their home county fellows face-to-face. To be a part of Tan Street community is obviously also useful for its members, as expressed in members' posts regarding their comments towards Tan Street. They benefited from community participation, in such ways as obtaining information, having their opinions heard by others, an increased recognition and reputation, an enlarged social network, by a feeling of satisfaction for helping others, etc. For instance, for those who had moved to a new environment alone, seeking out online those of their home county fellows who were living in the same place, was an effective approach to combat loneliness and build a supportive network. For those who had difficulties with job search, career development, and other personal issues, the community offered them a platform to express their concerns and to receive help and support.

The criteria of "common interest" and "useful" illustrate the rise of the Chinese individual, who has gained a higher degree of freedom to pursue their personal interests and desires since the initiation of the reform and opening-up policy in the late 1970s. Over the last few decades, Chinese society has experienced an intense individualization process, where individuals are both compelled and enabled by institutional changes, such as the cancellation of rural communes, the privatization of state enterprises, the opening up of the labor market, and the connection with global markets, to take charge of their own lives (Hansen & Svarverud, 2010; Yan, 2009). As numerous rural-urban migrants, most of Tan Street participants have moved from an intimate and familiar lifestyle based on shared customs and bounded locality to a lifestyle characterized by high levels of heterogeneity. They have encountered both the advantages and disadvantages brought about by globalization and individualization: on the one hand, they have obtained more chances and options to organize their own life projects, but on the other hand, they themselves must face and deal with social risks and uncertainties, such as unemployment, unstable personal relationships, social isolation, crisis of identity and trust, and have to take more responsibility for the consequences of their own choices.

The risks and uncertainties place burdens and pressure on individuals, while at the same time impel them to create strategies to fight the risks. To turn to collectives to share worries and burdens with others, as Tan Street participants did, is the individual's active response to risk and insecurity. In fact, the sense of community is an enduring human need, and the search for community and fellowship has existed throughout human history (Nisbet, 1953/1990; Williams, 1975). In the global age, the search for community is intensified. Individuals who inhabit fluid, fragmented, and unpredictable global societies easily experience anxiety, loneliness, and a loss of direction, which thereby fosters a yearning for security and a sense of community and togetherness (Bauman, 2001a; Castells, 1997, pp. 27–67; Giddens, 1991, pp. 202–208).

Moreover, although communities retain their importance in individuals' social lives, they no longer prescribe the role-sets of individuals and unite individuals' orientations towards collectivity with ascribed ties. Rather, they can be described as "peg communities", as termed by Zygmunt Bauman (2001b, p. 151), carrying the characteristics of loose, transitory, and replaceable. In other words, these communities are invented and chosen by individuals on the basis of their own wishes, and may quickly collapse and be replaced by other communities if participants' expectations are not met. The Tan Street community for instance merely provides members with one option to fulfill their needs for togetherness. Members may have strong commitment to the community. Their commitment, however, is not forced by the community upon them, but rather a product of their own desire. They do not face punishment if they stop contributing to the community. The low cost of exiting Tan Street and high possibilities of inventing a new one undoubtedly have an influence on community management, including the management of political conversations.

Characteristics of political conversations online

It is widely believed that Chinese netizens, young people especially, are more inclined to seek out entertainment and lifestyle issues rather than participate in political discussions (e.g. CASS, 2007, p. v; Damm, 2007). A brief overview of the Tan Street website seems to support this assumption. Among the various topics of the discussion boards in Tan Street – photography, bicycling, music and movies, literature, eating, drinking, and having fun, investment, online shopping, etc. – none shows a connection with politics. Nevertheless, a closer look at the content of participants' posts and their everyday discussions reveals that the line between entertainment and lifestyle issues and political issues is not so clear-cut.

First, posts that focused on everyday life, lifestyles, and entertainment always touched upon government policies and management behavior. For instance, posts about housing often criticized the housing reform initiated by the government; posts concerning online videos complained about the policy the government implemented to regulate broadcasting websites; posts gossiping about movie stars discussed how they were punished by the government for bringing a negative impact on society; posts about football mentioned officials' corruption. In fact, in post-Mao China, where the party-state retains its supervision of all spheres of society to ensure that the practices of individuals and groups do not cross political boundaries, issues relating to many areas of individual life are intertwined with government policies and management behavior. Therefore, political discussion does not necessarily focus on formal political processes, political participation, or political parties. Rather, it can be derived from discussions of everyday life and be associated with entertainment topics and lifestyle issues.

Second, political issues are often displayed in a playful and creative way. Some posts explicitly criticize the Party and the government, while some others deliver criticism by artfully using language, imagery, and sound. In Chinese cyberspace, words, stories, images, satiric videos that parody and mock mainstream ideology, political events, and officials' behavior are pervasive (Esarey & Xiao, 2008, pp. 764–765; Yang, 2009, pp. 85–102; Yu, 2007, pp. 429–432). This type of comic and ironic production has also been adopted, produced, and reproduced by Tan Street members. A typical example is the word "harmonious" (*hexie* 和谐). This word has been widely used in official propaganda, ever since it appeared in the slogan "building a harmonious society" (*goujian hexie shehui* 构建和谐社会) proclaimed by the current Chinese president. As with many other slogans, this word is also widely imitated by Chinese netizens to satirize governmental management behavior. For instance, a Tan Street member posted a picture of a migrant worker who was going to jump from a building to kill himself because he had not received his salary. This member named the picture "Jumping show in a harmonious society" as a way to vent angry feelings about social inequality. When one of Tan Street's QQ chat groups was temporarily closed down by the company that provided the chat service, a member wrote a post entitled "Tan Street is being harmonized". Some respondents used the phrase "river crab society" to replace "harmonious society" ("river crab" 河蟹 is a homonym of the word "harmony" 和谐). Others simply posted the image of a crab as a response. The creative use of the word harmony is an implicit way to show dissatisfaction with Internet censorship. It is clear that when Chinese netizens engage in activities that appear to be entertainment, such as producing and distributing photographs, text, music, or videos, their production is likely to be satire on Chinese politics. The engagement in entertainment activities itself can be seen as a way to demonstrate resistance towards authorities.

Third, discussions that began from non-political topics sometimes developed into political discussions. One example is a thread on the initiation of a fund drive. In this thread the author of the first post suggested that the Tan Street founder arrange a donation for a man who spent all his money on organizing charitable activities. Discussion began on the topic of whether or not Tan Street should initiate the fund drive and evolved to complaints about the difficulties of running grassroots charitable organizations in the Chinese political context. When Internet users are enabled by new technology to become information producers rather than being audiences, they are also encouraged to work together to create a collective production through open discussion and debate. In a discussion forum, it is common that when one member publishes a post, the content he or she generates is commented on and reworked by others. Some may enrich the original topic with different perspectives, while some others may initiate a discussion of issues relevant to the original topic. Therefore, posts focusing on non-political issues can eventually provoke political discussion if one respondent links the topic to politics.

Fourth, political discussion is often aroused when certain political events occur in the physical world. For instance, the dismissal of Chen Liangyu, the former secretary of the Shanghai Municipal Committee of the Communist party, sparked discussions among Tan Street participants on corruption in China. The withdrawal of Google from China provoked discussions about freedom of speech. News about political events was transmitted by Tan Street participants from other media sources, such as newspapers, television, blogs, and other discussion forums. The intensiveness of discussions of one political event decreased after some days; however, a new round of intense discussion was stimulated when news about the event in question was updated. When a political event no longer attracted members' attention, the occurrence of another political event aroused their participation in discussions on this new event. Therefore, at first glance, discussions in Tan Street seemed to be about entertainment and lifestyle topics; political events were clearly not an everyday topic. From a longitudinal perspective, however, political events had been discussed continually from the time Tan Street was established.

In sum, it is true that Chinese people in the reform era have achieved more opportunities and options to exhibit their personal interests, including fun, entertainment, and lifestyles. The pursuit of personal interests, however, does not necessarily lead to a decline of politics, but rather, may strengthen political involvement. When Chinese people go online to talk about their personal interests and needs, they are often involved in conversations about state governance. This is largely due to the interference of the state – either through direct control or soft management – in all areas of people's lives for the sake of political stability. State interference, however, gives reasons for citizens to be political, in order to avoid the interference. Therefore, when Internet becomes an everyday communicative tool for Chinese citizens, and gives opportunities to each person to voice their personal stories and opinions, political discussion becomes an everyday reality in Chinese cyber communities. For community managers, dealing with political discussion is an important part of their daily management.

The practice of everyday self-censorship

Studies on Chinese Internet censorship generally focus on the struggles between individual users and the party-state: the strategies the party-state employs to control Internet use, and the tactics users devise to resist censorship. Few studies have centered on the meso level of cyber communities and their website providers, discussing how they are involved in the struggles between individuals and the state. Unlike face-to-face communication where information can be directly transmitted from one person to another, information circulated through the Internet is routed through websites that provide services for online publications and communication. At the same time, the party-state's Internet regulations target website providers directly, demanding that they take responsibility for users' practices on their websites. In the following, I shall use a behind-the-scenes perspective to examine the responses of Tan Street's managers towards governmental demand, especially in regard to their considerations of whether or not, how, and to what extent to conduct self-censorship. A detailed exploration of managers' response to censorship shall give an insight to the organizing logic of cyber communities in China.

Information control in cyber communities

It is common that cyber communities have a managers group, including administrators and moderators, to manage members' behavior. Tan Street is no exception. After the latest adjustment in 2009, Tan Street has had in total four administrators and 28 board masters, or *banzhu* (版主), a Chinese word corresponding to moderators. Two administrators are technical experts responsible for dealing with technical issues, and two take charge of the overall community management. The board masters are in charge of their own boards. They have the responsibility to encourage members to publish posts in order to stimulate group discussions, and at the same time, the obligation to manage members' posts when they deem these posts to be in violation of board rules.

According to Tan Street's "*Rules for board masters' management*", board masters could delete posts that (1) violate laws or regulations; (2) are politically sensitive; (3) insult or slander others; (4) violate others' privacy; (5) disseminate pornography, violence, or other immoral information; (6) are off-topic in regard to board themes; (7) are spam messages; (8) are advertisements. Penalties imposed upon those who break the rules range from the most common penalty, having their posts deleted, to the most extreme penalty, a permanent ban of their member account and IP address. In addition to board rules, which are mainly implemented by board masters, another regulatory system – keyword-filtering software – is operated by website administrators. A set of keywords deemed by the administrators to be sensitive, including politically sensitive words, profanity, and sexually suggestive words, are in the filtering system. If a post contains these keywords, the post would be completely blocked or the keywords would be automatically replaced with asterisks.

One main purpose in establishing community rules, as explained by the board master who authored them, is "to prepare for inspection by Internet regulatory agencies". The implementation of keyword-filtering software is also a requirement of the government. According to the administrator who was responsible for setting up keyword-filtering software in Tan Street, the Public Security Bureau with which the website registered, tried to test Tan Street's keyword-filtering software on one occasion by sending some meaningless words to the founder, requiring him to include these words as filtered words, in order to check whether or not the website had set up a filtering system, and how quickly it worked.

It is mostly up to managers to decide whether or not a post could be deleted and which word should be listed as banned keywords. In my interviews with Tan Street managers, they seemed to have developed "common knowledge" (*gongshi* 共识) – a term used by many of them – in regard to the prohibition of political topics. For instance, topics relating to June 4th, Falun Gong, Tibet, or Taiwan independence are "high-tension lines" (*gaoyaxian* 高压线), which means "very sensitive". To comment on specific governmental policies would normally not be a problem. To directly question the legitimacy of the Chinese political regime, and to criticize the central government and leaders are, however, normally prohibited. To denounce the government and leaders of the region where the website is registered will possibly bring troubles to the community. It is, however, often not a problem to show indignation toward the governments and leaders of other regions.

Although managers exhibited the awareness of common knowledge, they admitted that it was still difficult to "grasp the yardstick" (*bawo chidu* 把握尺度) when dealing with specific cases. The difficulties are largely due to the vagueness of the types of content prohibited. The official rules and regulations prohibit content that "instigates subversion of state sovereignty or the socialist system", "instigates division of the country or damages national unification", "instigates hatred or discrimination among nationalities, or damages the solidarity of nationalities", or "distorts the truth, spreads rumors, or disturbs social order" (Measurements on the Management of Safety Protection of Computer Information Systems, Article 5). These descriptions used to judge "inappropriate" content are "too general and vaguely written" and "difficult to implement", complained the administrator of Tan Street, who was in charge of setting up filtering words.

Managers, therefore, have to learn how to continually control political content. Board masters sometimes consult with administrators when faced with a post that is difficult to evaluate. Administrators sometimes observe bigger websites intentionally to find out how these websites treat particular issues, and which topics they do or do not cover. They also learn from ideology and thoughts disseminated by the central Propaganda Department, as well as from direct calls and warnings from the local Propaganda Department and Public Security Bureau. Even though Tan Street did not register with any governmental agency in Wen County, it was treated by the Wen County Propaganda Department and the Public Security Bureau as a website from Wen County, and was considered to be under supervision. The reason was that "the website focuses on things related to Wen County", as explained by an official in the local Propaganda Department who was responsible for administrating websites in Wen County. For instance, in 2007, the founder received phone calls from the Wen County Propaganda Department to delete a post that revealed that a Wen County police officer had killed someone in a car accident. This post was considered to have "tarnished the image of the Wen County government, and would negatively affect social stability", as the founder transmitted. In 2008, after the massive earthquake in Sichuan province in Western China, the Wen County Propaganda Department called the founder to demand that he delete posts that were deemed to have "destroyed an atmosphere of solidarity". No longer after Tan Street started operation, the Wen County Public Security Bureau sent a requirement for administrative privileges to the founder. Even though the founder did not want to follow the requirement, he gave the Bureau administrative privileges because, as he put it, "It is impossible to disagree!" According to the founder, the police officer had in fact never used his right to manage the website directly.

The creation of public and hidden transcripts

It is true that Tan Street managers follow the requirements of the government to set up filtering software and conduct post deletion. What lies behind their compliance with the demands is, however, more intriguing. In the following, I shall present three posts that exhibit how managers presented their perception of self-censorship in different contexts. All these three texts were posted on the management board.

The first text was written by an administrator in September 2007. The purpose of the post was to remind managers to be careful about their management behavior during the period up to and including the Seventeenth Party Congress. The title of the post was "Building a harmonious forum, launching a rectification movement". In this post, he wrote:

> In order to build a harmonious society, we would like to ask all administrators and board masters to hold your ground and adhere to the strictest criteria in monitoring posts during this period of time. If you are unsure of the appropriateness of any posts, just move them directly to the trash. We need to discover and resolve problems quickly. All unhealthy and illegal expression must be severely punished. A lot of website servers have been closed down lately. We need to learn a lesson from them. We must ensure that Tan Street can run smoothly and exist for a long time. We also want to remind administrators of QQ discussion groups to manage group discussions strictly during this period of time. Let us work together to follow the direction of Internet supervisory agencies to build a healthy and positive Tan Street, for the sake of welcoming the Seventeenth Party Congress!

The second text was published only three days after the first, and was a speech excerpt. This speech was given by a manager at a conference organized by the Wen County Propaganda Department prior to the Seventeenth Party Congress. The manager was sent by the Tan Street founder to represent Tan Street at the conference. At this conference, every website representative was required to give a speech to introduce his own website. The representative of Tan Street introduced the purpose, content, and main features of Tan Street. One of the features was summarized as follows:

> We manage our website strictly. We keep pace with the times, abide by Party and state policies and regulations, and focus on promoting mainstream values. Since the Internet is a platform with a high level of freedom, our management group pays much attention to supervising and managing Internet expression. We strictly prohibit pornography, violence, and reactionary content. Any content that damages the image of the Party and the State, or that is unhealthy or in violation of laws and regulations is strictly prohibited. We are building a healthy and positive website to welcome the convening of the Seventeenth Party Congress.

The third text was published by another administrator in August 2009. He transmitted a notification from the government to other managers and reminded them to be stricter in their post management:

> We just received an indication that there will be a check on discussion forums before October 1st 2009. From today on, all discussion forums that are discovered by Internet supervisory agency to contain illegal information will be closed down immediately, and are not allowed to reopen before October 1st 2009. Users who want to reopen their discussion forums have to resubmit an application to the Ministry of Industry and Information Technology after October 1st.
>
> Another round of the strike-hard campaign starts again. Board masters, you have to work hard again. Please try to guide sensitive topics. You can also move posts that contain sensitive topics to the management board first. We can deal with them later. We hope that every board master can check posts with strict criteria. The current themes of our discussion forum are: calm and keeping a low tone.

At first glance, these three texts delivered one common message: community managers would and should follow the official demand to conduct supervision of members' online communication. However, a closer examination and comparison of the contexts in which the message was delivered and the way in which it was described reveals that there exists two disparate types of speech, which could be categorized as what James C. Scott calls public transcript and hidden transcript. Scott (1990) points out that subordinates tend to show respect to dominators in public, while on the other hand they create hidden transcripts, such as poaching and pilfering, to show resistance towards dominators behind their backs. The above texts clearly exhibit the different ways in which community managers spoke in different contexts. The managers offered a performance of consent and loyalty in the context political authorities were present and generated a backstage discourse concerning what they could not and did not want to expose to the authorities.

As mentioned above, the second text – the speech excerpt – was presented by a Tan Street representative at the conference convened by the local Propaganda Department. The department's purpose in organizing the conference was to place pressure on local websites to conduct self-censorship. The first and the third texts were presented as internal messages, and merely circulated on the management discussion board which was not open to the public and was beyond the observation of the authorities. Even though managers emphasized that they should conduct self-censorship in both contexts, they displayed different motivations and criteria for practicing self-censorship.

In the conference speech, the motivation for conducting self-censorship was described as if it was generated by a desire to assist the party-state in achieving its goals and was based on service ethics and obligations to the party-state. The criteria for controlling information were presented as if they consistently and strictly followed official regulations. In this speech, the author adopted the rhetoric of state propaganda, such as "keep pace with the times" (*yushi jujin* 与时俱进), "promote mainstream values" (*hongyang zhuxuanlü* 弘扬主旋律), "healthy" (*jiankang de* 健康的), and "positive" (*jiji de* 积极的), to reassure the authorities that their activities were in line with Party ideology. When presenting which types of information community managers prohibited and how strictly they supervised Internet expression, the author also used official descriptions of Internet regulations to give assurance that they adhered to laws and regulations and posed no threat to political system. This speech shows how the Tan Street representative performed in a way he perceived was consistent with the expectations of the authorities, both in regard to himself and to Tan Street.

In the administrators' internal management notifications, the motivation to conduct self-censorship was clearly defined as to "ensure that Tan Street can run smoothly and exist for a long time". This motivation was generated by the desire to maintain community survival, and was based on the interests of the community itself rather than those of the party-state. Even though the author of the first text also used words such as "harmonious" and "rectification" which can be found in the Party propaganda, the way the words were used had the effect of making his post more humorous than harsh. "Building a harmonious forum" is an imitation of the new ideology of "building a harmonious society" (*goujian hexie shehui* 构建和谐社会) proclaimed by the Chinese president Hu Jintao. "Rectification movement" (*zhengfen yundong* 整风运动) is an imitation of a movement conducted within the Chinese Communist Party in 1940s, which aimed to rectify Party members' ideology, attitudes, and behavior. Chinese Internet users often imitate party-state propaganda rhetoric to criticize and make fun of the Party and the government.

The criteria for controlling information as defined by the administrators were obviously not as strict and consistent as they were presented to the authorities. One obvious indication is that when the administrators specifically wrote the notifications to remind managers to be stricter during the period of the Party Congress and the Strike-Hard (*yanda* 严打) Campaign, they hinted that managers were allowed to operate with more relaxed management criteria before and after these events.

It is important to note that in order to tell the entire story about power relations, it is not enough to focus exclusively on the public transcript; one must also examine the hidden transcript to uncover how subordinates speak and practice behind the backs of power holders (Scott, 1990, p. 3). In this respect, the study of how exactly cyber communities practice self-censorship is of special importance. The discrepancy between the public and hidden transcripts exhibits the agency of the community in attempting to deal with the dilemma generated by the conflict of market and politics in the Chinese context.

Cyber communities in China cannot survive if they do not obey governmental regulations. Neither can they survive if they do not respect members' needs. With the introduction of market mechanisms, the Internet industry has grown rapidly and market competition has become increasingly harsh. In a cyber community, members are under the regulation of community rules; however, they also have the ability to change the regulation and influence the operation of the community. If the regulation of the community becomes harsher, members might choose to exit the community to evade regulation. Therefore, when faced with the intervention of the state, cyber communities and their website providers may try to protect the options they provide for participants and to strategically loosen the regulations and soften penalties placed on individual members. The public transcript of Tan Street managers demonstrates the power of the party-state in manipulating individuals and societal organizations. It can also be interpreted as a tactic community managers devised to protect the community for the sake of survival. The hidden transcript further shows the intention of community managers to provide more opportunities for individuals to express themselves.

Self-censorship as an everyday form of resistance

It is normal that Chinese netizens conduct everyday forms of resistance towards censorship through creative jokes, satire, songs, and other types of "weapons of the weak" (Scott, 1985). The hidden transcript created by cyber communities, as presented above, reveals that communities also have the intentions to design everyday forms of resistance to bypass censorship. What are the weapons communities devise to respond to Internet control? How do they use these weapons? And what makes it possible for them to conduct everyday forms of resistance?

I argue that it is exactly the self-censorship policy that makes it possible for communities to conduct everyday forms of resistance. As introduced above, website providers are required to set up keyword-filtering software to block posts and words. However, the words and phrases to be filtered are normally chosen by website providers themselves. Cyber community managers are required to delete illegal and inappropriate posts. However, to judge whether or not a post is illegal or inappropriate largely depends on the opinions of the managers themselves. The self-censorship policy leaves some room for communities to circumvent state intervention and to maximize their own interests. The following are some specific tactics that Tan Street managers devised to evade governmental control.

First, official regulations are not always implemented, or sometimes the implementation is relaxed and lacks monitoring procedures. This makes it possible for websites to evade regulations. For instance, according to the regulations, websites that have discussion forum services should apply for a special license and are required to arrange for full-time managers to monitor their screen round the clock. Tan Street did not have this license, and from my interview with the founder it seemed that he did not intend to apply for it, mainly due to the difficulty of obtaining the special license and the expense of hiring full-time managers. He also did not show any concern about violating the regulations and the possibility of being punished. "We have a 'relationship' (*guanxi* 关系) with the provincial Industry and Information Technology Bureau," he explained, and "those bigger websites don't have any trouble, let alone such a small site as Tan Street".

Second, the implementation of regulations often does not follow consistent criteria. Regulations are strictly enforced to begin with followed by a lax period, and then strictly enforced again when something happens, and when the government feels it needs to issue a warning (Tsui, 2001, p. 28). Examples include the events of the Party Congress in 2007 and the national day in 2009, as illustrated in the above three texts. The way the government implements regulations can be interpreted as a way to warn Internet users that they are being monitored and to remind them that there are boundaries they should not overstep. These same warnings could, on the other hand, be exploited by website managers to relax their management when the "sensitive period" (*mingan shiqi* 敏感时期) – as they put it – was past. The above notifications written by Tan Street administrators to remind other managers to be strict during special events clearly exhibit this adaptive tactic.

Third, although official regulations prescribe what kind of information is prohibited online, descriptions of prohibited information are vaguely formulated and can be interpreted and implemented in different ways by different interest groups. It is quite common for a single post to be treated differently on different websites, or on different discussion boards within one website, or even at different times within one discussion board. In Tan Street administrators set up banned words in its keyword-filtering software, but the blocking of some words was sometimes cancelled due to members' questions and protests. Managers also often took advantage of the vagueness of prohibited content to "play line balls" (*da cabianqiu* 打擦边球) – as they put it – to push the boundaries of what was politically acceptable.

Fourth, regulations are applied in all types of Internet-related communicative forms. Different forms are, however, covered by different regulators and regulatory means. This makes it possible for website managers to create relatively unmonitored spaces for users. For instance, compared to the two main forms Tan Street offered – discussion forums and QQ chat groups – the chat group was obviously less censored. I was surprised by bold expressions in Tan Street's chat groups, such as a picture of a naked female body with former president Jiang Zemin's head, humorous words added to serious images of current president

Hu Jintao, and some extremely harsh doggerel satirizing anti-corruption officials. These expressions would very likely be deleted by Tan Street managers, if they were posted on the discussion forum. Even though both discussion forums and QQ chat groups were under political supervision, they had the following differences: in the discussion forum, the party-state does not only use technology to automatically check posts but also appoints officials to scrutinize posts personally; in the QQ chat groups, the party-state merely uses keyword-filtering software to supervise group discussion. It is too complicated on a practical level to arrange for officials to supervise millions of chat groups and to control the huge amount of daily chat material.

Managing daily political discussion

Not only Tan Street managers, but also ordinary members exhibited a clear comprehension of the difficulties of running a website in China. In my interviews with the founder, he used a community member living in Taiwan as a typical example to illustrate members' support and understanding, and appreciated the fact that this member reminded managers to delete his posts if they were inappropriate. My interviews with community members also show that many of them were aware of government sanctions on a website and were cautious not to create problems for the community. As one member put it, "Tan Street is after all a spontaneous, private, and self-financing website. We should cherish and protect it".

Many members also seemed to develop a sort of common sense approach similar to that of the managers regarding the kinds of topics they could or could not touch upon. Those who were not aware of the yardstick generally became more cautious after being reminded by community managers. In fact, many members were not only cautious about their own behavior, but also watched the behavior of others – even of the managers – and tried to remind them to "grasp the yardstick" if necessary. Earlier, Tan Street had an online forum called "Tan Street evening talk", which provided an opportunity for members to gather in a QQ chat group and discuss "hot topics in the sphere of culture, economy, society, commerce, well-being, current affairs, etc.", as it was described in the activity proposal. A transcript of the discussion was then published on the Tan Street discussion forum. On one occasion when a board master, who had taken charge of "Tan Street evening talk", proposed a discussion about the fact that many Chinese government officials used the services of prostitutes, members reminded him that this topic was "too sensitive", and was likely to result in "serious consequences", especially during the current "tense situation".

However, there are also conflicts between members and managers in terms of political posts and discussion. The following case is a typical example that shows how ordinary users and managers negotiated in regard to the publication of political content.

This case began when a member posted a thread entitled "Questioning the People's Government of Wen County" in December 2005. This thread revealed that the local government had decided to allow the construction of a factory building in a residential area, and criticized the government for ignoring the health and lives of local residents. When the community founder discovered that the author had repeatedly commented on his or her own post in order to attract attention, he locked the thread to prevent follow-up responses. His treatment of this post irritated the post author, who immediately created another post, angrily requiring an explanation. The following text is the entire conversation, including the author's questions, the founder's responses, and comments from other participants. A refers to the post author, B, C, D, E, F, G, H, and I are other participants. It is possible that some of the participants were actually the post author A him or herself; A may have created other usernames and pretended to be a different person to support him or herself.

A: Why was the thread "Questioning the People's Government of Wen County" locked?! Who locked it? I strongly protest!!!!!!

THE FOUNDER: Sorry, I locked the thread. One reason is because everybody knows who is right and who is wrong in regard to this issue. It is meaningless to repeat it. The other reason is that I want to avoid trouble. It is very difficult for ordinary people to establish discussion forums. Hope for your understanding and forgiveness!

B: I support the thread starter! Who pushed the administrator to lock the thread?

C: I support the thread starter.

THE FOUNDER: Let me explain again. Nobody pushed me to lock the thread. A few days ago, one of the discussion boards in The Window of Wen County (another cyber community in Wen County) was forced to close down. I do not want to have the same problem. Hope everybody can understand.

A: Locking the thread is not convincing, you will lose the support of the people. . . . Since this issue has happened, why should we hide it? What's wrong with letting the victims voice their claims. . . . The disadvantaged group voice their claim because their lives and health are threatened. For the other party, the only thing they could possibly lose is their official career. . . . The disadvantaged group comes here to seek support. Even this is not allowed?!

D: If people from ZF (the government) come here to express their opinions, will they be prohibited? No!

E: I personally think it makes no difference whether or not the thread is locked. It is useless just to complain. We've offered suggestions before, but we don't see that anybody put them into practice. There are two ways to choose: either act or wait!

F: I support the above poster.

G: In my opinion, members of this forum have provided many suggestions. It is up to the litigants themselves to solve the problem. . . . However, if our public servants can put the brakes on their interest in fame and gain, and are aware of what they should and should not do, why should they be afraid of the grumbling of netizens?!

H: Is a forum a place for people to write and respond to posts, or a tool for the government to keep up appearances? If this place does not allow people to express themselves freely, can it be called a discussion forum?

I: For a nation, if there is no freedom, there is nothing else. . . . Freedom of speech is what human beings long for. However, it must never be a dream. To change an undemocratic political environment to democracy is the goal that a nation should continually struggle for.

THE FOUNDER: Hehe, I give up! I have already unlocked the thread. But I hope everyone will be careful about the words he chooses. Please do not use extreme expressions. I believe that you also don't want this website to be closed down. Thank you!

D: Thank you!

The Internet has offered more opportunities for Chinese disadvantaged individuals and groups to voice their grievances and to assert their rights and identities to the public (Tai, 2006, pp. 255–286; Yang, 2009; Zhao, 2008, pp. 245–285). In the above conversation it is clear that post author A's purpose in joining the community was not to make friends and exchange opinions, in contrast to many other members. A was among those who used the Internet as a weapon for fighting the authorities, and expected that by publicizing the injustice he encountered and expressing his grievance in Tan Street he would garner support, which would place pressure on the local government. Unlike some members who simply left the community when they were dissatisfied with post management or who chose alternative means of communication without openly questioning management, A chose "voice" strategy as the way he or she used to deal with managers. He or she published a new post to openly voice his or her indignation and demand an explanation. I do not know whether or not he or she finally had his or her wishes realized in the physical world. This voice strategy he or she used in Tan Street obviously succeeded in persuading the founder to change his original decision.

The success of the above protest illustrates that the community founder was open to questions and challenges, and was willing to develop an open communication and a friendly relationship with ordinary members. Even when faced with post author A who could possibly cause problems for the community, the founder showed understanding and tolerance, and patiently explained his reasons for locking the thread instead of ignoring the author's protest. In Tan Street, rules and sanctions were established and implemented to constrain activities that were deemed to be deviant, and to maintain community order. However, when dealing with members' questions and challenges towards community management, managers were not allowed to use coercive methods, but rather were required to adopt the strategies of negotiation and dialogue. If they decided to delete, move, or lock a post, they had to send a message to give an explanation to the post author in advance. In this case, the Tan Street founder conceded to the post author in the end. It is very likely that the founder would still lock the thread if the government demanded that he did so. Nevertheless, regardless of the result, the attitudes the founder held and the approach he used to negotiate with the post author would be the same.

The above conversation also clearly shows that the founder was confronted with the dilemma of preserving the community's openness and obeying the government's rules simultaneously. Although he showed a strong fear of the government's political censorship, he tried to balance this conflict and did not want to constrain members' self-expression completely. During the negotiation the founder emphasized the difficulties of running websites in China, and asked for members' understanding and forgiveness. By using this approach, he transmitted a message that the community was also the victim of governmental control, and that whether or not the community could survive was closely tied with users' practices. Making censorship transparent could easily generate understanding and sympathy from members, who wish to have a place for self-expression.

Conclusion

This article has explored the organizing logic that sustains the productivity of cyber communities in China. My data show the abilities of communities to balance the conflict between market and politics. Communities adhere to governmental requirements of the supervision of political discussions among members. At the same time, however, they take advantage of self-censorship policy to encourage members' self-expression, in order to retain them in the communities. The opportunities that communities have obtained to maximize their own interests are largely due to the opening up of the social space created by economic reform and the partial withdrawal of the party-state from the management of societal collectives. The opening up of social space has also generated competition among numerous communities. Communities, that provide services such as discussion forums and blogs for members to express themselves and to communicate with each other, are in competition with others that provide similar services. When members are not satisfied with a community, they are very likely to leave or turn to other communities to seek other options. Just as with firms or organizations, cyber communities' chances for survival and development depend to a great extent on their members. An exodus of members, especially those who have gained a reputation due to their active participation and high-level posts, is a great loss to the community. Communities must therefore consider how to improve their ability to attract and retain members in order to succeed.

The importance of members to cyber communities illustrates a type of individual-collective relationship: it is not that individuals are subject to the community, but rather that the community serves the needs of individuals. These communities are invented by individuals on the basis of their personal interests and needs, and may be replaced by other communities when these needs are not met. This new type of individual-collective relationship is the result of the individualization process that is occurring in post-Mao China, where individuals are forced by institutional changes to create communities to deal with risks and insecurities that are placed on their own shoulders. At the same time, this relationship facilitates individualization, by widely and officially acknowledging individuals as the basic unit of society. It is undoubtedly true that the connection between individuals and this type of community is not as strong and close as in traditional communities, which emphasize obligation, morality, and loyalty. However, in the current globalized and individualized Chinese society, one community may quickly collapse, and the possibilities of creating a similar one is intensified.

References

Bauman, Z. (2001a). *Community: Seeking safety in an insecure world*. Cambridge, UK: Polity Press.
Bauman, Z. (2001b). *The individualized society*. Cambridge, UK: Polity Press.
CASS. (2007). *Surveying Internet usage and its impact in seven Chinese cities*. Beijing: Center for Social Development, Chinese Academy of Social Sciences.
Castells, M. (1997). *The power of identity*. Malden, MA: Blackwell.
Damm, J. (2007). The Internet and the fragmentation of Chinese society. *Critical Asian Studies, 39*(2), 273–294.
Esarey, A., & Xiao, Q. (2008). Political expression in the Chinese blogosphere: Below the radar. *Asian Survey, 48*(5), 752–772.
Giddens, A. (1991). *Modernity and self-identity: Self and society in the late modern age*. Stanford, CA: Stanford University Press.
Hansen, M. H., & Svarverud, R. (2010). *iChina: The rise of the individual in modern Chinese society*. Copenhagen, Denmark: NIAS Press.
Nisbet, R. A. (1953/1990). *The quest for community: A study in the ethics of order and freedom*. San Francisco, CA: ICS Press.
Scott, J. C. (1985). *Weapons of the weak: Everyday forms of peasant resistance*. New Haven, CT: Yale University Press.
Scott, J. C. (1990). *Domination and the arts of resistance: Hidden transcripts*. New Haven, CT: Yale University Press.
Tai, Z. (2006). *The Internet in China: Cyberspace and civil society*. New York, NY: Routledge.
Tsui, L. (2001.) *Big mama is watching you: Internet control and the Chinese government* (MA thesis). University of Leiden, Leiden.
Williams, R. (1975). *The country and the city*. St. Albans, Australia: Paladin.
Yan, Y. (2009). *The individualization of Chinese society*. Oxford, UK: Oxford University Press.
Yang, G. (2009). *The power of the Internet in China: Citizen activism online*. New York, NY: Columbia University Press.
Yu, H. (2007). Blogging everyday life in Chinese Internet culture. *Asian Studies Review, 31*(4), 423–433.
Zhao, Y. (2008). *Communication in China: Political economy, power, and conflict*. Lanham, MD: Rowman & Littlefield.

10 The role of Chinese Internet industry workers in creating alternative online spaces

Bingqing Xia and Helen Kennedy

In most of the discussion about the Internet as an alternative space – a space which allows for greater freedoms than other spaces, a space of liberating potential – the focus is usually on "ordinary" Internet users. Indeed, the rising importance of such ordinary users has been the subject of a great deal of academic attention around the globe, for example in Henry Jenkins' (2006) discussion of convergence culture, and in the widespread discussion of the possibilities for participation opened up by Web 2.0 platforms and technologies and their user-generated content (for example, Benkler, 2006; Bruns, 2008; Ornebring, 2008; Thurman, 2008, amongst others). In contrast, this chapter focuses on a group of Chinese Internet actors who have not been the subject of much scholarly attention: the actual producers of the Chinese Internet. In so doing, the chapter follows the argument made by a number of scholars (such as Gill, 2007, 2010; and Kennedy, 2012) that in order to fully understand online cultures, it is necessary to examine the important role played by the professional producers of those cultures. While research into the producers of online and other cultural products is expanding (for example Banks, 2007; Hesmondhalgh & Baker, 2010; Kennedy, 2012), there is little research that analyzes the contributions made by workers in Chinese Internet industries to the production of "online China". This chapter fills that gap.

The chapter draws on empirical research carried out by one of the authors (Bingqing Xia) in two Chinese Internet industries, one which focuses on online gaming and another which offers social networking services (SNS). In the chapter, we reflect on the ways in which the practices of workers in these industries can be seen to represent acts of agency, negotiation or resistance, which, in turn, open up the possibility of creating meaningful, expressive and resistant spaces. We do not focus on the consequences of such practices in this chapter, but rather highlight their potential for realizing some of the liberatory ideals associated with the Internet, such as giving voice to a more diverse population than has previously been able to access media technologies. The chapter proposes that the potential of Chinese Internet industry workers to contribute to the transformation of online China can be traced in their negotiations with the gaze of the allegedly authoritarian state. Thus this essay also argues that a focus on workers in Internet industries contributes a valuable perspective to exploring the shaping of the emergent socio-cultural space of online China.

The chapter introduces the contemporary Chinese Internet industries before proceeding to discuss workers' practices in detail. We highlight the difficult conditions of many workers in this sector and the ways in which some of these conditions are a result of state intervention. Such detail illuminates the conditions in which acts of agency take place, and the difficulties that workers face in their efforts to create alternative online spaces. We then go on to discuss the various ways in which workers mobilize their agency, drawing on Hodson's definition of this concept, with specific reference to his understandings of worker resistance. We point out that in addition to the tradition of organizing resistance into two categories, collective/organized or individual/routine level, a third category of resistance can be identified, at the level of the individual firm or company. Thus, we add to existing understandings of types of worker resistance. But we do not only talk about worker resistance in this chapter. We identify other forms of agency, which might be characterized as negotiation or hope, which, in different ways, open up possibilities for online China.

Chinese Internet industries

Since the policies of economic reform were introduced into China in 1978, Chinese society has been variously characterized as neo-liberal (Harvey, 2005; Huang, 2010; Wang, 2003), crony communist (Andreas, 2010; Dickson, 2003; 2011), and post-socialist (Chun, 2006; Zhao, 2003, 2007, 2011). Despite fierce disagreement about which of these terms best characterizes China today, all of them share a recognition of the growing importance of the market, whilst some acknowledge the close entanglement of the market and the state (such as crony communism and post-socialism) more than others (such as neo-liberalism).

It is in this context of the growth of markets and the strong hand of the state that the Chinese Internet industries emerge as an important economic sector. As Andrew Ross (2005) stresses in his book *Fast Boat to China*, most of the industries which are strongly influenced by the state are "technology-driven and skill-intensive" (p. 91), like the Internet industries. Eighteen years on from their initial development, the Internet industries now contribute significantly to China's fast-paced economic development. According to the CNNIC (China Internet Network Information Centre), in 2011, Chinese Internet users had risen in number to 505 million (nearly 38 per cent of the total population), and the profit of the industries had reached 80 billion RMB (Renmin Youdianbao, 2012), growing at a pace which was nearly five times faster than Chinese gross domestic product in the past 10 years (Liang, 2012). Online gaming is a particularly striking sector, worth around 50 per cent of the total Internet industry market (41.43 billion RMB, around £4.15 billion, in 2011). The convergence of Internet industries with the mobile phone market, through the provision of their services via apps or other mobile-enabled technologies, has served to consolidate the sector. For example, Sina Weibo, China's primary microblogging service, has been extended to all mobile phone systems, which has resulted in an increase in the number of microblog users. At the time of writing, 21 large companies dominate the Internet industry sector, as listed in Table 10.1.

Table 10.1 Main players of the Chinese Internet industry (Hulianwang, 2012, trans. by the authors)

Rank	Name of companies	Services provided by companies	Profits in 2011 (in billions of dollars)	Market value on 26th June 2012 (in billions of dollars)
1	Tencent	Portal & instant message	4.52	51.75
2	Baidu	Search engine	2.3	38.78
3	Netease	Portal	1.2	7.4
4	Sohu	Portal	0.85	1.53
5	SNDA	Online entertainment	0.77	1.13
6	Ctrip	Online travel agency	0.59	2.37
7	Dangdang	Online bookstore	0.52	0.49
8	Sina	portal	0.48	3.46
9	Changyou	Online travel agency	0.48	1.08
10	Wanmei	Online game	0.43	0.37
11	Soufun	Online real estate	0.34	1.3
12	Ztgame	Online game	0.26	1.06
13	51job	Online recruitment	0.22	1.18
14	M18	Electronic commerce	0.22	0.06
15	Qihoo 360	Software (antivirus software)	0.17	2.04
16	21 Vianet Group	Carrier-neutral Internet data centre services	0.16	0.63
17	Kongzhong	Online entertainment	0.16	0.22
18	Jinshan software	Sofware (antivirus software)	0.15	0.53
19	Youku	Online video	0.14	2.4
20	Ifeng.com	Online news	0.14	0.38
21	Renren	Social networking services	0.12	1.79

Internet industries have become sufficiently significant for the state to play a strong hand in their governance, through the development of policies which impact on this sector. For example, in the executive Meeting of the State Council in 2011, Premier Wen Jiabao set out a blueprint for the Internet industries. This was the first time that the state focused on the new Internet industries in its policy-making practices (Liang, 2012). On May 4, 2011, the National Internet Information Office was set up to manage the industries (Liang, 2012). There are also other policies corresponding to various Internet services, such as those that relate to SNS and microblogging. For instance, at the end of 2011, the Beijing government issued a policies (Beijing Municipality, 2011) forcing Internet users registering on microblogging platforms to use their real names and identity cards, in order to facilitate the monitoring and control of Internet users' online activities. These policies give an indication of the involvement of the state in the newly developing Internet industries. However, as we indicate below, it is not simply the case that such policies operate without resistance or negotiation from Internet industry workers.

At the same time, as the sector develops at a high speed, the Internet is increasingly seen as an important space for freedom of expression and even resistance in contemporary Chinese society, because it is perceived to facilitate debate amongst ordinary Chinese people. At the annual conference of the Internet industries in 2011, one of the top ten influential issues that year was seen to be the development of microblogging (Renmin Youdianbao, 2012). Because of microblogging, it is claimed, ordinary Chinese people have the chance to discuss public issues and push the state to improve public services, such as in the case of the 723 Wenzhou train crash, where criticism in microblogging platforms is believed to have led to a change in government strategy. On July 23, 2011, two high-speed trains collided in the suburb of Wenzhou, Zhejiang Province, China. Several hundred people were injured or died in the accident. It was the first high-speed train crash in China. Officials in the Ministry of Railways blamed the crash on technological problems and hastily ordered the derailed cars to be buried, which elicited strong criticism from Chinese people, both online and offline. As a response, the government restricted media coverage, but could not control the online forums where much debate was taking place. Eventually, some officials in the Ministry of Railways were forced to resign, allegedly because of the strong criticism they received from some Chinese netizens. At the same time, local governments have been pushed to be transparent about certain issues, with over 10,000 local government departments setting up microblogging accounts to make their services transparent (Renmin Youdianbao, 2012). As we suggested in the introduction to this chapter, online platforms like microblogs, social networks and other forums are designed and built by Chinese Internet industry workers, so it is important to consider the role they play in the construction of these alleged spaces of freedom.

One of the authors, Bingqing Xia, carried out empirical, at times ethnographic research, in two Chinese Internet industries to study the workers in this sector. The first we call Grand here. This company focuses on online entertainment, such as online gaming and online fiction. The second one we call Campus. This provides social networking services. We used observation and in-depth interviews as our primary methodology. Bingqing conducted in-depth interviews in three periods in Campus: seven interviews in February 2010; nine interviews in August 2011; and five interviews in December 2011. She also spent three months in Grand conducting participant observation, where she worked as an intern to observe and keep a journal about workers' daily practices. We also invited one worker at Campus, who we call Galeno, who participated in our interviews in two periods in 2011, to conduct self-observation, by keeping a journal about his working life during the period of September 2009–December 2011. We had hoped that more workers would agree to engage with this process, but in the event, they did not. Through these mixed, qualitative methods, we examined the working conditions within the Chinese Internet industries, which we discuss in the next section, and workers' acts of agency, negotiation and resistance, discussed in the subsequent section.

Bingqing's participant observation in Grand was covert, for a number of reasons. First, because Chinese companies tend to reject requests for access to do academic research, unless the research could bring them commercial benefits. Such rejection would certainly have been the case for our research into worker agency and resistance. Second, we felt that we would be able to witness more "genuine" acts of worker agency through covert research. However, covert research necessarily brings with it ethical concerns. Bingqing felt that she was deceiving "participants" as she simultaneously built personal friendships and gathered their stories. Participants told Bingqing their personal stories because they saw her as a friend; friendship therefore helped Bingqing to gather data. This then presents us with a dilemma regarding sharing the stories that participants confided in Bingqing. This dilemma and feelings of deception remain, yet we choose to write about the research in this public domain, because we feel that it contributes to understanding Chinese society and the role played by Internet industry workers in that society. Indeed, this is why we chose to pursue the research through what might be seen as an ethically problematic means. We hope that if our participants read this chapter and recognize themselves in it, they understand our motivations for carrying out covert research and the benefits it may bring, and that they do not feel deceived by us.

Working conditions in the Chinese Internet industries

Working conditions in the Chinese Internet industries are not good, and workers in these industries face numerous barriers in their efforts to create alternative online spaces. The first problem relates to working hours. One of our participants, working in Grand, indicates that she rarely has dinner with her boyfriend, even though they live together, because he works in another Internet company and always works overtime. Another highlighted how working a 16-hour shift is not unusual.

> I always work until 10 PM, which is nearly twice the normal working time . . . (August 25, 2011, Davis, Campus)
> Look at the record of my clock on and off, one day I worked 16 hours without any break. (December 11, 2011, William, Campus)

Even though these workers devote themselves to their industries with such long working hours, they are not rewarded with salaries comparable with workers in state-owned enterprises or companies borne out of foreign investment. Overtime work in the Internet industries is rarely rewarded, compared to the double or triple overtime pay that is on offer in other industries. William, who develops social networking services on mobile phone platforms in Campus, said:

> My salary is £13,000 per year (£1,000 per month multiplied by 13 months) with the endless hard work, while my friend who works in the state-owned enterprise, earns around £20,000 per year (salary of £800 per month multiplied

by 16 months, and bonus of £200 per quarter multiplied by 4 quarters) without any overtime.

(December 11, 2011, William, Campus)

Work in the Chinese Internet industries takes place in an era of intense global competition. Andrew Ross (2005) claims that in the globalized economy, China is not guaranteed of its role as the world's factory, as its high-tech industries face competition from both home and abroad, with countries like India competing for outsourced work in the high-tech sector. As our fieldwork indicated, workers in both of the companies in which we undertook our study are made aware of and are anxious about the threat from such competition. Galeno, the Campus employee who kept a work journal for us, said:

My leader always reminds me to keep myself in a highly competitive status. For example, to think about who will be fired if the company needs to reduce staff, if I were the person, it means I need to work harder.

(August 24, 2011, Galeno, Campus)

Some of the difficult conditions that workers in these two companies experience result directly from state intervention in the sector. Officials from the Propaganda Department, the Ministry of Culture and the General Bureau of Radio, Film and Television regularly make contact with Internet companies, in order to monitor and intervene in the daily practices of workers. According to Leo (February 27, 2010, Beijing), whose department is responsible for developing online games at Campus, one of the most popular games was withdrawn by the Ministry of Culture, because the game contains thematic content relating to gangs and gambling, which was deemed undesirable. During the participant observation at Grand, the manager of the department responsible for the production of online novels, Sarah, told us that workers in her department were worried about news stories which were circulating about teenagers' addiction to network cultures. They were concerned, she said, that if the news attracted the attention of the relevant government departments, such as the Ministry of Culture, some of their novels would be deleted and some of their related services would need to be adapted, or even withdrawn. All of this creates labor for the people working in these companies, and impacts on the extent to which they can dedicate their energies to the creation of alternative online spaces.

Another way in which the state intervenes in the practices of workers in these industries relates to key word filtering. Such well-known strategies do not only influence Internet users' experiences, by prohibiting them from posting sensitive content online, but it also affects workers' conditions, for example in relation to working time. Take the Tian'anmen Square incident as an example: every year, near the 4th of June, the anniversary of the Tian'anmen Square incident, workers in the security department of Campus receive a list of sensitive keywords, such as word of "explosion", from the Ministry of Culture (Louis, February 27, 2010, Campus). All workers are then on duty day and night to monitor and filter "sensitive" texts and pictures from Internet users' posts to various online forums. At other times, only three teams, rather than all workers, would undertake such tasks. In this sense, workers' already extensive hours are extended yet further as a result of state intervention.

The high pressure caused by the long working hours, low pay, heightened competition and limitations to workers' autonomy and creativity, which results in part from state intervention, drives some workers to *karoshi*, a Japanese term meaning "death by overwork" or to suicide. On November 14, 2011, a staff member in the online game department of Baidu died from exhaustion (Xiao, 2011). The average age of workers dying from karoshi in the industries is just under 38. As Ross (2005) notes, these and the other difficult conditions highlighted in this section are in urgent need of academic attention. We add to this, by arguing that research into the creation of meaningful online public spaces in China needs to pay attention to the conditions in the Internet industries in which these online spaces come into being. This is necessary not only in order to enhance our understanding of these spaces, but also to help us understand the adverse conditions that Internet workers need to overcome in their endeavors to create alternative spaces.

Internet idealism

It is within this context of long hours, low pay, heightened competition, state intervention and serious burn-out that workers in the Chinese Internet industries attempt to create meaningful, alternative public spaces. Without question, these difficult conditions limit workers' capacities to do so. And yet, despite these conditions, it is possible to identify acts of agency amongst workers that result in the possible opening up of such spaces. This phenomenon can be understood by drawing on two schools of thought. First, as scholars working in the emergent field of cultural industries studies have acknowledged (for example Banks, 2007; Hesmondhalgh & Baker, 2010; Kennedy, 2012), there are many rewards for working in this sector, despite widespread difficult conditions. For example, Hesmondhalgh and Baker's (2010) model of good and bad work includes amongst the characteristics of good work in the creative/cultural industries the following: interest, involvement, autonomy, self-esteem, self-realization and the production of products that contribute to the common good. Thus the writers referenced here argue for the need to produce accounts of work in the cultural and high-tech sectors which balance critique (of the difficult conditions such as those described here) and hope (about the rewards of working in these sectors, and the possible outcomes of the labor undertaken). These positive characteristics, then, account to some extent for the acts of agency that can be traced in Internet industry workers' practices.

A second explanation for the acts of agency that we observed in our research comes from meanings attached to the Internet itself. As one of us has argued elsewhere (Kennedy, 2012), Tim Berners-Lee's original vision of the web often orients Internet workers towards certain ideals and orients idealistic individuals towards Internet work. In Berners-Lee's vision, the web would be an open, interoperable and accessible medium, whose power would be in its "universality", and to which access by everyone was "an essential aspect" (Berners-Lee, 2003). Although this vision had its geographical home on the west coast of the United States, in what came to be known as the Californian ideology, its influence had global reach. As one of the participants in our research, Galeno, puts it, "Most people working in the industries are idealists". According to Galeno, idealistic Internet workers are concerned about contributing to the creation of a politically open and free space accessible to everyone, which is used to keep the state under surveillance, by commenting on its actions, and even pushing it to self-reform.

Internet producers are as interested as Internet users in the freedoms that the web and the Internet are said to offer. For many of the participants in our study, a number of freedoms were perceived, which in turn serve to explain their acts of agency and their related efforts to create alternative online spaces. For example, the Internet industries serve as a hopeful space for ordinary people in contemporary Chinese society, bad working conditions notwithstanding. Compared to other work opportunities, such as state-owned enterprises and civil service posts, work in Internet industries is seen to provide more possibilities for success to ordinary people. It is widely believed that to work in state-owned enterprises and the civil service, it is necessary to be the offspring of officials, while people from ordinary families have few chances in these sectors. By contrast, in the Internet industries, many workers are from ordinary families, and the belief exists that promotion and success are possible through hard work. One worker, Lara, working in the advertising department at Campus, said:

> It is said that we (the offspring of poor) could work as civil servants, but we would have no chance to get promotion, since we don't have a parent who is rich or an official . . . Whilst in the Internet industries, at least, we could get some of the same chances (as the offspring of the rich and officials). So, sometimes, I think working in Internet industries is better for us, the children of the ordinary people . . .
>
> (December 19, 2011, Lara, Beijing)

And our diarist, Galeno, said:

> Since I came to Beijing, several of my friends in the Internet industries, who are younger than me, have started their own businesses. So it means everyone in the industries could be successful at any time . . . My boss became a VP (Vice President) in his 20s . . .
>
> (August 24, 2011, Galeno, Beijing)

The Internet industries, then, are seen to provide a chance of success to ordinary Chinese people, and so to provide an alternative to the dominant social hierarchy in contemporary Chinese society. This might be seen as a modest transformation of offline, as well as online, China.

The quote from Galeno above also points to another freedom that the Internet industries are believed to offer: that is, the freedom to develop skills and then set up one's own business. Many participants suggested that they dreamt of running their own businesses, as indicated in the two quotes below:

> All my pals are doing different technical jobs in different Internet companies. We plan to study in these companies for 5 years, then we will group together to run our own business . . . I came here [Campus] just to learn all the things necessary for starting my own business in future . . .
>
> (August 26, 2011, William, Beijing)

> Everyone in the industries has a dream of setting up their own business. I am one of them. I'm just waiting for my pals, who are technical workers in other companies. I will leave here [Campus] and we'll start our own business as long as they learn enough in their areas . . . You cannot identify yourself as a member in the Internet industries if you have not started to run your own business in your 30s.
>
> (August 24, 2011, Galeno, Beijing)

For some, the motivation to do this is financial. As William puts it:

> To be honest, one of my main motivations (for starting my own business) is to earn more money than now. It is because of the common understanding in Chinese society nowadays: you can get anything, such as social status and respect from other people, when you are rich. And I believe it will not change in the coming 30 years, so it forces me to earn as much money as I can . . .
>
> (August 26, 2011, William, Beijing)

But this is not the only motivation, and other reasons for wanting to go it alone build much more explicitly on the "Internet idealism" identified earlier in this section. Another motivation expressed by William is autonomy:

> Another motivation is to control all the resources myself. As an employee in a big company, I am only working for my boss, say, selling my labor to my boss. But if I set up my own business, it means I could control all the things myself . . .
>
> (August 26, 2011, William, Beijing)

Two other respondents, Walter and Galeno, expressed the belief that running their own companies would make it possible for them to develop products that contribute to the common good, one of the characteristics of "good work" in the cultural industries identified by Hesmondhalgh and Baker (2010). Walter said: "The freedom brought by running my own business is quite important to me. I could develop any program that I think is valuable, rather than waiting for approval from the company I am working now" (August 26, 2011, Walter, Beijing).

Galeno spoke much more directly about the public benefits that might result from the products that he could develop in his own company. He wrote: "The most exciting thing to me is finally I have a platform to realize my dream of changing millions of people's lives" (Self-observation journal, October 26, 2009, Galeno, Campus).

Of particular concern to Galeno was the ways in which technologies were developed with little regard to what he described as "vulnerable communities". He expressed a sense of shame that the screen reader, an assistive technology used by people with visual disabilities to read out text content from websites, was developed by a blind person, rather than a sighted person sensitive to the needs of such vulnerable communities. He expressed the hope that in the future, able-bodied Internet workers would turn their attention to developing new assistive devices, suggesting that his company might do so: "I hope they (blind people) will be able to open their eyes online and embrace the Internet like other users in the future, as a result of our help. . . ." (Self-observation journal, June 29, 2011, Galeno, Campus).

The Internet idealism expressed in these quotes gives an indication of why workers persevere in the Internet industries, despite the difficult conditions they encounter. It also highlights how working in the Internet industries not only provides the opportunity to create alternative spaces online, but also constitutes an offline alternative space for Internet industry workers, a space which they believe offers them the possibility for professional success which would not be available in other sectors, and which offers as a path to other freedoms, such as self-employment. The Internet idealism evident here is also what motivates workers in their acts of agency, negotiation and resistance, as they strive to create alternative spaces. The following section discusses these acts in detail.

Worker agency and the creation of alternative spaces

In this section, we draw on the work of Randy Hodson, amongst others, to discuss the acts of agency amongst Internet industry workers that we witnessed during our fieldwork. Coming at the concept from a sociological perspective, Hodson (2001) discusses agency in the context of safeguarding dignity at work. He defines agency as "the active and creative performance of assigned roles in ways that give meaning and content to those roles beyond what is institutionally scripted" (p. 16). He proposes that agency can be divided into four categories of behavior, which he describes as "resistance, citizenship, the pursuit of meaning, and social relations at work" (p. 17). His first category, resistance, is of particular interest here. In Hodson's formulation, resistance at work is made up of the subtle and subdued practices actively and passively enacted by workers against unequal "abuse, over-work and exploitation" (p. 17). It usually relies on "small-scale actions involving a subtle withdrawal of cooperation or a banking of enthusiasm" (p. 17). Hodson

(2001) defines worker resistance in the workplace as individual or small group acts which "mitigate claims by management on employees or to advance employees' claims against management" (p. 42).

In research on resistance, there has been a tradition of dividing acts of resistance into two forms: collective/organized resistance (for example, Bodnar, 2006; Edwards, 1979; Friedman, 1977); and individual/routine resistance (for example, Fiske, 1992; Fleming & Sewell, 2002; Fleming & Spicer, 2003; Knight & McCabe, 2000; Prasad & Prasad, 2000; Scott, 1985). The former usually happens in the form of "unions, strikes and coordinated output restrictions" (Fleming & Spicer, 2003, p. 159). The latter frequently materializes in forms such as sabotage or "careful carelessness" (p. 159). Scott's research into peasant resistance in Malaysia focuses on the latter form of resistance, as the subtitle of his 1985 book indicates: *Weapons of the Weak: Everyday Forms of Peasant Resistance*. Here, Scott emphasizes the individual and covert resistance of subordinate groups. He argues that subordinate groups frequently resist in ways that "require little or no coordination or planning", "represent a form of individual self-help", and "avoid any direct symbolic confrontation with authority or with elite norms" (p. 29). More recently, as Prasad and Prasad (2000) claim, the main focus in workplace resistance research has shifted from formal and collective resistance to informal and routine resistance.

But these concepts of everyday, routine and informal forms of resistance cannot explain all forms of small-scale resistance, especially in the context of Chinese society, where resistance is complex. A number of scholars have identified forms of resistance which take place in the Chinese context which fall between these two polls of routine/individual/micro and organized/collective/macro. For instance, Smith and Pun (2006) explore the collective protests carried out by Chinese "dormitory labor", laborers who work in factories and live in factory dorms, and whose lives are thus dominated by their work. These protests usually happen in a single factory and focus on issues relating to the working conditions in that factory, such as "plant closure, unpaid wages, bankruptcy or relocation" (p. 1468). None of these protests are "covert" or "individual", to use Scott's terms, but neither could they be defined as macro-level resistance. Qiu's (2009) discussion of the resistance of subordinate groups in Chinese society is helpful here, as he points out that group acts of resistance can be characterized as small-scale, collective resistance, based on networks of families or small communities of what he calls the "information have-less". In other words, some acts of resistance in the Chinese context are undertaken collectively, but are small scale, not macro level.

In our research, we identified acts of resistance that were both small-scale and larger in scale. We rarely identified individual acts of resistance, as most practices were enacted by multiple workers. In this sense, the category of the individual act of resistance was somewhat redundant to us. What's more, we also identified acts of agency which we categorize as *negotiations* of particular working conditions, constraints or government policies, rather than acts of resistance. We use the term negotiation here to refer both to discussion and circumvention of particular working conditions. We also identified the complex ways in which Internet industry workers interact with ordinary Internet users in these acts of negotiation and resistance, sometimes acting as users, sometimes mobilizing their professional knowledge to negotiate systems and structures in ways which were unavailable to ordinary users without access to this knowledge. We map out some of the examples we encountered below, and reflect on the ways in which they contribute to the creation of alternative Chinese spaces, online and offline.

Chinese Internet industry workers engage in collective discussions of issues relating to their working life, a fact which may not be significant or unusual in other national contexts, but one which marks a fundamental shift in attitudes to worker agency in the Chinese context. For example, in an Election Meeting of Candidates of the National People's Congress in Shanghai, which took place during our fieldwork, representatives of workers in Grand expressed discontent about current working conditions and made a case for more work-related benefits. They asked the local government to build a new kindergarten near the company in order to benefit workers with children. They also raised the issue of overtime in the industries. In authoritarian and centralized China, these representatives' acts at the conference could be regarded as acts of agency which aim to improve working conditions. We see these acts of agency as negotiation, rather than resistance, and here we understand negotiation as discussion. Below, we present other examples where negotiation is understood as circumvention.

In another example, this time of resistance rather than negotiation, at Campus, Internet workers engaged in group acts to resist unfair working conditions. In December 2011, there was a new rule in Campus requiring workers to come to work before 10 AM, in place of the flexible working time arrangements that had previously existed. Meanwhile, the right to a free dinner for people working overtime, the only reward for working overtime in the previous system, was removed. Instead, the new rule stated that only people working over 12 hours per day could benefit from a free dinner. As a result, many workers chose not to work overtime, choosing instead to leave early after coming to work before 10 AM, and giving up the chance of a free dinner by working less than 12 hours per day. As Galeno said: "We leave earlier to show our discontent and resistance to it (the new rule) . . ." (December 10, 2011, Galeno, Beijing).

This example reflects neither individual acts nor collective, macro level, organized resistance. Rather, it represents resistance (not negotiation) amongst groups of workers in a single company. It might not be as influential as macro-level resistance, but it also should not be ignored, as it points towards the potential for changing working conditions in the Internet industries in the future, to make these "good", "alternative" spaces of work.

In some ways, Internet workers are like ordinary Internet users – they see the Internet as offering up the potential for an alternative public space, and they work towards realizing that potential. In other ways, they are different, as their professional positions equip them with greater skills, knowledge and possibilities for creating such spaces. A number of Internet workers expressed their awareness of this fact, and described the ways in which they mobilized these opportunities in acts of creative agency. For example, Galeno said:

> We (workers in Campus) know where the bottom line of the state is, and we know how to balance requirements of the state against the creation of free space for users. For example, we could highlight May 4th, but could not mention June 4th; we could criticize the local government, but could not say anything about the central government . . . It is admitted that the Ministry of Culture usually forces us to delete some issues, but if there were too many users focusing on the issues, then, the related departments would be pushed to solve problems . . . Some recommended topics are planned to push local governments to be concerned about certain issues and show their abilities in solving problems . . .
>
> (December 20, 2012, Galeno, Beijing)

Workers, then, negotiate (or circumvent) the limitations posed upon them by the state in terms of creating "free" spaces in which Internet users can speak out. Such negotiations contribute towards the creation of alternative spaces for Internet users.

It became apparent in our fieldwork that many Internet workers share the same concerns as Internet users. However, they differ in that the former group's "inside" knowledge allows them to navigate and negotiate the limits imposed upon what they post by key word filtering systems:

> We are the same as Internet users in terms of posting sensitive content. Sometime our sensitive posts are also deleted by our own company. But since we know more about how the filtering system works, we are more likely to write acceptable posts. Acting creatively, we use indirect methods to discuss issues . . . I like applying my creativity to post sensitive issues . . . It's more about individual acts rather than collective behaviour . . .
>
> (August 27, 2011, Carl, Bejing)

> We are more skilled than most users so we can access many foreign websites. Then, we have more information about the "real China" (compared to the image of China produced by official media), and are more eager to discuss some sensitive issues against the state (we usually discuss these issues on Campus and microblogging platforms . . .)
>
> (December 20, 2011, Galeno, Beijing)

These quotes give examples of Internet workers' negotiation/circumvention of state-imposed limitations on what can be discussed in online spaces, which Carl describes as "individual acts rather than collective behavior". In this sense, these acts fit with the traditional understanding of individual resistance. However, these workers are talking about acts in which large numbers of Chinese Internet workers engage, so that whilst the acts may not be organized, they might be considered to be collective. Indeed, as most of the acts of agency discussed here are carried out by multiple Internet workers, it is hard to identify any acts that can be classified as individual. This calls into question the frequent conflation of individual and micro level resistance (for example in the work of Scott, 1985, and Fleming & Sewell, 2002), for the forms of resistance discussed here might be micro level, but they are not individual. The acts discussed here show how Internet workers work alongside ordinary Internet users in the creation of alternative spaces to discuss sensitive topics. Arguably, they are more successful in their efforts than ordinary users, because of their insider knowledge. Therefore Internet workers make a significant contribution to the production of new forms of online freedom in contemporary China. It is not only Internet users who do this, despite the fact that most existing debate focuses on them (Kenneth, 2011; Lei, 2011; Lu & Webber 2009).

Thus Chinese Internet industry workers use their professional knowledge and expertise to create online spaces in which ordinary Internet users can talk about sensitive issues. Workers try to create new online products to encourage Internet users to speak out within the limited "free space" permitted by the state. For example, Campus created a public page, named "Status Sovereign", which aims to encourage Internet users to freely discuss popular and sensitive issues, such as Google's withdrawal from the Chinese market because of online censorship in 2010. Through examples such as this, workers attempt to create free public spaces for ordinary users.

Some high level workers within the Chinese Internet industries worked in liberal newspapers before joining this sector and are known for the public positions that they take against the state, in relation to particular social problems. Some of them are said to have joined the Internet industries in order to create free spaces for ordinary Chinese people to speak out. As Galeno said:

> A lot of executives in Internet companies are opinion leaders and against the state. For instance, Ho is quite a famous opinion leader, who is in Tencent now, taking charge of editing. Lots of workers in liberal media choose the Internet as a space to speak out and give voice to different voices.
>
> (December 20, 2011, Galeno, Beijing)

Galeno then went on to give the specific example of Netease, which is a widely used Chinese web portal, and is considered to be comparatively liberal. He said:

> The most famous case is Netease, where plenty of famous opinion leaders are gathering. Some of my net friends, who worked in Southern Weekly before, then changed to Netease. Netease has been created as one of the most influential liberal portals in China, and some of its columns are quite critical and radical . . .
>
> (December 20, 2011, Galeno, Beijing)

These workers' acts are not only providing spaces for Internet users to discuss social problems, but, more significantly, they directly open up space for discussion of radical topics, building on increasing social tensions to gather Internet users to directly criticize the state. For instance, in 2011, the education section of Netease edited a special report about the rise of university tuition fees, which was based on an online survey conducted among its users. It directly criticized problems in the education system and hundreds of Internet users responded to the topic with their own experiences. For example, compared to university students in the 1980s and 1990s, university students in 2000s claimed to suffer from higher tuition fees, faster growing living expenses and no guarantee of future employment after graduation. In the report, the difficulties students encountered paying high tuition fees, the need to borrow money from relatives and problems paying it back after graduation (because of limited employment opportunities) were highlighted. As a result, the editors concluded the report by directly criticizing the problematic development of the Chinese education system and the related economic system. Although less direct than the resistance to the new overtime rules at Campus, discussed above, this act clearly has wider reach and, like the other acts of agency discussed here, aims to create an alternative space in both online and offline China.

Internet workers also co-operate with Internet users in acts of resistance which sometimes take the form of protest, as can be seen in some of the examples we have already discussed. According to our interviewees, in some big media events, Internet workers not only organize varied online activities, but also participate in offline activities. Such events include participation on microblogging platforms in activities against child abduction (*weibo daguai*), prompted by a father of a 3-year-old abducted child who posted his story on a microblogging platform, calling for help online. Subsequently, millions of Internet users focused on the abduction of children and helped to find some of them, including the child of the man who initiated this action. Another example is the Xiamen PX protest. In November 2006, a new plant which would produce 800,000 tonnes of paraxylene annually was planned for Xiamen. The dangers of the plant in terms of environment and health were made public in March 2007 by a professor in Xiamen University, which initiated the anti-PX factory protest. In the beginning of June 2007, tens of thousands of citizens in Xiamen were organized through the Internet and mobile networks to protest against this planned project. The protest alarmed officials in Beijing and eventually forced the local government to suspend the construction of the PX factory.

Galeno's friends worked in some of the major Internet companies and participated in the Xiamen PX protest. Galeno told us that some Internet workers purposefully organized online activities, such as producing videos and organizing Internet users to post critical comments on some government official websites. These workers therefore played an important and influential role in the online activities, because of their professional knowledge of how to use the Internet for these purposes. As Galeno put it: "In mainland China, only few people, who are mainly in Internet industries, could give voice to the varied opinions and voices . . . " (December 20, 2011, Galeno, Beijing). At the same time, some of these Internet workers directly participated in the offline protests. Thus the cooperation between Internet workers and Internet users created spaces both online and offline for varied voices to speak out and for ordinary people to show discontent, in what could be described as a traditional form of collective, organized resistance.

Conclusion

In this chapter, we have highlighted both the difficult working conditions and hopes and ideals of workers in the Chinese Internet industries, in order to piece together a picture of working life in this sector, which provides a basis for understanding how workers in these industries contribute to the production of alternative spaces in online and offline China. We have shown how the Internet industries serve as hopeful and meaningful spaces for ordinary Chinese workers, bad working conditions notwithstanding, because they are seen to provide chances and possibilities of success to varied classes of Chinese people. In this sense, hope provides a pathway to agency. We have focused on worker agency in this chapter, but it is not our view that agency "trumps" bad working conditions, nor do we arrive at primarily optimistic conclusions about Internet industry work in China. As Andrew Ross points out, problematic working conditions in Chinese high-tech industries need urgent attention, academic and otherwise. Furthermore, elsewhere, one of us asks whether good working conditions in the Western world depend on bad conditions in other countries like China (Xia, forthcoming). We offer this disclaimer here as we are aware that this chapter, with its focus on worker agency and its location in a section about the production of alternative spaces, may be read as overly and simplistically optimistic without this contextualization, or as romanticizing worker agency (Mumby, 2005).

Nonetheless, in this context of problematic working conditions, acts of agency by workers in these industries contribute to the production of alternative online spaces. These may, in time, bring about possible transformations in offline China. We have highlighted individual, collective, small-scale and large-scale acts of negotiation (both discussion and circumvention) and resistance which contribute towards the building of these alternative spaces. These include, for example, worker engagement in collective negotiation relating to their working life; worker creation of online spaces which builds on professional knowledge and expertise to negotiate constraints; and worker participation in online and offline resistance, as in the case of the Xiamen PX protest. Many of these acts are simultaneously individual and collective – there are no examples of practices that can be understood as purely individual acts of everyday resistance cited here. Despite Carl's view that Internet industry workers' posts about sensitive issues are individual acts, as soon as more than one worker engages in this activity, it ceases to be individual. In this sense, the individual/collective distinction is somewhat redundant. Much more interesting, we suggest, are the numerous ways in which various forms of resistance and negotiation come together in the complex process of creating an alternative China. With these varied forms of resistance and acts of negotiation, Internet workers are influential in their contribution to the creation of a resistant online space giving voice to diverse classes in China. Thus a focus on the workers in Internet industries who shape the production of *online* China is both productive and necessary, in order to arrive at rich and rounded understandings of potential transformations in *offline* China.

Some China scholars have asked the question of what is the best route to a better China. Gradualists such as Huang (2008) suggest China further liberalize the market and weaken the intervention from the state in order to strengthen capitalist development. But in Andreas' (2010) discussion, it is the free market that resulted from the market reforms of 1978 that has caused social problems in contemporary China. From his perspective, further reforms to the free market proposed by Huang (2008) will only make things worse. As Andreas (2010) concludes, social problems can only be solved through the efforts of the state to stop the exploitation of workers and of smaller local companies by "powerful capitalist companies" (p. 85). Reformists provide an alternative answer. For example, Chun (2006) claims that transformation in China will not be achieved by mimicking a Western-style society, but rather through "recapturing the state from within the state and party through a hegemonic 'war of position'" (p. 220). In other words, the transformation of China does not relate to how independent the market becomes or how much the state intervenes, but rather, it relates to "what the state does (performance), aims to do (nature), and can accomplish (capacity)" (p. 221).

By contrast, Zhao (2011) is more radical. She realizes the important role that will be played by the resistance of Chinese peasants and workers, what she calls "agencies and alternatives" (p. 559). Bottom-up agency of the kind discussed by Zhao has also been examined in the work of Qiu (2009), who investigates the experiences of subordinate groups, the information "have-less", in their "daily struggles and participation in the class-making and history-making process" (p. 18). Qiu regards new media events, to which the information have-less make a significant contribution, as "an important harbinger of change" (p. 226) in Chinese society. These events provide opportunities for ordinary Chinese people to discuss "the reality they experience" (p. 226) before bringing about social change by taking significant and effective action, argues Qiu. Thus Qiu proposes that a new working class is emerging and being empowered through the development and diffusion of information and communication technologies (ICTs), which, he hopes, will bring Chinese society into a new era. In Qiu's vision, as in Zhao's, an alternative China results from resistance from below. Such a pattern could perhaps be mapped onto the picture we have painted here: ordinary Chinese workers equip themselves with ICT skills, knowledge and power, and play a role in the creation of alternative online spaces which may, in time, lead to the potential transformation of offline China.

References

Andreas, J. (2010, September/October). A Shanghai model? On capitalism with Chinese characteristics. *New Left Review*, 63–85.

Banks, M. (2007). *The politics of cultural work*. Basingstoke, UK: Palgrave Macmillan.

Beijing Municipality. (2011). Several provisions of the Beijing Municipality on the administration and development of microblogging in Beijing. *Lawinfochina.* Retrieved July 31, 2014, from http://www.lawinfochina.com/display.aspx?lib=law&id=9215

Benkler, Y. (2006). *The wealth of networks: How social production transforms markets and freedom.* New Haven, CT: Yale University Press.

Berners-Lee, T. (2003). Web Accessibility Initiative (WAI). Retrieved July 31, 2014, from http://www.w3.org/WAI/

Bodnar, C. (2006). Taking it to the streets: French cultural worker resistance and the creation of a precariat movement. *Canadian Journal of Communication, 31,* 675–694.

Bruns, A. (2008). *Blogs, Wikipedia, second life and beyond: From production to produsage.* New York, NY: Peter Lang.

Chun, L. (2006). *The transformation of Chinese socialism.* Durham, NC: Duke University Press.

Dickson, B. J. (2003). *Red capitalists in China: The party, private entrepreneurs, and prospects for political change.* Cambridge, UK: Cambridge University Press.

Dickson, B. J. (2011). Who consents to the "Beijing Consensus": Crony communism in China. In S. P. Hsu, Y.-S. Wu, & S. Zhao (Eds.), *In search of China's development model: Beyond the Beijing consensus* (pp. 189–203). London, UK: Routledge.

Edwards, R. (1979). *Contested terrain: The transformation of workplace in the twentieth century.* New York, NY: Basic Books.

Fiske, J. (1992). Cultural studies and the culture of everyday life. In L. Grossberg, C. Nelson, & P. A. Treichler (Eds.), *Cultural Studies* (pp. 154–173). New York, NY: Routledge.

Fleming, P., & Spicer, A. (2003). Working at a cynical distance: Implications for power, subjectivity and resistance. *Organization, 10*(1), 157–179.

Fleming, P., & Sewell, G. (2002). Looking for the good soldier, Svejk: Alternative modalities of resistance in contemporary workplace. *Sociology, 36*(4), 857–873.

Friedman, A. (1977). *Industry and labour: Class struggle at work and monopoly capitalism.* London, UK: Macmillan.

Gill, R. (2007). *Technobohemians or the new cybertariat? New media work in Amsterdam a decade after the web.* Report for the Institute of Network Cultures, Amsterdam. Retrieved July 18, 2012, from http://networkcultures.org/wpmu/portal/publications/network-notebooks/technobohemians-or-the-new-cybertariat/

Gill, R. (2010). Life is a pitch: Managing the self in new media work. In M. Deuze (Ed.), *Managing media work* (pp. 249–262). London, UK: Sage.

Harvey, D. (2005). *A brief history of neoliberalism.* Oxford, UK: Oxford University Press.

Hesmondhalgh, D., & Baker, S. (2010). Creative labour: Media work in three cultural industries. Abingdon, UK: Routledge.

Hodson, R. (2001). *Dignity at work.* Cambridge, UK: Cambridge University Press.

Huang, Y. (2008). *Capitalism with Chinese characteristics: Entrepreneur and the state.* Cambridge, UK: Cambridge University Press.

Huang, Y. (2010, September/October). The politics of China's path, A reply to Joel Andreas. *New Left Review,* 87–91.Hulianwang shangshi gongsi yingshou yu shizhi tongji guanggao he youxi shi zui zhuyao yingli moshi [Statistics on Internet companies' revenue and market value, games and advertisement are the most profitable model]. (2012). *iResearch.* Retrieved July 31, 2014, from http://www.iresearch.com.cn/View/175398.html

Jenkins, H. (2006). *Fans, bloggers, and gamers: Exploring participatory culture.* New York: New York University Press.

Kennedy, H. (2012). *Net work: Ethics and values in web design.* Basingstoke, UK: Palgrave Macmillan.

Kenneth Y. (2011). The aborted Green dam-youth escort censor-ware project in China: A case study of emerging civic participation in China's internet policy-making process. *Telematics & Informatics, 28*(2), 101–111.

Knight, D., & McCabe, D. (2000). "Ain't misbehaving"? Opportunities for resistance under new forms of "quality" management. *Sociology, 34*(3), 421–436.

Lei, Y. (2011). The political consequences of the rise of the Internet: Political beliefs and practices of Chinese netizens. *Political Communication, 28*(3), 291–322.

Liang, H. (2012). Zhongguo hulianwang shinian chuanqi [The ten-year legend of the Internet in China]. Retrieved from http://www.banyuetan.org/chcontent/sz/szgc/2012824/55916.html

Lu, J., & Webber, I. (2009). Internet software piracy in China: A user analysis of resistance to global software copyright enforcement. *Journal of International & Intercultural Communication, 2*(4), 298–317.

Mumby, D. K. (2005). Theorizing resistance in organization studies: A dialectical approach. *Management Communication Quarterly, 19*(1), 20–44.

Ornebring, H. (2008). The consumer as producer-of what? User-generated tabloid content in the Sun (UK) and Aftonbladet (Sweden). *Journalism Studies, 9*(5), 771–785.

Prasad, P., & Prasad, A. (2000). Stretching and iron cage: The constitution and implications of routine workplace resistance. *Organization Science, 11*(4), 387–403.

Qiu, L. J. (2009). *Working-class network society: Communication technology and the information have-less in urban China.* London, UK: The MIT Press.

Renmin Youdianbao. (2012). Zhongguo hulianwang chanye huigu yu zhanwang. *Zhongguo Xinxi Chanyewang.* Retrieved March 24, 2014, from http://www.cnii.com.cn/index/content/2012-01/13/content_949853.htm

Ross, A. (2005). *Fast boat to China: High-tech outsourcing and the consequences of free trade: Lessons from Shanghai.* New York, NY: Vintage Books.

Scott, J. (1985). *Weapons of the weak: Everyday forms of peasant resistance.* New Haven, CT: Yale University Press.

Smith, C., & Pun, N. (2006). The dormitory labour regime in China as a site for control and resistance. *The International Journal of Human Resource Management, 17*(8), 1456–1470.

Thurman, N. (2008). Forums for citizen journalists? Adoption of user generated content initiatives by online news media. *New Media & Society, 10*(1), 139–157.

Wang, H. (2003). *China's new order: Society, politics, and economy in transition.* Cambridge, MA: Harvard University Press.

Xia, B. (forthcoming). *Labour in Chinese internet industries* (PhD thesis). University of Leeds, UK.

Xiao, B. (2011). IT hangye cheng wuda jibing zhongzaiqu: Guolaosi pingjun 37.9 sui [IT industries become the death area: Average age of workers dying of *karoshi* is 37.9]. Retrieved July 19, 2012, from http://tech.qq.com/a/20111124/000177.htm

Zhao, Y. (2003). Transnational capital, the Chinese state, and China's communication industries in a fractured society. *The Public, 4,* 53–74.

Zhao, Y. (2007). After mobile phones, what? Re-embedding the social in China's "Digital Revolution". *International Journal of Communication, 1,* 92–120.

Zhao, Y. (2011). The challenge of China: Contribution to a transcultural political economy of communication for the twenty-first century. In J. Wasko, G. Murdock, & H. Sousa (Eds.), *The handbook of political economy of communications* (pp. 558–582). Malden, MA: Wiley-Blackwell.

Index

Note: Pages in italics indicate figures and tables.

For Product Safety Concerns and Information please contact our EU
representative GPSR@taylorandfrancis.com
Taylor & Francis Verlag GmbH, Kaufingerstraße 24, 80331 München, Germany